John William Burgon

Ninety Short Sermons for Family Reading

Vol. 1

John William Burgon

Ninety Short Sermons for Family Reading
Vol. 1

ISBN/EAN: 9783744742313

Printed in Europe, USA, Canada, Australia, Japan

Cover: Foto ©Lupo / pixelio.de

More available books at **www.hansebooks.com**

NINETY SHORT SERMONS

for family reading:

FOLLOWING THE COURSE OF THE CHRISTIAN SEASONS.

BY THE AUTHOR OF
A PLAIN COMMENTARY ON THE GOSPELS.

IN TWO VOLUMES.
VOL. I.

OXFORD AND LONDON:
JOHN HENRY AND JAMES PARKER.
MDCCCLXV.

PRINTED BY MESSRS. PARKER, CORN-MARKET, OXFORD.

TO

THE BLESSED MEMORY

OF MY MOTHER.

Houghton-Conquest,
 Sep. 7th, 1855.

PREFACE.

The object which the writer had in view when he took in hand the following Sermons, is almost sufficiently explained by the title prefixed to his Work. Many who observe the practice of occasionally reading a sermon aloud to their household, are heard to declare that they can scarcely find anything quite suitable for that purpose. The *length* of most Sermons is a fatal objection. Some are thought too abstruse; and some, too polemical. Other Sermons, because they were written for large and mixed congregations, are found unsuitable for private use. For whatever reason, discourses written for pulpit delivery seldom seem to be altogether in harmony with the calm tone of a Christian man's fireside.

It appeared therefore to the present writer that he might be rendering a useful service if he attempted a series of plain, practical Sermons for the Sundays and Saints' Days of the Sacred Year, of about half the length of ordinary Sermons.

He has been careful to urge such topics, (suggested generally by the Epistle or the Gospel for the Day,) as appeared most obviously to tend to edification: avoiding everything of a controversial, or a party character. He is not conscious of having either intentionally borrowed his thoughts from others, or of having gone out of his way in order to be original. To be practically *useful* has really been throughout the chief object of his concern.—Two of these short Addresses, (the fifty-ninth and the sixtieth,) are the kind contribution of an abler hand.

It may not be improper to point out, that although Discourses written for a mixed congregation are generally not suitable for domestic reading, short Sermons like these, expanded and rendered somewhat more *hortatory* in their character, may easily be rendered available for the pulpit. Their usefulness, (if they are found useful,) need not be confined to the domestic circle.

Oxford,
October 15*th*, 1855.

CONTENTS OF VOL. I.

	Page
SERMON I. *THE ADVENT SEASON.* The First Sunday in Advent. (St. Matthew xxi. 5.)....	1
SERMON II. *COMFORT OF THE SCRIPTURES.* The Second Sunday in Advent. (Romans xv. 4.)........	9
SERMON III. *THE UNEXPECTED MANNER OF CHRIST'S COMING.* The Third Sunday in Advent. (St. Matthew xi. 2, 3.)...	17
SERMON IV. *CAREFUL FOR NOTHING, BUT IN EVERY THING BY PRAYER.* The Fourth Sunday in Advent. (Philippians iv. 6, 7.)...	25
SERMON V. *THE WORD MADE FLESH.* Christmas-Day. (St. John i. 14.).........................	33
SERMON VI. *NO ROOM FOR CHRIST.* The Sunday after Christmas-Day. (St. Luke ii. 7.)......	41
SERMON VII. *THE BIRTH OF CHRIST GLORIOUS.* The Epiphany. (Isaiah lx. 1.)	49
SERMON VIII. *THE WISDOM OF LITTLE ONES* The First Sunday after the Epiphany. (St. Lu. ii. 46, 47.)	57

SERMON IX. *THE MIRACLE AT CANA OF GALILEE.*
The Second Sunday after the Epiphany. (St. John ii. 1.) ... 65

SERMON X. *THE FAITHFUL CENTURION.*
The Third Sunday after the Epiphany. (St. Matt. viii. 5,6.) 65*

SERMON XI. *THE DEMONIACS OF GADARA.*
The Fourth Sunday after the Epiphany. (St. Matt. viii. 28.) ... 73

SERMON XII. *THE PARABLE OF THE TARES.*
The Fifth Sunday after the Epiphany. (St. Matthew xiii. 24—30.) ... 81

SERMON XIII. *LIKENESS TO GOD, THE CONDITION OF SEEING GOD.*
The Sixth Sunday after the Epiphany. (1 St. John iii. 2, 3.) ... 89

SERMON XIV. *HEAVENLY PAYMENT.*
The Sunday called Septuagesima. (St. Matth. xx. 9, 10.) 97

SERMON XV. *THE PARABLE OF THE SOWER.*
The Sunday called Sexagesima. (St. Luke viii. 5—8)... 105

SERMON XVI. *CHARITY, THE GREATEST OF VIRTUES.*
The Sunday called Quinquagesima. (1 Cor. xiii. 4—8.) 113

SERMON XVII. *LENT, THE SEASON OF CONVERSION.*
Ash-Wednesday. (Joel ii. 12.) ... 121

SERMON XVIII. *MAN SHALL NOT LIVE BY BREAD ALONE.*
The First Sunday in Lent. (St. Matthew iv. 4.) ... 12

CONTENTS.

SERMON XIX. *THE WOMAN OF CANAAN.*
The Second Sunday in Lent. (St. Matth. xv. 21, 22.)... 137

SERMON XX. *THE RELAPSED DEMONIAC.*
The Third Sunday in Lent. (St. Luke xi. 24—26.)...... 145

SERMON XXI. *THE FEEDING OF THE FIVE THOUSAND WHEN THE PASSOVER WAS NIGH.*
The Fourth Sunday in Lent. (St. John vi. 4—6.) 153

SERMON XXII. *THE ONENESS OF OUR LIFE.*
The Fifth Sunday in Lent. (St. John viii. 51.) 161

SERMON XXIII. *THE TIME OF VISITATION.*
The Sunday next before Easter. (St. Luke xix. 44.) ... 169

SERMON XXIV. *THE BLIND AND THE LAME.*
Monday before Easter. (St. Matthew xxi. 14.) 177

SERMON XXV. *NOTHING LITTLE IN GOD'S SIGHT.*
Tuesday before Easter. (St. Luke xxi. 2.) 185

SERMON XXVI. *SIN A HARDENER OF THE HEART.*
Wednesday before Easter. (St. Matthew xxvi. 14—16.) 193

SERMON XXVII. *LONG-SUFFERING AND FORBEARANCE.*
Thursday before Easter. (Hebrews xii. 3, 4.) 201

SERMON XXVIII. *CHRIST CRUCIFIED.*
Good-Friday. (St. John xix. 30.) 209

SERMON XXIX. *CHRISTIAN SORROW A PRELUDE TO CHRISTIAN JOY.*
Easter Even. (Psalm cxxvi. 5.) 217

CONTENTS.

Page

SERMON XXX. *THE EASTER ANTHEM.*
Easter-Day. (1 Corinthians v. 7.).......................... 225

SERMON XXXI. *BELIEVING WITHOUT SEEING.*
—(PART I.)
Monday in Easter-Week. (St. John xx. 29.) 233

SERMON XXXII. *BELIEVING WITHOUT SEEING.*
—(PART II.)
Tuesday in Easter-Week. (St. John xx. 29.) 241

SERMON XXXIII. *THE VICTORY THAT OVERCOMETH THE WORLD*
The First Sunday after Easter. (1 St. John v. 4.)...... 249

SERMON XXXIV. *THE SHEEP KNOWN AND KNOWING.*
The Second Sunday after Easter. (St. John x. 14.) 257

SERMON XXXV. *THE SORROW OF GOD'S SAINTS.*
The Third Sunday after Easter. (St. John xvi. 20.).... 265

SERMON XXXVI. *OUR BODIES, TEMPLES OF THE HOLY GHOST.*
The Fourth Sunday after Easter. (1 Cor. vi. 19.)....... 273

SERMON XXXVII. *ANSWERED PRAYER.*—(PART I.)
The Fifth Sunday after Easter. (St. John xvi. 23.) 281

SERMON XXXVIII. *CHRIST'S DEPARTURE AND RETURN.*
The Ascension-Day. (Acts i. 11.)........................... 289

SERMON XXXIX. *ANSWERED PRAYER.*—(PART II.)
Sunday after Ascension-Day. (St. John xvi. 23.) 297

CONTENTS. xi

Page

SERMON XL. *GRIEVING THE SPIRIT.*
Whit-Sunday. (Ephesians iv. 30.).......................... 305

SERMON XLI. *THE SOUL'S THIRST.*—(PART I.)
Monday in Whitsun-Week. (St. John vii. 37.) 313

SERMON XLII. *THE SOUL'S THIRST.*—(PART II.)
Tuesday in Whitsun-Week. (St. John vii. 37.) 321

SERMON XLIII. *THE SUGGESTIONS OF TRINITY SUNDAY.*
Trinity Sunday. (Psalm xc. 12.)........................... 329

SERMON XLIV. *THE PARABLE OF LAZARUS.*
The First Sunday after Trinity. (St. Luke xvi. 19.) 337

SERMON XLV. *THE PARABLE OF THE GREAT SUPPER.*
The Second Sunday after Trinity. (St. Luke xiv. 16.) 345

First Sunday in Advent.

THE ADVENT SEASON.

St. Matthew xxi. 5.

Behold thy King cometh unto thee.

To any one who has learnt to appreciate, even in a slight degree, the beautiful arrangement and lofty purpose of the Christian Seasons, the return of Advent cannot but be a source of real comfort and satisfaction. We seem to have been too long estranged from Him whose Ascension into Heaven we celebrated more than six months ago. Up to that period, how constantly was He brought before us! How much of Humiliation indeed, yet how much of Glory was there in the varied history of Christmas and Epiphany, Lent, and Easter; until Whit-Sunday gathered up all into one glorious Festival! But from that moment, all has appeared to be at an end; and we seem to have been only more and more losing sight of Him who died for our sins, and rose again for our sanctification. The Apocryphal lessons which have been read in Church for the last two months have conduced not a little to sever the links which connected us, at least in memory, with our LORD. We have missed those far-sighted allusions to the Day of the Gospel,—those typical histories,—those familiar prophecies,—which are for ever recurring in the Old Testament Scriptures, and which help to keep the History of Redemption before our eyes when what may be called the sacramental half of the year has come to a close. Even on Sundays, the first Lessons from the book of Proverbs have helped to produce the same general impression that we were becoming daily further and further removed from the heavenly Canaan,—the Land of our promised inheritance: for it is hard to see CHRIST in the book of Proverbs, though we know for certain that He *is* there.

In the meanwhile, it is not fanciful to point out that the very decay of external Nature contributes an element of unconscious despondency and regret. While Summer was with us in its leafy pride, and Autumn in its exquisite variety, there was something outward for the eye if not for the heart to rest upon with pleasure. But Summer and Autumn have already been gathered into the grave of Winter. The air is chill, and the sky is dark, and the days grow visibly shorter. The trees have become bare, and the gardens empty. Every thing preaches to us unmistakably of decay and death. The kingdom of Nature therefore, is now beginning to partake in the decline which we have so long witnessed in the kingdom of Grace; and its phenomena affect us in a somewhat kindred manner.

At such a time does Advent surprise the inattentive, and cheer the wakeful, by its heart-stirring approach. This Day's Collect, (which is founded on this Day's Epistle,) is like a trumpet-blast to awake the spiritually dead, to arouse the sleeping, to produce activity and attention in all. Well may we pray for grace to 'cast away the works of darkness,' if indeed 'the Night is far spent and the Day is at hand.' At the same time the mention of armour suggests the idea of an enemy to be encountered, and a victory to be won: while the allusion to our LORD's second Advent sets before the mind at once the great reality of this,—the first of the sacred Seasons; and establishes its purpose to prepare the Church for what is yet future, no less than to remind her of what is already past.

This indeed is the great object of all our sacred anniversaries. Their obvious effect is to inform us concerning the History of our LORD; but their actual purpose, their true office, is thereby to conform us to His Divine image. Advent, which is intended to prepare us for the worthy celebration of His Nativity, is also intended to fulfil the yet higher office of preparing us to behold His face with joy when He shall come again in His glorious Majesty to judge both the quick and dead.

When the natural year therefore has come to a close, the spiritual year begins; and as the one grows darker, so does the other increase in glory; only slackening in its course of brightness with the return of Summer. And the spiritual year breaks upon us, in all its brightness, to-day,— the Festival of St. Andrew being as it were the star which ushers in the dawn of the first morning. Four Advent Sundays in succession now prepare us for the worthy celebration of the Nativity of JESUS CHRIST; just as six Sundays will hereafter prepare us for the worthy celebration of His Death and Resurrection, and as many more for our Christian Pentecost. In this manner the Israel of GOD have their three great yearly Festivals, no less than Israel after the flesh had theirs; and the season of preparation which precedes each is a solemn witness of our need of preparation and self-discipline in order that we may profit adequately by the Festival which is to follow.

Unspeakably cheering after the long interval already noticed, during which such sounds have been kept as it were in abeyance, is the full Gospel-note which falls upon the ear on this day. The two first Lessons are the i^{st} and ii^{nd} chapters of the evangelical prophet: while the Epistle and Gospel exhibit our SAVIOUR CHRIST as not merely remotely approaching, but as already arrived at our very doors. It would seem to be impossible to hear the well-known Collect without a thrill of emotion and of pleasure; or to avoid being struck by the solemnity of its daily repetition until Christmas-Eve: a perpetual witness of our SAVIOUR's first coming in the flesh, and a constant warning to us of His second Advent yet future.

Some such remarks as these force themselves upon us at this season. It is right to pause before we enter on the bright series of Sundays which await us, and to remind ourselves of the greatness of our danger no less than of the largeness of our privileges: for a danger it is to pass through such seasons, to hear such words, and to witness such awful transactions, and yet to remain unchanged, still less to remain wholly unaffected by them. But the privilege is vast also; nor does it seem possible to over-estimate its preciousness. For how can a Christian man be more blissfully employed than in the contemplation of the Christian mysteries; not merely in the privacy of his chamber, or amid the distractions of a secret mental review; but in the congregation of the faithful, and in concert with the Holy Church throughout all the world? Surely, it is little short of Heaven upon Earth, to be so engaged! This is none other than the beginning of our Everlasting Service!

And the practical aspect in which this solemn season will present itself to every serious man will be,—that Advent, instead of being a mere name, is a great reality. Our SAVIOUR comes to us now, with the same suddenness, the same secrecy, as when He came at first to the Jewish nation. Do we run no corresponding risk of overlooking His approach, and so of sharing *their* condemnation? What reason have we for hoping that when He comes to judge the world, we shall be more prepared for His Divine presence? better able to behold His face with joy?

'Tell ye the Daughter of Sion, Behold thy King cometh unto thee!' These were the words which the HOLY SPIRIT by the mouth of Zechariah the prophet addressed to the Jewish nation. It was a message which every individual of the crowd might have taken home to himself: 'Behold, thy King cometh *unto thee.*' And the message is still the same. It is a private, and an individual appeal. Let it be explained in a few words how this comes to pass; lest it should unhappily appear to any that such words are but conventional, have no distinct, definite meaning.

What we would convey then amounts to *this:*—that our Church Services are a great reality; and that the temper which can view them without interest,—see them pass without sympathy,—receive their lessons without an endeavour, or even without a wish, to profit by them,—*that* temper would be unmoved even were CHRIST Himself to appear again on earth, and to stand among us. Such an one would have been unmoved had his lot been cast in the days of MESSIAH. It is not too much to say, that he who, understanding the meaning of the Advent services, can yet hear them without any kind of emotion, interest, or pleasure,—*that* man is in a fearful state to live and die in. His summons will come at last; and assuredly it will find him unprepared to meet his King, when 'behold, He cometh!'

For the very purpose of these solemn anniversaries, as already hinted, is to bring in a living manner before the heart the events of our LORD's Life. 'What, could ye not watch with Me *one hour?*' is the question asked of us in Lent: 'Watch and pray, that ye enter not into temptation[a].' 'Is it nothing to you, all ye that pass by? behold, and see if there be any sorrow like unto My sorrow[b],' is the message to us all during Holy Week. St. Paul told the Galatians that JESUS CHRIST had been 'evidently set forth crucified *before their eyes*[c]:' and what less can be said to *us* on every recurrence of Good Friday? Surely, *we* 'handle' Him at Easter, and 'see that it is He indeed' who has triumphed over Death and Hell! Surely, while *we* are gazing after Him, He is 'carried up into Heaven;' and it is *our* faults if He 'leaves us comfortless' after He hath Himself departed! . . . Even so, at the present holy season, it is said to every one of us, 'Behold, thy KING cometh unto thee!' Shall we disregard the announcement, like those foolish ones who 'slumbered and slept?' or shall we rather strive to do as *they* did, who forthwith trimmed their lamps, and went forth with awful joy to meet the Bridegroom[d]?

[a] St. Matth. xxvi. 40, 41.
[b] Lamentations i. 12.
[c] Gal. iii. 1.
[d] St. Matth. xxv. 6.

Second Sunday in Advent.

COMFORT OF THE SCRIPTURES.

Romans xv. 4.

Whatsoever things were written aforetime were written for our learning, that we through patience and comfort of the Scriptures might have hope.

Most of our Collects, it is well-known, are of immense antiquity, many of them being traceable back to within three hundred years of the Apostolic age. Some few, (and those certainly not the least exquisite,) are comparatively modern. To-day's Collect, for example, appeared for the first time in the first reformed English Book of Common-Prayer; namely, in 1549. It is quite unlike every other Collect, and seems at first sight to stand without any particular fitness or propriety in the place where it is actually found; being, in effect, nothing else but a prayer preparatory to the reading of Holy Scripture. As such, we find it printed inside the cover of many of our Bibles; nor can we perhaps approach the study of God's Book with a better 'form of sound words' upon our lips. Let us make it our business, on this occasion, to offer a few remarks illustrative of the matter thus brought before our notice. Wherein consists the fitness of this day's Collect, and to what train of thought does its insertion in the present place guide us?

First, it will be perceived at once that it is formed out of the Epistle for the day; which, like the present Gospel, has been used by the Church of England ever since Christianity was first planted in these kingdoms. By singling out St. Paul's reference to Holy Scripture however, in preference to any of the numerous striking *Advent* allusions which the Gospel for the day would have supplied, it is impossible to avoid suspecting that our compilers were eager to vindicate for the newly recovered Treasure of GOD's Word, its true dignity and importance. They placed the mention of it on the very threshold of the Church's Book of Devotions, as if in perpetual memorial of what 'was lost and is found;' and deep indeed must have been the fervour with which every pious heart will have joined in a prayer so scriptural in its tone, so truly comfortable and edifying in its general tenor and purpose. Difficult, or rather impossible is it for us at this distance of

Time to appreciate what must have been the feelings of our forefathers in this respect. The free use of the sacred volume, which had been so long proscribed, must have seemed to them like little else than Life from the dead,—the very Advent of CHRIST Himself.

But this is evidently only an imperfect account of the matter. There must have been a profounder motive which induced our Reformers to construct such a Collect for the Second Sunday in Advent; and it appears to have been of the following nature. They seem to have wished to draw attention to the singular manner in which the Epistle and Gospel for the day are contrasted: the latter telling of alarm, the former of consolation: the one, drawing an awful picture of the convulsions in Heaven and Earth which will be witnessed in the latter days; ('signs in the Sun, and in the Moon, and in the Stars; and upon the Earth, distress of nations with perplexity, the sea and the waves roaring; men's hearts failing them for fear;') the other, preaching words of Patience, and prompting thoughts of Comfort, and whispering lessons of Hope. Take notice of the concluding words of the Epistle: 'Now the GOD of Hope fill you with all Joy and Peace in believing, that ye may abound in Hope, through the power of the HOLY GHOST.'

What then, is it implied, should be the Believer's stay in the Day of Terror? On what shall he anchor his heart, and fix his thoughts, with confidence? The Collect suggests an answer to this question. Besides Patience, (which is required at the hands of all GOD's children,) there is *the comfort of GOD'S Holy Word;—* whereby we embrace, and by GOD's help, ever hold fast the blessed Hope of Everlasting Life which He has given us in our SAVIOUR JESUS CHRIST. *This* is the soul's stay in the hour of adversity. *This* will be the prop of failing hearts in the great and terrible Day of the LORD!

And that all this is indeed so, must appear to any one who shall be at the pains to consider how unspeakable will be the consternation which our LORD describes; when, amid strange sights, and sounds unutterable;—amid the conflagration of this Earth, the interruption of the course of Nature, the disorganization of this entire visible frame of things;—'The Son of Man' will be seen 'coming in a cloud with power and great glory.' Surely, in that tremendous hour, (an hour which we shall every one of us witness!) the terror-stricken soul will reach out for something whereby to sustain itself. And on what shall it lay hold, if not on GOD's sure mercies in CHRIST? Where shall be its confidence, if not in those everlasting promises which, we know, *cannot* fail?

Not only amid the terrors of the Great Day, but during all those darker hours through which we have to pass in the course of our mortal pilgrimage,—'among all the changes and chances of this mortal life,'—Holy Scripture is our appointed comfort. And this in truth is one of the chief reasons why, during the season of health and prosperity, the Sacred Volume should be much in our hands, the subject of our constant and assiduous study. Out of that heavenly armoury we shall thereby know how to furnish ourselves with an appropriate weapon in the hour of our greatest need. The Enemy will assail us with disquieting thoughts; but we shall know how to beat him back with 'the Sword of the Spirit, which is the Word of GOD.' The manner in which the Almighty One has constantly brought positive Good out of seeming Evil; has overruled events in themselves disastrous, to a blessed issue; has kept His people long waiting for an answer to their prayers, yet has ever answered them abundantly in the end; has had patience with them notwithstanding their repeated sins; has proved to be a GOD of Mercy on their sincere repentance and amendment; — all these 'comforts of GOD's Holy Word,' may well rejoice the believer's heart, and sustain his hopes amid adversity. CHRIST's Holy Nativity and Circumcision, His Baptism, Fasting, and Temptation, His Agony and Bloody Sweat, His Cross and Passion, His precious Death and Burial, His glorious Resurrection and Ascension, together with the Coming of the HOLY GHOST,—all these blessed truths, faithfully received into 'an honest and good heart,' cannot but be productive of Heavenly Comfort: heralds are they of that Peace which the world can neither give nor take away.

The connexion of such a doctrine as this with the present solemn Season will be felt at once, when it is remembered that whatever the historical date of CHRIST's Second Advent may prove to be, He comes to every individual believer at *the hour of Death ;* and *that* hour cannot be very far distant from any of us; while it may be very close at hand in the case of some. This is a matter which deserves to be kept clearly before us at all times, and especially at this time. Let us not perplex ourselves with any speculations about the historical question, which really concerns us but little. The immense variety of opinions which have been expressed on this subject by the most learned writers, is enough to convince such as we are that we have not the necessary faculties for investigations of this class. It may well content us to fall back on the unmistakeable statements of the SPIRIT in connexion with our LORD's ultimate appearance. 'Behold, *I come quickly*[a],' He says; and the words occur in the concluding portion of the Book of Life. As if to give additional emphasis to that great announcement, He repeats, ere He permits His servant John to close the sacred record,— '*Surely I come quickly.*' This is in fact the very last statement of the SPIRIT. The New Testament may be said to conclude with those words.

What then is the Church's office and the believer's duty in this respect? The Church's office is to bring the thought of Judgment to come, vividly before the minds of all her children: to tell them of its terrors, and to warn them at once of its certainty, and of its nearness. She is not faithful unless she makes them feel that this is a strictly private and personal concern; a matter which comes home to the inmost con-

[a] Rev. xxii. 12.

science of every one of them. And it cannot be said that the Church has neglected this duty. The Advent Season is a perpetual record of her faithfulness. May we not add that the Church of England has evinced her own tender care of her children in a very special manner in giving the earliest place she could to the 'comfort of *the Scriptures*,' in connexion with this Doctrine; and reminding us, (as she so earnestly does in this day's Collect,) that thereby we may (GOD helping us,) 'embrace and ever hold fast the blessed hope of everlasting Life?'

Our own duty is gratefully to accept her warning, and gladly to follow her counsel. If we have never yet been methodical and earnest in our study of the Bible, why should we not strive to become so from to-day? Should many words be needed to induce men to embrace their truest good? 'Remember the word unto Thy servant, upon which Thou hast caused me to hope,'—was the exclamation of the Psalmist in his hour of trouble; and can we doubt that the Almighty allowed his plea? Have we not his express testimony in the very next verse,—'This is my comfort in my affliction, for Thy word hath quickened me?'

Third Sunday in Advent.

THE UNEXPECTED MANNER OF CHRIST'S COMING.

St. Matthew xi. 2, 3.

Now when John had heard in the prison the works of Christ, *he sent two of his disciples, and said unto Him, Art Thou He that should come, or do we look for another?*

It has been the subject of considerable discussion what was the Baptist's purpose when He sent two of his disciples to our Lord with this inquiry. Some have supposed that John himself doubted: others, with more reason, have thought that his purpose was to satisfy his disciples. Perhaps a yet more satisfactory explanation of the matter might be suggested. For example, the Baptist, immured in a prison, may have wished for that *confirmation of his own Faith* in our Saviour as the Messiah, which he was sure that our Saviour would instantly afford him. And when all the circumstances of the case are considered, this will perhaps seem the most satisfactory explanation of all.

For it should be borne in mind that the Baptist's Ministry was not certainly of more than one year's duration; and that when it was drawing to its close, our LORD came to him for Baptism, in the manner described by all the Evangelists. Three days after that event, our SAVIOUR departed into Galilee; and for aught that appears to the contrary, neither beheld the face of the other any more. John was immediately thrown into a dungeon; and at the end of two years, was barbarously murdered. The first year of the Baptist's imprisonment had elapsed when the incident recorded in the text took place. Is it extraordinary that he should have desired to ask such a question at such a time? Surely; the wonder would rather have been if he could have endured to linger out all the tedious period of his captivity in the darkness of a dungeon, without once seeking for a ray of Light from Him who is the source of all Light and Glory!

The only subject however which it concerns us to observe for our present purpose is that need was felt of some Testimony which might be for the confirmation of belief, if not for the actual dispersion of doubt, in *some* quarter: and we will not dispute by whom the feeling was entertained. We will but point out that the uncertainty must clearly have arisen out of the strange and unexpected manner of CHRIST's Coming. CHRIST's Coming did not correspond with, it did not come up to, the notions which men had formed to themselves of it. Certain expectations were entertained, and the reality did not altogether correspond with these expectations. This is the point on which we propose now to say a few words.

For it is much to be feared that something of the self-same kind is very apt to befal ourselves; that it may be befalling us even now. Advent has arrived; or rather, the sacred Season is half ended. Are we at all affected by it? Do we make any effort to realize the solemn truths so often brought before us, that behold, our 'King cometh?' that 'the LORD is at hand?' that 'the Judge standeth at the door?' It is to be feared that, in the case of a good many, nothing of the kind takes place. And the reason is plain; namely, because it is hard to persuade ourselves that this *is* 'Advent;' or rather, that 'Advent' is anything more than a mere name. We secretly think that surely when CHRIST shall indeed 'stand at the door and knock,' it will not be in *this* gentle way, in this strange and unexpected manner; speaking by the mouth of His unworthy servant, or using the silent eloquence of the Calendar and Collect, the Epistle and Gospel. We form to ourselves a particular notion of the way in which CHRIST will come to us. We persuade ourselves that His Coming in the way of warning,—the last chance He will give us,—will be under very different circumstances from these.

For instance, one person chooses to assume that the day of his death is far distant; and flatters himself that his warning will take place in a very solemn and affecting manner; in old age, and after the due preparation of illness.

Another person determines that when the Judge is really at the door, He will knock so loudly that conscience shall be *unable* to slumber. He resolves that there shall be a strong pang of entire Repentance on his own side; prompt and hearty forgiveness on the side of GOD.

A third person makes up his mind that it will be in some strange place, and on some out-of-the-way occasion;—not certainly in the Parish Church, or by his own fire-side, and in the regular course of the Advent-Service,—that the voice of warning will come to *him!*

Then, there are persons everywhere who form their notions of what GOD will do for their soul, by what they have heard from other persons that

God has been pleased to do for theirs. It seems not to be believed to any practical purpose that we are very bad judges of this matter: that we are by no means competent to decide *how* God will come to us. We are loth to accept the simple certainty that in our own place, in our own Church, on the well-known day, in the familiar season, by the instrumentality of ordinary human lips, He *does* come, *does* knock, *does* stand at the door. . . . The self-same causes therefore of doubt or uncertainty exist now which existed of old, and which led to the mission of the two disciples. They stood in the very presence of our Saviour, and yet they asked their question. Why was it? Because then, as now, His Coming was not what men had expected. There were no such miracles performed as men hoped. The Forerunner had been bound. Surely, (said they,) Jesus of Nazareth, and John the son of Zacharias, will soon depart, (as indeed they soon did,) and then, where will be the promise of His Coming? Even so, men say *now*. We looked not for this, (they exclaim;) we see no signs; the grace which should have gone before in our hearts is inactive. Advent, Christmas itself, will soon be over. Where then will be the reality of His 'Coming,' of which we heard so much?

However true therefore it may be that CHRIST comes to us in divers manners; however true that He calls to us at divers seasons; the point now insisted on is that He most likely comes to each one of us in the manner we least expect: and further, that one of His seasons of visitation is the present season; one of His manners of coming, the present manner. In the Advent services,—in the words prayed, read, preached throughout this solemn time of Advent,—(O let us be well persuaded of it!),—each is called to repentance, invited to holiness, urged to newness of life. If we disregard the call because, uttered by human lips, it sounds feeble; neglect the visitation because it comes not to us with circumstances of outward awe and peculiar solemnity;—what do we else, (in Scripture phrase,) but 'take offence' at CHRIST's Gospel, and miss that blessing which He pronounced on the opposite characters, on this very occasion, in the hearing of the two Disciples;—'Blessed is he whosoever shall *not* be offended in Me!'

Finally, the convincing signs that it was He indeed, the things which the Disciples were commissioned by our SAVIOUR Himself to go and tell John that they heard and saw, were such as the following: 'The blind receive their sight, and the lame walk, the lepers are cleansed, and the deaf hear, the dead are raised up, and the poor have the Gospel preached to them.' Are we so little acquainted with the wonders of Grace as not to be aware that these marvels are being daily transacted under our very eyes, and therefore are proofs of CHRIST's presence,—to as many at least as have eyes to see and ears to hear,—among us *now*? What else did the cure of Blindness typify but *that* gift which enables a man to discern the way that he should walk in, and to see the wondrous things of GOD's Law? the cure of Dumbness, but that opening of the lips which enables our mouths to shew forth GOD's praise? An ear attentive to the Gospel, feet eager to run in the way of GOD's commandments, a state of death in trespasses and sins, forsaken, or rather escaped from, at the strong call of CHRIST;—all these shew what was meant by miracles performed on the deaf, and the lame, and the youth borne out to burial. These are the *true* Gospel miracles: these are the works which when *we* 'do hear and see' them, are meant to convince us that our SAVIOUR CHRIST is indeed He that 'was to come,' and that we need look for no other: that He hath indeed come; that He is even now in the world; that in this very place, at this very time,—disguised indeed as in the days of the Gospel, yea, unseen as then,—He is making His Advent 'in great Humility' to every one of ourselves.

Let not the strangeness of this matter veil it from us. Rather let us, with a generous effort of Faith, strive to see the mysteries of CHRIST's Religion as they really are; and seek to make the foremost of the Christian seasons, (which is meant to be a preparation as well as a guide to all the rest,) no empty name, but a great reality.

Fourth Sunday in Advent.

CAREFUL FOR NOTHING, BUT IN EVERY THING BY PRAYER.

PHILIPPIANS iv. 6, 7.

Be careful for nothing; but in every thing by prayer and supplication with thanksgiving let your requests be made known unto GOD. *And the peace of* GOD, *which passeth all understanding, shall keep your hearts and minds through* CHRIST JESUS.

THIS is one of those passages in Holy Writ which gather up in a few plain words the substance of many exhortations, and many promises. And why are command and promise here put forth in language so simple? Surely it is because by the help of words like these, (whatever our age, or rank, or opportunities may happen to be,) we have to steer our way across 'the waves of this troublesome world' when the storm lies most heavily upon us. Parts of GOD's Word are dark and mysterious indeed; but those parts do not concern *practice:* whereas the passage before us is meant to be our help and guide in a matter which belongs to the history of every day; informing us how GOD wills that we should act in a case which, as long as life lasts, we know will be one of constant occurrence.

Surely, it was Almighty Love which guided the Apostle to write those words of counsel, 'Be careful for nothing;' for they imply GOD's foresight that many an occasion will arise in the course of a man's life when he will be tempted to be *exceeding* careful. The thing implied is in other words, 'Suffer none of the casualties of life to trouble you *over-much.*' And these are the words of Love. It is as if, foreseeing the terrors of a journey, one were to warn a child how to proceed when those terrors overtook him.

1. Now concerning this command, what we have first to point out is, that it is altogether absolute: 'Be careful for *nothing.*' This is much to be noticed. For all are ready to admit that most of the things which vex and trouble us are not really deserving of the thought and anxiety which we bestow upon them. But then, men always reserve to themselves the right of distressing themselves about some *other* thing. Thus, either disappointment in a cherished scheme of happiness, or continual bodily suffering, or the sight of distress very close at home,

or severe reverses of fortune,—some one of these things is deemed by most men a reasonable ground of 'carefulness.' But the HOLY SPIRIT, speaking by the Apostle, makes no exception whatsoever: 'Be careful for nothing.' As if it were said, 'All that can by possibility befal the sons of men hath been fully foreseen and provided for. Sorrow will sometimes assume dire shapes, assailing thee in unexpected ways and embittering all thy cup. But be thou careful for *nothing*. I have provided for thee a remedy. I have overcome the world.'

What then is to be the Christian's course when he is most severely tried? In everything, he is to let his requests 'be made known unto GOD.' That is, 'prayer and supplication' is the prescribed remedy. The two words come together in other places of Scripture[a]; and though they seem to mean one and the same thing, ancient writers say that the word we translate 'prayer,' means properly the petition offered up for obtaining a blessing; while 'supplication' is the entreaty which we make that we may be released from affliction. And surely, if Love it was which forbade carefulness, it is Love which recommends the cure; so easy to be obtained

[a] As Ephesians vi. 18, and 1 Timothy ii. 1.

that no one, however circumstanced, in the hour of his extremity, need pine for lack of it.

2. This suggests a second remark on the very remarkable wording of the text. It is not simply said, 'In every thing by prayer and supplication let your requests be made known unto GOD:' but it is added,—'*with thanksgiving.*' So then with prayer and supplication are always to be mingled words of thankfulness. Why so? Partly, because GOD loves a thankful spirit: partly, because He has so mingled sweet with bitter, so heaped blessings upon us, so comforted us on every side, that we cannot omit words of 'thanksgiving' without base ingratitude, even amid our deepest affliction. Let the occasion of carefulness be the severest that it may, still should the Psalmist's language be ours,—' Bless the Lord, O my soul, and all that is within me bless His holy Name. Bless the LORD, O my soul, *and forget not all His benefits*[b].'

Now Prayer is a leaning upon the Everlasting Arms; a casting of our whole burthen upon *Him* who invites all that labour and are heavy laden to come and He will give them rest. Prayer is not the mere saying of a collect, or reading of a Psalm; not the mere repetition of

[b] Ps. ciii. 1, 2.

any form of words,—as if it were a charm to drive away evil spirits. Even this is better than nothing, doubtless; but Prayer, properly speaking, is far more than this. It is the desire of the soul made audible. We are directed instead of fretfully entertaining that desire, — locking it up in our bosoms, and brooding over it in silence,—to pour it into the ears of our Heavenly FATHER, who heareth as well as seeth in secret.

3. And this suggests a third remark upon the language of the text; which proves, on inspection, to be brimfull of heavenly teaching. We are not here invited, (as elsewhere we are,) to earnest, unwearied supplication; but, (as one may say,) simply to a transfer of the thing which vexes us, to GOD. 'Let your requests *be made known* unto GOD.' This is a remarkable, as well as an unusual, way of enforcing the duty of Prayer. Instead of distressing ourselves with that which we can neither avert, alter, nor overcome; instead of a fretful, anxious investigation of possibilities and chances; instead even of a restless endeavour to achieve our own deliverance, or to attain the gratification of our wishes in our own way;—instead of all this, we are commanded simply *to make our requests known*

FOURTH SUNDAY IN ADVENT.

to Him in whose Hands are the issues of Life and Death, who orders and governs all things, who shapes all our ends, who bringeth Light out of Darkness, yea, bringeth all things as it pleaseth Him, to pass..... So much then for the manner of our prayer; whereby we are reminded of the pious language which concludes our Morning and Evening Service: 'fulfil now, O LORD, the desires and petitions of Thy servants — *as may be most expedient for them.*' *That* calm committal to GOD of our supposed wants and our most ardent wishes, is the very language of Faith and Hope. It is to make our requests known unto GOD. Not indeed as One who needeth to be told any thing; (for to *Him* the very secrets of our hearts are known;) but as One who is pleased to make *our petitions* the very condition of *His benefits*.

And this, as before observed, is a leaning upon the Everlasting Arms; a staying ourselves upon Him who alone is a sufficient support and stay. It is an admission that we have a Rock, and a Fortress, and a Deliverer, and a place of Refuge,—all which is CHRIST. We put our trust in Him, and we no longer fear what Man can do unto us. We build our nest in Heaven, and grow comparatively careless as to the things of earth.

IN EVERY THING BY PRAYER.

4. For lastly, it is to be observed that not a word is here said about the fulfilment of petitions. Elsewhere, the promise is,—'Whatsoever ye shall ask the FATHER in My Name, He will give it you.' But it is not said so here. The promise made is that Peace,—'the Peace of GOD which passeth all understanding,'—shall take up its abode in the hearts and minds which before were filled with an unreasonable amount of corroding anxiety and care. O the blessed change! and O the blessed promise, which is much stronger in the original than in our English Version. It is declared that the Divine Inmate will take up His abode in our heart and mind, (the seat of our affections, as well as the faculty whereby we think,) and keep His dwelling-place as soldiers keep a garrison. 'The Peace of GOD which passeth all understanding shall *guard* your heart and mind,'—for the Greek word means as much as that. This is the sum of the whole matter. The disturbing Spirit will be driven out, and the Spirit of Peace will enter in its place. This is the great gift which the Prince of Peace hath pledged Himself ever to bestow in answer to prayer... 'Great peace have they which love Thy Law[c],' says the Psalmist. It is

[c] Ps. cxix. 165.

a peculiar sign of a holy life that the heart and mind should be at peace.

Peace then, the Peace of GOD, let us learn above all things, in prayer, to look and long for. More even than the fulfilment of our petitions, let us covet this,—which is surely good for us: whereas we may chance, in our blindness, to ask for that which, if bestowed, would be our very ruin. Thrice happy are we in the promise that our affections shall thus become sanctified, our very reasonings about the present, past, and future rendered calm and holy! Well may such a precious gift be made the subject of many a collect, many an ejaculation, many a solemn benediction in the Prayer-Book! How is that word (Peace) the very key-note of the Gospel also,—the constant theme of the Spirit!... The Angels, on the night when CHRIST was born, proclaimed, 'On earth, '*Peace!*' When He was about to leave the world, this was the legacy which He bequeathed to His Church,—'*Peace* I leave with you: *My Peace* I give unto you.' And when He rose from death, 'Peace' was the first word which the ten Apostles heard His blessed lips pronounce. He said,—'*Peace* be with you!'

Christmas-Day.

THE WORD MADE FLESH.

St. John i. 14.

The Word *was made flesh, and dwelt among us.*

Christmas-Day, as it is the foremost of our great Christian Festivals, so is it the foundation of all the others also. On the Incarnation, (or the Coming of Jesus Christ in the flesh,) is built the entire fabric of our hopes as Christian men. The two Sacraments of the Gospel grow out of it, and are altogether indebted to it for their meaning, force, and value. To establish this great doctrine, St. John declares that he wrote his Gospel[a]; and the purpose of the whole New Testament is clearly no other. On our acceptance or rejection of it, our eternal happiness may be truly said to depend. Let us then, at this time, seek to bend our thoughts dutifully on this solemn subject. The contemplation of a doctrine may not be so entertaining to the mind, as the discussion of a history; or so affecting to

[a] St. John xx. 31.

the heart as an appeal directly made to the feelings; but it is at our peril that we turn away with impatience from the great doctrines of Religion when in the course of the Sacred Year they are brought before our notice. It is quite monstrous that we should deem it a weariness to be reminded of the Rock whereon we are built; while it is not to be believed that we can view with unconcern the great 'mystery of Godliness,' (as the Apostle terms it,)—'GOD manifest in the Flesh[b].'

'In the beginning was THE WORD,' says the beloved disciple: by that Name, in conformity with the approved tradition of his people, denoting the Only-Begotten SON. He is called 'THE WORD,' because as words are the very image of the thoughts of our minds, so is the Only-Begotten SON 'the express Image' of the Eternal FATHER. He was *uttered* by the FATHER, somewhat as a word is uttered from the mind: and He 'declared' the FATHER,—who is accordingly said 'in these last days' to have '*spoken* unto us by His SON[c].' '*With* GOD' from all eternity, and Himself very GOD, 'all things were made by Him; and without Him was not anything made that was made.' Yet this was

[b] 1 Tim. iii. 16.   [c] Heb. i. 2.

He who in the fulness of time was 'made flesh.' 'THE WORD,' (says St. John,) 'was made flesh, and dwelt among us:' that is, He was made Man, and in the tabernacle of our common Human Nature was content to make His dwelling. Accordingly, the great truth which we now have to contemplate is the wondrous humiliation of the Second Person in the glorious Trinity, who, being in the form of GOD, thus 'made Himself of no reputation, and took upon Him the form of a servant, and was made in the likeness of man.' We have to remind ourselves of the unspeakable mercy, the wondrous love, of Him who, forsaking the highest Heaven where He dwelt in Light unapproachable, visited this lower world for so amazing a purpose as to become a partaker of our fallen nature. By taking Manhood into eternal union with His own Godhead, He provided a means for making us partakers of His triumph over Sin and Death; for restoring us to that condition from which our first Parents fell. He became, in short, *the new Man,*— 'the Second Adam,' — the beginning of the New Creation. He was to make a fresh beginning of Mankind. As in Adam all had died, so in Him were all to be made alive. Our first father naturally begat an offspring in his own likeness: but the second Father of Mankind was spiritually to beget a new and heavenly race, 'created anew in grace, and therein abiding, and multiplying through all nations and ages to the glory of GOD.'

The more we think of this great wonder, the more does the strangeness of it seem to grow upon us. Before the event took place, *who* could have imagined the method which GOD would adopt to fulfil His Divine promise and most gracious purpose? MESSIAH was to be the seed of the Woman: yet had His goings forth been from of old, from everlasting[d]; and His generation, who was to declare[e]? He was to come forth out of the stem of Jesse[f]: yet was He to grow up as a root out of a dry ground, despised and rejected of men[g]. He was to be 'GOD with us[h]:' yet was He to be 'a worm and no man[i].' How could these things be?

The event came about secretly and silently; and every contradiction was reconciled by a single miracle of Divine Love. Of the substance of the Blessed Virgin, by the influence of the HOLY SPIRIT, was born the Man, CHRIST JESUS; and that wonderfully created Manhood,—that

[d] Micah v. 2. [e] Is. liii. 8. [f] Is. xi. 1.
[g] Is. liii. 2, 3. [h] Is. vii. 14: viii. 10. [i] Ps. xxii. 6.

Human Soul and that Human Body,—was taken into mysterious union with the GODHEAD. Mysterious union indeed! for the Second Person in the Blessed Trinity, in thus taking the Manhood into GOD, retained His GODhead and His Manhood, each distinct and entire; yet of two was made *One Person*. The union of soul and body in man may help us to understand how GOD and Man are one CHRIST: but it is only an illustration of that unrivalled mystery. The differences of the two cases are numerous. Body and soul are alike created: but GOD is uncreate. The soul influences the body, and the body the soul: but the Human Nature does not affect the Divine, in CHRIST's Person. Soul and body may be disunited: but the Manhood may never more be severed from the GODhead in the One Person of CHRIST. The GODhead and Manhood were not for an instant severed, even in death, in His Divine Person. Lastly, He has carried our glorified Human Nature with Him into the highest Heaven. And the design of all this was that He might prepare a place for those who love Him; that He might enable them to behold the glory which He had with His FATHER before the World was[k]; that our fallen race might regain

[k] St. John xvii. 24, 5.

that happiness which had been forfeited by the sin of our first Parents.

We shall do well to gaze steadily at this great mystery, until the wonder of it really strike us; for we perceive not all that we are capable of perceiving in it, at first. It should be noticed that our SAVIOUR did not take upon Himself the nature of Adam *before* the fall; but it was our *fallen* nature that He bore,—the likeness, (not the reality, GOD forbid! but the *likeness*) of our *sinful* nature[1]. And the reason of His stooping so wondrous low was, that we might not 'have an High-Priest which cannot be touched with the feeling of our infirmities; but was in all points tempted like as we are, yet without sin[m].'

This was the first stage of that dispensation to which all prophecy, and all type, had been pointing for four thousand years. Everything everywhere had been tending to this. The history of GOD's chosen people, the provisions of the Mosaic Law, the very rise and fall of the great empires of the world,—all had been preparing the way for the Coming of CHRIST in the flesh. And when at last He came, though Man gave little heed to the event, how much of rapture is it found to have supplied to all the heavenly

[1] Rom. viii. 3.   [m] Heb. iv. 15.

host! The Angels sing carols in the sky: they look into the Work of Redemption with curiosity, awe, and wonder[n]: they are brought into closest brotherhood with that race which CHRIST came to save[o]: they are for ever ascending and descending upon the Son of Man[p]!

Let these, or the like of these, be our Christmas thoughts. They will not be found enemies to our Christian joy,—to that social happiness which belongs to the present season. Well may we rejoice on 'the Birth-Day of CHRIST,' for it is the birth-day of all our hopes likewise: but let our rejoicing be the rejoicing of Christian men; our festivity, let it be *that* of 'the sons of GOD,' and heirs of future glory. Between thoughtless gluttony, and boisterous mirth, and frivolous amusements, on the one hand,—gloom, and severity, and moroseness, on the other,—there is surely a mighty difference. Both alike dishonour the season, although in vastly different ways. *How* often must it be repeated that Religion alters none of the relations of life, though it sanctifies them all? Our duties and our joys, our private pursuits and our social pleasures, will yet continue; but they will be ennobled and hallowed by being mixed up with the thought of

---

[n] 1 St. Pet. i. 12.   [o] St. Luke xv. 10.   [p] St. John i. 51.

Him who ought to be the End of each : of Him who is the Author of our life, the well-spring of our happiness : of Him who came as at this time, in the meekness and helplessness of infancy, to be our SAVIOUR; but who, in the Last Day, will come in His awful Majesty to be our Judge.

The Sunday after Christmas-Day.

NO ROOM FOR CHRIST.

St. Luke ii. 7.

There was no room for them in the Inn.

It is a striking and instructive fact that the collect for Christmas-day is simply *repeated* on this, the sunday after Christmas-day. The reason is plain. Our Lord's Incarnation is so great a doctrine,—Christ's Coming in the flesh is so important an event,—that the Church would have us fix our hearts upon it day by day for a week and more; in order that so she may assure herself that the only foundation which can be laid,—*has been* duly laid; that the corner-stone of Man's Salvation occupies its due place in that building which every following sunday helps to build up, and make glorious.

The words of the text in like manner are meant to carry our thoughts back to the birth of Christ. They remind us in the most striking manner of the 'great humility' in which, as at this time, He deigned 'to visit us.' Let us recal, in a few words, what happened; in order that we may fill our minds with the thoughts which the collect for the sunday after Christmas brings back.

It was so contrived by the providence of GOD, that when the time came for CHRIST's Birth, there went forth a decree from Cæsar Augustus that all the world should be taxed; and in consequence of this order, Joseph, the husband of the Blessed Virgin, (who was the companion of his journey,) came up from Nazareth in Galilee to Bethlehem in Judæa, (for to Bethlehem they belonged,) to be taxed or enrolled *there*.

Now it seems when this holy pair reached Bethlehem, there were so many other persons pressing into 'the City of David' for the same purpose with themselves, that the Inn was full. We cannot but picture these humble persons asking the favour of a lodging; and we feel in our degree both amazed and shocked to remember how the Virgin Mother, in her hour of greatest need, was informed that she might not obtain what she sought. There was 'no room' for them. Some one must have come forth, and told them so. Whereupon, we see them withdrawing to that humbler spot where the ox and the ass found a shelter, and were provided with food. *There* the Virgin brought into the world her first-born and her only Child,—'wrapped Him in swaddling-clothes, and laid Him in a manger.' ... Such is the history of the Birth of CHRIST. It was in this manner that the Eternal SON,—the WORD, who 'was in the beginning with GOD,' and who 'was GOD,'—was born into the World.

Every part of this wonderful history supplies a great lesson: but above all, we seem to need a solemn warning against the danger which the people of Bethlehem incurred;—namely, of being so bent on the things of this life,—its business or its pleasures,—as to exclude CHRIST Himself from our society, when He comes among us and claims to be admitted. The SAVIOUR of the World was born in a manger because there was *no room for Him* in the Inn; and we shall do well to consider in how many ways we seem prone to be guilty of shewing by our actions that neither can *we* find room for Him. Thus, who does not know what it is to be so very busy as to fancy that he cannot find time for daily prayer? or again, how often have we suffered whole days to go by,—*weeks*, it may be,—without ever finding time to study a portion of GOD's Word? Surely, this is to banish our LORD from among us, on the plea that we cannot make room for Him! We may not confess that this is the reason. But if we ask ourselves *how* it has come to pass that lately we have been so unfrequent in prayer, such careless readers of the Gospel, and the like,—we shall probably have but one answer to render. It will be, in the main, that we have not been able to *find room* for Him whom we confess to be our greatest good, and whom we declare to be our greatest joy. It may not perhaps be that we have been *too busy;* but the effect produced may be exactly the same, though the cause may be quite different: for example, we may have been too happy, or too sad: we may have been too anxious, or too entirely free from care: too well, or (as we fancied) too ill, to pray, read, think upon GOD. . . . Surely, in all such cases, we say (as the men of Bethlehem did of old) 'we have no room for Him!' *They* said it of their *Inn*. *We* say it of our *hearts*.

This may be done in many ways besides those already mentioned. Alas, in how many ways is it done daily! Those who are engaged in Trade know well what it is, every now and then, to be tempted to overlook the duty of strict honesty. They say to themselves,—'In matters of this kind, one cannot afford to obey the strict law of the Gospel.' Ah, what is this but to say,—'One cannot afford room for CHRIST?' Is it so indeed? Shall He, every now and then, be banished from our Trade,—as if it had been found out that there is 'no room for CHRIST' in the market? ... The young and thoughtless are prone to think that it will be high time to regulate their lives by GOD's Word when they are older, sadder, steadier. What? Is He then such an intruder upon our joys,—is the thought of Him such a burthen for youth,—that it should be assumed that neither in early life nor in happy hours there can be found any room for *Him?* .. Just so, though for an opposite reason, labouring folk have been known to be so taken up with the cares of this sad life, that they put off for a day which may never come at all, the care of their immortal souls,—thoughts of Death, of Judgment, and of CHRIST. Can a lowly estate be supposed to have no room for Him? It cannot be! At every time, and in every place,—at all ages, and in all stations,—there must be room for *Him*, without whom nothing is strong, nothing holy.

A very few words will suffice to remind you how large is the warning which we are seeking to gather from the text.—In the disposal of money, how many persons find room for everything and everybody but *Him* who is the Author and Giver of it all! For CHRIST's service they set apart nothing.—Others shun the Sacrament of CHRIST's Body and Blood, even at this solemn season; shewing thereby that they cannot make room in their hearts for Him who comes to them in that blessed mystery: that they are careless, in short, whether they end the year with CHRIST, or *without* Him!

For indeed, though thoughts like these can scarcely ever be mistimed,—yet, how solemnly do they come home to us at *this* season; and on this, the last sunday of the year! *He* must be made of very rugged stuff indeed to whom the end of the year does not bring a harvest of solemn thoughts. Very happy is he, if no bitter regrets mingle with the memory of the past. Very unhappy, (or rather, very forgetful,) if he cannot recal a thousand undeserved blessings,—countless mercies which have been heaped upon him throughout the days which are fled; and for which he desires to falter forth his praises at the throne of Grace, before the year which brought them has quite departed. How many days of peace, and health, and pleasure! How many hours of sunshine, both inward and outward! How many acts of human kindness enjoyed!

How many consolations, secret and sacred, but not the less real, which call for grateful remembrance *now!*

Heavy affliction may have fallen to the lot of some of us. It cannot be needful to exhort one another to the recollection of that which is never for a moment absent from the memory. But it may be right to insist on the claims of Sorrow to a calm and humble review at the close of the year. The Hand of Love was doubtless clearly discerned throughout. The precious memory of the Past yet remains. Of nothing can we afford to be unmindful.

And the season brings with it solemn thoughts about ourselves. Pass a few short years, and *we* also shall be missed from our accustomed place. Now, to die, and to be with CHRIST, are one and the same thing. But how shall we face *Him* in Heaven, for whom we found *no room* on Earth? How dwell eternally with Him, whom *here* we looked upon as an intruder on our joys? . . . Shall we not, on a day like this, call ourselves to exact account, and build ourselves up with godly resolutions, and pray for strength to keep them too? . . . 'My soul!' (let us say,) 'we have many a time neglected His sweet service because we fancied that our health or our engagements, our pleasures or our anxieties, afforded no room for Him. We will do so no longer. Henceforth, we will watch ourselves more closely. When we are hurried, and inclined to omit our morning devotions, we will ask ourselves,—What! no room for CHRIST? At night, when we are weary, and tempted to leave our souls uncared for, we will still ask ourselves,—What! no room for CHRIST? In our worldly calling, whatever it may happen to be, we will be jealous for His honour; and often inquire,—Am I *making room* in all this, for *Him?* At our meals, in our friendships, during our studies, amid our pleasures; abroad, and at home; when we walk by ourselves, or when many are with us; in the crowded room, and when we lie awake at night; many a time, O my soul! let us ask ourselves the question. And the test of our state, the sign that we are not forsaken, shall be that we delight in the thought of His goodness,—rejoice above all things in His presence,—can always, let what will betide, can *always find room for Him.*'

The Epiphany.

THE BIRTH OF CHRIST GLORIOUS.

Isaiah lx. 1.

Arise, shine, for thy Light is come, and the Glory of the Lord *is risen upon thee.*

At the last Review of the Book of Common Prayer, (in 1662,) it was thought advisable to add the explanation of the names of certain Festivals of the Church. 'Epiphany' is one of the names so explained: and in consequence, we never turn the pages of the Prayer-Book, without being reminded that on that festival, the Church celebrates *the Manifestation of* Christ *to the Gentiles.* Out of this announcement, certain considerations seem naturally to arise, which it may be worth while to set forth somewhat in detail.

The great Humility, in which our Lord and Saviour Jesus Christ, as at this time, 'deigned to visit us,' is indeed a remarkable circumstance; so remarkable, that it may well be dwelt upon, and made much of, by mankind.

THE EPIPHANY.

To the humblest of our Brethren, the circumstances under which the Holy Babe was born at Bethlehem,—the station of society to which His Blessed Mother and her wedded protector belonged at Nazareth,—may well prove a source of consolation unspeakable. Yet is it much to be feared that one aspect of this wondrous history is dwelt upon to the exclusion of another, which it equally concerns us to keep steadily in view. We must beware how we make too free with our CREATOR, REDEEMER, JUDGE. We may not presume on His unspeakable condescension; and treat the narrative of His Holy Birth,—or Life,—or Death, with vulgar familiarity, because for our sakes He made Himself very poor. To speak of His having been born 'in a stable,' and being the son of 'a carpenter;' to say that He 'worked at the trade of His reputed Father;' and that He was 'a houseless wanderer;' and that He was attended by 'twelve poor fishermen:'—sayings of this kind, though some of them may perhaps be true; and *all* of them perhaps are true *in a certain sense*,—are yet, one and all, liable to grave objections, when they are dwelt upon *exclusively;* and supposed to represent *the whole* of the matter. We venture, by way of contrast, to state the opposite side of the case: to say a few words concerning our Blessed SAVIOUR's Birth, and Life, and Death, as we think the sacred story may, *with equal truth,* and *far more profitably,* be considered.

And first, to dwell on the estate of Poverty, as if it were in itself a kind of disgrace, is surely a somewhat unchristian proceeding; and shews a wondrous wrong estimate of that condition which CHRIST Himself pronounced 'blessed.' Neither ignorance, nor stupidity, nor vulgar sentiments, nor coarse expressions, nor low habits, nor filth, nor rags,—none of these things, (as every one who loves the poor knows very well,) *none* of these are the *necessary* adjuncts of Poverty. Exceeding munificence; perfect honesty; the very keenest sense of whatsoever things are true, honest, just, pure, lovely, of good report; great proficiency in what GOD, speaking by the mouth of the wisest of mankind, calls *wisdom,*—(and we may suppose that the Author of Wisdom knows more about this matter than ourselves;) added to *the best* natural gifts:—all these things are observed to be quite *consistent* with Poverty. We do not, of course, say that they are observed always to attend it: nothing of the kind. But they are *not inconsistent* with it.—And thus much concerning the station in society to which

Joseph and the Blessed Virgin, (our LORD's reputed Parents,) belonged. Let us next think of the Nativity; regarding it with the eyes of Faith and Love,—not in the cold carnal spirit which can see no splendour except in ermine; no nobility except in wealth.

The lowly pair, on reaching Bethlehem, find that there is 'no room for them in the Inn.' We have already dwelt on the grievous circumstance, in a separate sermon. Accordingly, they withdrew to that humbler enclosure where the cattle were provided with a shelter and with food. There, in all the helplessness of infancy, the Divine Babe was laid,—surrounded, (like Adam in Paradise,) by the brute creation: and there, (as painters love to remind us,) the ox will have known his Owner, and the ass his Master's crib, —though Israel did not know; though GOD's people did not consider[a].

Meanwhile, such a glorious spectacle as was never before revealed to mortal eyes, is passing in the immediate neighbourhood. Shepherds, who are keeping watch over their flocks by night, behold the Angel of the LORD suddenly stand before them,—girt about with that wondrous Glory which belongs to the Divine Presence.

[a] Is. i. 3.

After announcing to these lowly swains the SAVIOUR's Birth,—suddenly, there is seen 'with the Angel a multitude of the heavenly host, praising GOD, and saying,—Glory to GOD in the highest, and on earth Peace, good will towards men[b]!' It was the Birth-day of the New Creation, and the Morning-stars must needs again sing together: all the Sons of GOD must needs again shout for joy[c].

The Holy Family had come up to 'the city of David,' to be enrolled, in obedience to the Imperial edict; and lo, when they are asked by the appointed officer concerning their descent, they make answer that they derive their birth by *a double line* from King David himself! That little Babe which slumbers on His Mother's pure breast, is the offspring of a long line of Kings. Poor, He is indeed. The family has declined since the day of Zerubbabel, ('him of the dispersion of Babylon,' as his name implies;) but they retain the written record of their lofty origin.—Can a prouder tale have been told by any?

The special event of to-day, is the adoration of the Wise Men, or, (as they are called in the Gospel,) *the Magi.* Eastern sages were they, of

---

[b] St Luke ii. 8—14   [c] Job xxxviii. 7.

priestly and of royal race; to whom it had been revealed in a far country that the splendid meteor which they beheld in Heaven betokened the Birth of MESSIAH,—'the Desire of all nations,'—'the King of the Jews.' It conducted them from their own Land to Jerusalem; and lo, on their arrival, they inquire where the newly-born King is to be found? The interview with which pictures have made us familiar from our infancy, followed. And how truly royal must the scene have been! Those noble strangers, arrived from the land of gold and frankincense and myrrh, bowing down before the Infant King with their costly gifts; while His Blessed Mother and Joseph look on with wonder and adoration; and ask themselves whereto all this will grow?

It shall suffice to have thus dwelt on some of the chief events of the Nativity. Let it not be forgotten that this mysterious Birth was heralded by the Angel Gabriel: that the spiritual Elijah had already come 'to prepare His way:' and that now, while the Infant CHRIST withdraws into Egypt, He leaves at Bethlehem a band of infant martyrs behind Him. Let it be observed that holy Simeon has poured out his burning hymn of prophecy, at His presentation in the Temple; while aged Anna has borne prophetic witness to

His Advent, also. After which, it will probably be admitted that the Birth of CHRIST was indeed an event of much splendour; and felt, that it may not be spoken of as an obscure or an inglorious transaction.

And to dismiss the subject, we would observe that the real *earthly* dignity which is found to have attended our Blessed SAVIOUR's Life and Death, is far too considerable to admit of being overlooked. A houseless and homeless portion, the Son of Man did indeed choose for Himself: to suffering and hardship, pain and privation, He was indeed no stranger: yet surely, when He traversed the Land which by traversing He made Holy, attended by an adoring crowd,—waited upon by the Twelve and the Seventy,—ministered to by the loving female hearts whose names are written in the Book of Life,—there was something even of state in His humble outward Life! We will not here dwell on the long line of Prophets,—all pointing steadily to His Coming: the many foreshadowings of the days of MESSIAH by Psalms, and Types, and Histories:—of all this, we now say not a word. Nor do we call attention to His astounding miracles,—the stilling of the storm, the feeding of the five thousand, the calling of Lazarus, three days buried, from the grave. No, nor will we speak of the Angels 'ascending and descending upon the Son of Man[d],' at His Temptation, His Agony, His Resurrection, His Ascension into Heaven. No. We are content now to discourse of His outward and visible honours. Anointed to His burial with precious odours,—witnessed to, during his Passion, by so many of His very enemies,—confessed by the darkened Sun, and rocking Earth, and opened graves,—and finally laid in the rich man's new tomb, where none had ever been laid before:—was not the Death and Burial of our SAVIOUR rescued, by its very outward dignity, from the risk of contemptuous notice? Let it not at least be said that *we*, His disciples, make too free with what concerns Him so nearly; and overlook the Majesty and the Glory which attended Him from the cradle to the grave.

[d] St. John i. 51.

The First Sunday after the Epiphany.

THE WISDOM OF LITTLE ONES.

St. Luke ii. 46, 47.

It came to pass, that after three days they found Him in the Temple, sitting in the midst of the Doctors, both hearing them, and asking them questions. And all that heard Him were astonished at His understanding and answers.

The Epiphany, or Manifestation of Christ, was effected partly by a Star, which brought Wise Men from the East to worship Him: partly, by a Voice from Heaven, which proclaimed Him to be the Beloved Son of God: partly, by the wisdom He displayed in His questioning with the Doctors, when twelve years old: partly, by His miracles. Accordingly, we find all these things brought into prominent notice in the Gospels, or in the Lessons, for this solemn season. On the Feast of the Epiphany itself, the Star, the Voice, and the 'beginning of miracles,' come before us. On this, the first sunday after the Epiphany, our attention is invited to that memorable transaction with the Doctors in the Temple which St. Luke alone records, and which is the only incident related of our Blessed SAVIOUR from the season of Infancy until the period when His Ministry commenced.

It seems impossible to dwell attentively on any of the events of our LORD's Life, without being made sensible at once of their exceeding beauty; and of our own very limited knowledge of the Divine Being to whom they relate. Thus, the incident which is specially brought before our notice to-day cannot but perplex, even while it so exceedingly delights us. Let us first briefly call to mind the event itself, as it stands recorded in St. Luke's Gospel.

After informing us that 'the Child grew, and waxed strong in Spirit, filled with Wisdom; and the grace of GOD. was upon Him;'—and after stating that 'His Parents went to Jerusalem every year at the Feast of the Passover;'—the Evangelist proceeds to relate how, at the age of Twelve years, the SAVIOUR went with them. The Days of the Feast being ended, the holy pair prepared to return into Galilee; and had got to the end of their first day's journey, before they discovered that the youthful JESUS was not with them. Such a circumstance seems to us extraordinary, even with the Evangelist's explanation; namely, that Joseph and Mary supposed the adorable Being who stood towards them in the relation of a Son, to be 'in the company,'—that is, to be travelling with them, but to have joined Himself to the more immediate society of some of 'their kinsfolk and acquaintance.' This, however, is only one of the many instances where the scanty amount of our information is the true cause of our perplexity. Joseph and Mary returned to Jerusalem; and on the third day, (which is ever the day of relief in Holy Scripture,) they find our SAVIOUR 'in the Temple, sitting in the midst of the Doctors, both hearing them and asking them questions.' In reply to the Virgin's amazed inquiry, 'Son, why hast Thou thus dealt with us? behold Thy Father and I have sought Thee sorrowing,'—our SAVIOUR calmly reminds them that a long and sorrowful *search* for Him ought to have been unnecessary; that they had found Him where a Son may reasonably be looked for, and even expected to be found; namely, *in His Father's House:* (for so the words should probably be translated). In which saying of our Blessed LORD, the contrast which His words present to those of His Virgin

Mother, is very striking. 'Thy Father and I,'—she had said; and, according to the Jewish method of speech, she spoke advisedly and well. Yet could Joseph in none but a legal sense be called the *Father* of JESUS CHRIST: and of this, He seems to remind them both. 'How is it that ye sought Me? Did ye not know that I ought to be,' (or 'must needs be,') 'in My FATHER'S House? .... And they understood not the saying which He spake unto them.'

St. Luke adds,—' And He went down with them, and came to Nazareth, and was subject unto them: but His Mother kept all these sayings in her heart.' The most striking statement of all, follows;—' And JESUS increased in wisdom and stature, and in favour with GOD and Man.'

Thus are we reminded, and in the most striking manner, of the truth of our Divine LORD's human nature,—very Man as well as very GOD. He submitted to the ordinary laws of growth; both of Mind, and Body. *That* sinless Temple of fallen Humanity in which He was divinely pleased to dwell, went through every stage of developement, from helpless infancy to robust manhood. His pure Mind increased in power, from year to year; while by diligent study, He added to its stores of acquired knowledge... We stand upon the edge of a great and inscrutable mystery while we thus speak; for the union of the Two Natures in the One Person of CHRIST is what we may not hope *to understand.* Quite safe, however, while we keep close to the inspired record of the Evangelist, we should not fail to observe that He whom St. Luke describes as '*filled* with Wisdom,' is also related to have '*increased* in Wisdom;' and indeed to have given astonishing proofs both of His natural powers, and of His acquired proficiency, when in the Temple He sat in the midst of the learned Doctors of Jerusalem; 'both hearing them, and asking them questions.'

And how can we read this statement without feeling our heart burn within us, at the thought of such a questioning on the part of our REDEEMER while yet a little child? How assiduous again must His previous studies have been, to have enabled Him, at such a tender age, to solve the curious doubts of men so deeply versed in sacred lore as these learned Rabbis of Jerusalem! For if His 'both hearing them, and asking them questions,' reveals Him as *a Learner* on this occasion, the astonishment which He is said to have created by ' His *understanding* and *answers,*' is a sufficient proof that He was called upon to become *their Teacher*, in turn: and we are reminded of that saying of the Psalmist, (which seems indeed to supply a clue to what we most desire to know in connexion with this subject,)—' I have more understanding than My teachers, *for Thy Testimonies are My study*[a].' The Book of God's Law must have been alike in our Saviour's youthful hands, and in His heart. Not only must He have talked of it when He sat in the House, and when He walked by the way, and when He lay down, and when He rose up[b]; but it must have been the constant subject of His studies likewise.... To have touched slightly on such a matter, shall suffice. We forbear to press the speculations which so naturally arise when it is remembered that the Holy One was reading in every page about Himself; (for Christ is declared to be ' the end of the Law[c]:')—all Types,—all Histories,—all Prophecies, — all Psalms,—pointing silently to *Him;* 'the Spirit of Christ' which was in their blessed authors 'testifying beforehand the sufferings of Christ, and the glory that should follow[d].'

The entire spectacle thus set before us, brings to mind that those whom Christ calls ' little

[a] Ps. cxix. 99.
[b] Deut. vi. 6, 7.
[c] Rom. x. 4.
[d] 1 St. Pet. i. 11.

ones,'—(which are not so much 'children in understanding,' as 'in malice[e],')—practically are ever found to be wiser than the worldly wise; the men whom the same SAVIOUR calls 'the children of this world[f].' They have a peculiar wisdom of their own; a kind of divine instinct, whereby they escape the snares which entangle subtler wits; see through the doubts, which yet they cannot solve; and find their way out of difficulties, which are daily baffling the more ingenious. CHRIST's little ones walk amid dangers, but it is as if a hedge were made about them[g]. They go unharmed upon 'the young lion and the dragon:' they are delivered 'from the snare of the hunter, and from the noisome pestilence:' 'a thousand fall beside them, and ten thousand at their right hand, but it comes not nigh *them*[h].' . . . All must have been struck, at some time or other, with the truth of what we are saying; and felt even tempted to envy CHRIST's 'little ones' their security.

The wisdom of these men, (for 'wisdom' theirs is, though the worldly-wise deny it, and are ever inclined to call it 'foolishness' instead;)—this wisdom of CHRIST's little ones, we say, is not to be

[e] 1 Cor. xiv. 20.
[g] St. Luke xvi. 8.
[f] Job i. 10.
[h] Ps. xci. 13, 3, 7.

learnt in the crowded thoroughfare of life, nor indeed in any human school. It comes 'from above[1];' and betrays its heavenly origin in a thousand ways. One great principle, (the Love of GOD,) is with the little ones of whom we speak, the fruitful source of almost every action.

Perfect truth, and rigid honesty, are their only guides. They affect not to be possessed of wisdom: deeply convinced on the contrary, that they lack it, they 'ask of GOD, who giveth to all men liberally, and upbraideth not[k].' They are *men of prayer*. . . . With human learning they have, or seem to have, but very slender acquaintance. They are not familiar with many books. One only Book, (with which, however, they are thoroughly familiar,) contains their rule of life; but that book is—*the best.*

GOD give us the mind of 'little ones' in the hour of doubt, the hour of trial! GOD grant us that while 'in understanding' we seek to be 'men,' we may above all things prize 'the Wisdom that is from above,'—*that,* namely, which St. James describes as 'first pure, then peaceable, gentle, and easy to be intreated, full of mercy and good fruits, without partiality and without hypocrisy[l].'

[1] St. James iii. 17.   [k] St. James i. 5.   [l] St. James iii. 17.

The Second Sunday after the Epiphany.

THE MIRACLE AT CANA OF GALILEE.

St. John ii. 1.

There was a marriage at Cana of Galilee.

THESE words introduce the account of our SAVIOUR's first recorded miracle, which forms the subject of this day's Gospel. The miracle of the water made wine is brought before us at this season, because it is one of the three great Epiphanies, or *Manifestations* of CHRIST. To the Gentiles, He was manifested by a Star: to the people, at His Baptism, by a voice from Heaven: to His Disciples, He manifested forth His Glory by the present miracle. Accordingly, all these three events come to view on the Feast of the Epiphany itself. The last, which obtains repeated notice to-day, we should consider a little in detail.

While our LORD and His Disciples are said to have been '*invited*' to this marriage, it is related that the Mother of JESUS '*was there.*' The difference of expression deserves notice. Coupled with all that follows, (the words she addressed to our LORD, and the directions she gave to the servants,) it creates a suspicion that the Blessed

SECOND SUNDAY AFTER THE EPIPHANY.

Virgin was in the house of some near relative; and that the miracle which we are about to consider graced the marriage of one of her kinsfolk. . . . For whatever reason, the want of Wine, as soon as it was discovered, seems to have been made known to *her*. Her remedy we find was to appeal to her Divine Son. Not that her words, as they stand, contain a request; but they certainly *imply* one. Nay more, they amount to a command; for when a Mother makes a request to her son, she does virtually lay a command upon him. 'They have no wine,' must have meant,—' Therefore do *Thou* supply their need.' And *that* is why our LORD addressed to her who spoke, those words of rebuke: 'Woman, what have I to do with thee? Mine hour is not yet come.'

The mode of address, ('Woman,') was of course respectful and affectionate. We find our expiring REDEEMER so addressing the same Mother, from the Cross. But 'What have I to do with thee?' was the language of *reproof*. And why? Because a mere woman was here seeking to control GOD. The rights, even of a Mother, could not extend so far: rather was it here entirely out of place. 'What have *I* to do with *thee?*' The question, so considered, is unanswerable; and scarcely seems to require explanation. The HOLY ONE disclaims His Mother's control, the instant that it becomes necessary to vindicate His Divine Nature;—'very GOD, as well as very Man.'

And the words which follow, ('Mine hour is not yet come,') are most probably an intimation that *when He saw fit,* He would work: which may be the reason why the Virgin said unto the servants, 'Whatsoever He saith unto you, do it;' —as if understanding, even from His discouraging reply, that it was His gracious intention to fulfil the desire and petition of His servant, not only *as* might be most expedient for her, but also *when* the proper time should arrive. . . . And here let us pause to point out that it is no proof whatever that our prayers will not be answered, because they are not answered immediately. Our Divine LORD could make His own Mother wait.

To proceed: 'There were set there six waterpots of stone, after the manner of the purifying of the Jews.'—St. John explains the Jewish practice of washing before meals, because he wrote his Gospel at a distance from the Holy Land. Here then were six large vessels which had been used for this purpose. Our LORD, at last, bids the servants fill those large vessels with Water. Now this was, seemingly, a very useless proceeding; certainly not the right way, to all human appearance, of remedying the want of Wine. But what signifies the unpromising earthly appearance, when GOD commands? 'Hath He said, and shall He not do it?' O my soul, in our hour of greatest need, we will remember that the Church says unto us, as *then* the Blessed Virgin said unto the Servants,—' *Whatsoever He saith unto you,* do it!' We will ask no questions; but only obey! *That* is the counsel which is sure to guide us to blessedness at last.

JESUS said,—' Draw out now, and bear unto the governor of the Feast. And they bare it.' The person here spoken of, had the entire management of the Festival; hence, ' the water made wine' is first conveyed to *his* lips. He is surprised at its wondrous goodness. It is not of the same quality as the wine they have been hitherto drinking. There is no mistaking the one for the other. At the same time he has no idea whence the new supply has come. He thinks that, surely, it must all be a device of the Bridegroom: a graceful specimen of hospitality; so rare, indeed, as to be unknown. for who, when men are satisfied and all but gone, thinks of producing something better still, (if such there be,) that he has? It is against reason. We bring forth our *best* at once. Not only in respect of meat and drink, but in respect of manner, feature, sentiment, we seek to shew our best, *first*. We fall away on trial. When better known, we set forth in each respect ' that which is worse.' But what said the man who tasted the cup which *He* had filled whose ways are not Man's ways, and who doeth all things *well?* He calls the Bridegroom; and before all the guests, pays him a compliment which belongs to *another* Bridegroom, (even to Him who took for His Spouse the Church,) and who then received the speaker's unintended homage from a distance, and in silence. 'Every man at the beginning doth set forth good wine; and when men have well drunk, then, that which is worse. But *Thou* hast kept *the good wine until now!*'

This is the end of the history of *that* which St. John calls 'the beginning of miracles;' the miracle whereby JESUS first 'manifested forth His Glory;' and by reason of which, ' His Disciples believed on Him.' . . . How does it set forth the blessedness of having His presence among us; the blessedness of having *Him* for a guest! . . . How does it teach us again that the events of our daily life are not too lowly, nor too earthly, nor too private, to share His notice; to engage His sympathy; to claim His presence! By becoming a guest at this marriage-feast, our SAVIOUR gave His sanction to all similar joys; teaching us that if they be but consecrated by Him, (without whom *nothing* is strong, *nothing* is holy,) festive meetings are capable of becoming holy things; so holy as to endure His presence; yea, *so* holy as to become the very occasions of the special manifesting of Himself in power!

On so sacred a theme we cannot dwell too particularly. Holy men have seen prophetic outlines, dimly yet surely, in the Miracles and Parables of our LORD. We do believe that they have not been deceived; and when the relation in which CHRIST stands to His Church is recollected, (the Bridegroom and the Bride,) can we fail to see the singular fitness of the occasion selected by our LORD for His first great miracle? Surely, at 'the Marriage of THE LAMB,' the great features of this wedding-feast will be all restored; although in grander shapes, in countless ways, and by even more stupendous acts of Power! There will be then assembled all the Christian Church, from first to last, from Adam to the remotest of his posterity; not a few guests in a far village, but the Church Catholic gathered out of all lands, at once guests and Bride, rejoicing in the presence and in the power of her LORD. He had all along, (she will then confess it,) in divers ways, been exhibiting in her what He displayed in type at Cana of Galilee. How had He converted the weak ordinances of the Jewish Law, into the strong sanctions of the Christian Covenant: *that* good wine of the Gospel which, at His coming into the world, He was careful to pour into 'new bottles!' How, further, had He converted the unstable joys of earth, the poor delights of this mortal being, (which like water ever runneth apace,) into that which can alone quench the soul's thirst, satisfy its passionate longings, and gladden the heart of man for ever!

'Thou hast kept the good wine until now:' *that* is surely the language of a heart exulting in untold blessedness! the very cry of Saints in bliss! .... We thought the sights and sounds of earth pleasant and lovely; but here they are sweeter far. 'Eye hath not seen, nor ear heard, neither hath it entered into the heart of man to conceive it.' Thou hast kept the best until now!—We knew that we were surrounded by many excellent wonders; and while we rejoiced in those we knew of, we gloried in the thought of more. Ah, but we little dreamed of the reality: we suspected nothing like this! 'Thou hast kept the best until now!'—And we thought the happiness of our homes a great happiness, and the welfare of our little ones a rare delight, and the love of one another a joy unspeakable: but oh, to be thus re-united, without one pang, one anxiety; the pain unfelt, the tear unknown; beyond the reach of sorrow, the possibility of parting: verily, O LORD, Thou hast kept the best of all things until now!— *Then* we knew Thee by faith, but not as *now* we know Thee. In Thy Gospel, we saw Thee, only dimly: and the meaning of Thy wondrous sayings we perceived, only darkly. It was a great gift which Thou gavest us in Thy Word and Sacraments: Histories, foreshadowing *Thee,*—Types, displaying *Thee,*—Psalms, wherein we heard *Thy* voice: Discourses, which brought us into *Thy very presence:* Parables and Miracles, which taught us a thousand things about ourselves and *Thee:* yea, and Sacraments, whereby we were made partakers of *Thy very Nature,* and became *Thy children:* but oh, it was *nothing* to what we *now* enjoy! How hast Thou kept the best of all things until now! .... 'I have heard of Thee by the hearing of the ear, but now—mine eye seeth Thee.'

The Third Sunday after the Epiphany.

THE FAITHFUL CENTURION.

St. Matthew viii. 5, 6.

When Jesus was entered into Capernaum, there came unto Him a Centurion, beseeching Him, and saying, Lord my servant lieth at home sick of the palsy, grievously tormented.

At the Epiphany Season, clustered together in marvellous number and beauty, like the stars of Heaven, the Church brings before us Sunday after Sunday, in the Gospel, some of our Lord's chiefest acts of Power. The reason is plain: because He thereby *manifested forth His Glory*[a]. To-day, we are reminded of the healing of the Leper, and the cure of the Centurion's servant. Between two such instructive incidents it is hard to choose. We shall however say a few words about the latter,—which is full of interest and affecting beauty.

Our Lord on entering Capernaum was met by a certain Centurion, 'beseeching Him, and say-

---

[a] St. John ii. 11.

ing, LORD, my servant lieth at home sick of the palsy, grievously tormented.' Our SAVIOUR's answer was,—' I will come and heal him.'—We have scarcely entered on the history as related by St. Matthew, when we feel ourselves constrained to pause; and remark on the person who is thus brought before our notice.—He was a Centurion, (that is, the captain of a band of Roman soldiers,) stationed at Capernaum; and a proselyte to the Jewish religion, as we learn from St. Luke's account of the same transaction. The last-named Evangelist in fact informs us that, before coming in person to CHRIST, the Centurion sent 'elders' to Him, with the request 'that He would come and heal his servant.' These men, in vaunting the other's claims on our SAVIOUR's mercy, reveal the striking circumstance that, in token of the love which this Gentile soldier bore their nation, he had built the synagogue of Capernaum. And thus, a beautiful character is at once, in two words, set before us. A gentile convert,—an alien from the Commonwealth of Israel,—on coming to the knowledge of the true GOD, is impatient to display his love and zeal. What is it to him, that Capernaum is a city full of hard hearts, and unkindly natures[b]?

[b] Consider St. Matth. xi. 23, 24.

It is *GOD* whom he seeks to honour ; and therefore, (like David,) he resolves to 'build Him an House.' Yet is he not one whose acts of public munificence swallow up his private charities ; or whose love of strangers exhausts the love which is demanded first by the ties of kindred, and by the claims of a man's own household. His slave is sick, and must be healed at all hazards. The Centurion knows of our LORD's acts of Mercy ; and at a distance, has been a believer. In his hour of need, (or rather, in *his servant's* hour of need,) he draws near to CHRIST Himself ; and implores that He will display His gracious power on behalf of the humble dependent who is 'dear unto him.'

Our SAVIOUR's ready promise to 'come and heal him,' while it reminds us of the gracious love which is ever prompt to answer prayer, recals by the very force of contrast the different reception which the same SAVIOUR gave to the nobleman who came from the same city to JESUS,—beseeching Him 'that He would come down, and heal his son ; for he was at the point of death[c].' 'Except ye see signs and wonders, ye will not believe,'—were the words which our LORD addressed to this loftier applicant ; suiting

[c] St. John iv. 47.

His reply to the man's spiritual needs,—rather than to his supposed necessities. 'The nobleman saith unto Him, Sir, come down ere my child die!' Thereupon, our LORD healed the nobleman's son indeed, yet went not down.

How unlike was the Centurion's rejoinder to our LORD's gracious announcement that He 'would come and heal' his suffering servant! 'The Centurion answered and said, LORD I am not worthy that Thou shouldest come under my roof; but speak the word only and my servant shall be healed. For I am a man under authority, having soldiers under me : and I say unto this man, Go, and he goeth; and to another, Come, and he cometh; and to my servant, Do this, and he doeth it.' ... The meaning of which words may not perhaps strike every one at first. The Centurion, (who before had sent the elders because he did not think himself worthy to approach our LORD in person,) is lost in self-abasement at the idea of receiving such a Being under his roof. He therefore cries out with St. Peter,—' Depart from me : for I am a sinful man, O LORD!' At the same time, he has made up his mind how this miracle of mercy shall be achieved. The Almighty stranger, (for the Centurion's words prove that he recognised in Him nothing less than One endued with Almighty Power,) shall simply say to the palsy, 'Begone!' and the desire of his soul will be satisfied. He proceeds to make a marvellous confession of his faith :—*I*, (he says,) am a man *under authority*, (that is, subject to some, and having others, in turn, subject to myself;) and yet, even *I* utter my commands, and am instantly obeyed. How much more mayest Thou, who art subject to no one, but on the contrary art supreme,—with how much more effect mayest *Thou*, who art LORD of Heaven and Earth, command this palsy to retire,—which is after all a mere creature of Thine! . . . A sublimer confession, a more lofty notion of the Son of Man, is not to be met with in the Gospels. Accordingly, we are not surprised to read, that 'when JESUS heard it, He marvelled, and said to them that followed, Verily I say unto you, I have not found so great faith, no not in Israel!'

The pattern of Evangelical faith is thus furnished by a Gentile soldier: and Capernaum, which was to be brought down to Hell[d], proves to have been his home.—On that other occasion, already alluded to, when our LORD said to the nobleman, 'Go thy way; thy son liveth,'—we find the man anxiously retracing his steps to

[d] St. Matt. xi. 23, 24..

Capernaum, and on encountering his servants, curiously questioning them as to the hour when his son began to amend. It was not till he learned that 'yesterday at the seventh hour, *the fever left him;*' not till *then* was it that 'himself believed and his whole house[e].' Far different is the conduct of the faithful Centurion. 'Go thy way,' (our SAVIOUR said to him also;) 'and as thou hast believed, so be it done unto thee!' But what was the result? '*They that were sent*' returned to the house, and 'found the servant whole that had been sick[f].' The Centurion remained behind; and thus enjoyed a twofold blessedness,—first, the blessedness of being with CHRIST: next, the blessedness of '*not having seen, and yet having believed*[g].'

Some of the many lessons which arise out of this beautiful narrative, have been hinted at, already, in passing. None will fail to notice that *a devout soldier* is the Gospel pattern of Faith on *two* great occasions. Thus, besides the nameless Centurion of Capernaum, Cornelius, the devout Centurion of Cæsarea, is set before us even more conspicuously, in the Acts[h]: in whose person, (and in the persons of whose

[e] St. John iv. 50—53.   [f] St. Luke vii. 10.
[g] St. John xx. 29.   [h] Acts x.

friends,) the calling in of the Gentiles took place. And perhaps it may not be out of place in a time of war, like the present, that men of peace should be reminded that none of *their* callings, but *the calling of the soldier* supplies at once the model of lofty piety; and of *that* living faith in the unseen World which CHRIST most approves. We do not forget that the profession of arms is, to all appearance, a bad nursery for the highest Christian Graces: but we request our brethren to observe that those graces *may exist* there; nay, that they may flourish and abound —unsuspected.

Let it be only further pointed out, in conclusion, that if there be but a true and sincere love of GOD, men will be guided to the knowledge of the Truth, as it is in CHRIST JESUS our LORD. Little did the faithful Centurion dream of the rapid strides he was to make towards perfection, when he first 'set his heart to understand, and to chasten himself before his GOD[1].' He speedily beheld a synagogue arise in the city where he dwelt; and he grew in the knowledge of Divine things while he frequented its courts, and enjoyed the converse of the Jewish elders whom he had made his grateful friends. Sick-

[1] Dan. x. 12.

ness befals his servant; and lo, in one day he is brought into the very presence of the SAVIOUR of the World, and wins for himself everlastingly an honourable place in THE LAMB's Book of Life!

The Fourth Sunday after the Epiphany.

THE DEMONIACS OF GADARA.

St. Matthew viii. 28.

And when He was come to the other side, into the country of the Gergesenes, there met Him two possessed with devils.

This day's Gospel presents us with two stupendous miracles: the stilling of the Storm,—whereby our Saviour shewed His dominion over lifeless Nature; and the cure of the Demoniacs of Gadara,—whereby He controlled the evil spirits by His word. These two *Epiphanies*, or *Manifestations* of Messiah, suit the season well. It is proposed to make the latter of them the subject of a few remarks, on this occasion. If not the most wonderful of our Lord's miracles, the cure of the Demoniacs of Gadara suggests a larger number of curious thoughts to the mind, than almost any other.

Our Lord had crossed the Sea of Galilee with His Disciples; but scarcely had He set foot on its eastern shore, when two miserable men came rushing violently towards Him;—frantic in their gestures, and doubtless prepared to harm Him if they could. They were possessed with devils; and their violence was such, that the coast, in that part, was deserted: none dared to pass that way. St. Mark says that one of them was so exceeding strong that 'no man could bind him, no, not with chains: because that he had been often bound with fetters and chains; and the chains had been plucked asunder by him, and the fetters broken in pieces; neither could any man tame him. But always, night and day, he was in the mountains, and in the tombs; crying, and cutting himself with stones*.' There seems to have been a grave-yard close to the spot where our LORD landed. The graves however were not like ours; but chambers, resembling vaults, cut in the rock; and into those dwellings of the dead, these two afflicted beings loved to retire. According to GOD's ancient Law, to touch a corpse, or indeed anything thereto belonging, was accounted pollution;—the very reason, perhaps, why these men, possessed with devils, haunted the tombs. From the tombs, it was, that they ran, when our LORD first beheld them: and He accosted them with the solemn words,—'Come out, thou unclean Spirit!'

Thus addressed, the two men fell at His feet

* St. Mark v. 3—5.

and cried, saying,—'What have we to do with Thee, JESUS, Thou SON of GOD? Art Thou come hither to torment us before the time? I adjure Thee by GOD that Thou torment me not[b]!'

And here, several striking things call for notice:—First, that the devils *knew* our LORD: believed the Man who stood before them to be JESUS, the Son of GOD: believed—*and trembled*[c].

Next, that they knew how certainly torment awaited them. Their only complaint was that our SAVIOUR had come to torment them '*before the time.*'

Next, observe how, to the wicked, the very *presence* of CHRIST is *torment*. Learn hereby the folly of wishing for higher *privileges*, instead of striving after greater *holiness*. To be in Heaven, would be *misery* to the wicked. And let us be sure of *this*,—that if reading Holy Scripture is distasteful to us, and Prayer unpalatable; if the society of the good is a hindrance, and the House of GOD no joy;—let us be well persuaded that it is a sign that we are far from GOD, and desire to be yet farther from Him: that we exclaim with the two men of Gadara,—'What have we to do with Thee, JESUS, Thou SON of GOD?'

Observe lastly, that the time is fixed in GOD's

[b] St. Mark v. 6—8.   [c] St. James ii. 19.

foreknowledge when He will take vengeance on the disobedient among men, and angels also.

Then follows the short but striking dialogue which St. Mark and St. Luke, (not St. Matthew,) record. Our SAVIOUR inquired of the evil spirit his name. 'Legion,' was the answer; '*for* we are many.'—Now a legion was a division of the Roman army, containing several thousand men. Observe therefore what is implied by the very *name* of this unclean spirit; namely,—that boldness, and discipline, and violence, and skill; concert and order in making an attack; firmness and courage in maintaining an advantage; weapons also, and a leader, and a subdivision of ranks,—*all* these things, as being employed by devils, are implied in that short answer, 'My name is Legion, for we are many!'. . . . How can *we*, who know it, slumber at our posts,—be off our guard,—and give the enemy of souls so many advantages over us, as well as opportunities against us? How *can* we act thus, remembering that we have to do with one whose name is 'Legion'?

Next in order comes the very remarkable request of the unclean spirits. They besought our LORD not to send them into the bottomless pit. So St. Luke says,—for *that* is the meaning of 'the deep' in his Gospel; ('they besought Him that He would not send them out into the deep[b].') They further prayed that He would not send them out of the country. And yet, feeling certain that they must be expelled forthwith from the human temple in which they had violently taken up their abode, and which they were so terribly profaning by their presence,— they asked leave to enter into a great herd of swine which were feeding near the mountains, a good way off. Our LORD gave them permission. They availed themselves of it, at once; and, in another instant, the whole herd of swine, (they were about two thousand,) were seen violently running down the steep, falling over the precipice, and drowning themselves in the sea.

And here, the striking circumstance may not be overlooked, that next to the satisfaction of dwelling in an unclean human body, comes the pleasure of inhabiting swine. That most filthy of animals is the chosen dwelling-place of the unclean spirit: which had yet rather dwell in a human form; where the work of defilement may be even more complete, inasmuch as the imaginations of the heart and the powers of the body constitute nobler instruments wherewith to work his infernal desires and designs. *Nearest*, how-

[b] St. Luke viii. 31.

ever, to the impure and degraded man, comes the filthiest of the brute Creation,—the very by-word of uncleanness,—the *swine!*

Notwithstanding the fatal result, we venture to suggest that these accursed ones were perfectly well aware what it was they asked. They had not more than a few moments to deliberate: but *they availed themselves* of those few moments; and the result of their hurried, but most shrewd deliberation was, that the deadliest act of mischief yet within their reach would be to drown the swine which belonged to the people of Gadara. The keen foresight with which they had calculated the consequences of this act, fills the mind with wonder, when it is observed that the immediate consequence was that the swineherds fled to the city; told the people what had happened; 'and, behold, the whole city came out to meet JESUS. And when they saw Him,—*they besought Him that He would depart out of their coasts!*'

Let us attend therefore to what this stroke of infernal policy had achieved. The unclean spirits may no longer infest the country of the Gadarenes, beside the Lake; break into the sepulchral chambers of their dead; and by their violence make it unsafe for any man to pass that way. What remains but, in parting, to inflict upon them some signal mischief? 'Yonder, near the mountains, are their swine. Come,' (say the Legion,) 'let us destroy these; and so, bring severe temporal loss upon the people. The result will be yet more glorious. The SAVIOUR has come to visit them: but when they learn that He has been the cause of the destruction of their property, they will either offer Him violence; or at least, they will compel Him to withdraw from among them.'... And even so it came to pass! 'The whole city came out to meet JESUS: and when they saw Him, they besought Him that He would depart out of their coasts.'

O miserable men! to have beheld their SAVIOUR, and to have besought Him to depart! ...O miserable men! Life has come to them, Life and Salvation, and they have thrust it rudely away. They have almost repeated the language of the evil spirits,—'What have we to do with Thee? Art Thou come to torment us? We adjure Thee by GOD that Thou torment us not!' ...And the SAVIOUR, who constraineth none, but leaves men free to act; this pattern of Humility and Meekness,—*He* complies with their blind request, and grants their prayer... St. Matthew adds, that 'He entered into a ship, and passed over, and came into His own city.'

'When they saw Him, they besought Him that He would depart out of their coasts.' O that we may never do the like! Henceforth, let some mere worldly loss be to us a blessed token of His presence; a sweet pledge that He cannot be very far away! And if His drawing nigh may be obtained by the forfeiture of any earthly possession,—let us hold the price as of no account. Let us take warning from those ancient men, who have long since discovered their terrible mistake; long since deplored the blindness which could hanker after their lost swine in the very presence of the LORD of Glory; and, for the sake of the filthiest of His creatures, could spurn the SAVIOUR of the World,—even 'when they *saw* Him!'

'*When they saw Him*, they besought Him that He would depart'. . . Truly therefore had it been declared by the prophet of old,—' When we shall *see* Him, there is no beauty that we should desire Him'. . . GOD grant *us* the eyes, when we *behold* Him, to *discern* Him! Far more, may He grant us the heart, when we *discern*, to *desire* Him also!

The Fifth Sunday after the Epiphany.

THE PARABLE OF THE TARES.

St. Matthew xiii. 24—30.

The kingdom of Heaven is likened unto a man which sowed good seed in his field: but while men slept, his enemy came and sowed tares among the wheat, and went his way. But when the blade was sprung up, and brought forth fruit, then appeared the tares also. So the servants of the householder came and said unto him, Sir, didst not thou sow good seed in thy field? from whence then hath it tares? He said unto them, An enemy hath done this. The servants said unto him, Wilt thou then that we go and gather them up? But he said, Nay; lest while ye gather up the tares, ye root up also the wheat with them. Let both grow together until the harvest: and in the time of harvest I will say to the reapers, Gather ye together first the tares, and bind them in bundles to burn them: but gather the wheat into my barn.

THE Parable of the Tares, which has just been read to us, forms the Gospel for this, the fifth Sunday after Epiphany. Let us seek to derive from it three lessons,—the first, to be supplied by *the appearance of the Field:* the second, by *the inquiry of the Servants:* the third, by *the reply of the Householder.*

1. The appearance which the Field presented was very different from what an English reader would suppose. Our 'tares' are so unlike 'wheat' that the one can be distinguished from the other in a moment: but it is not so in Palestine, where our LORD lived, and where the Gospel was written. In that country there grows in the corn-fields a plant so very like wheat in appearance that a careless eye would hardly detect the difference. On closer inspection, however, it is discovered that the weed has no corn in the ear,—is a mere barren, bearded husk. This is the plant which is intended by the 'Tares' in the Gospel. We have to picture to ourselves a field of wheat overgrown with this mischievous weed, in order to have an exact notion of the sight which distressed the servants, and grieved the heart of the Householder in the parable.

Happily for us, there is no room for doubt as to what is taught hereby. 'The field is the World: the good seed are the children of the kingdom: but the tares are the children of the wicked one.' Thus, while the good and the wicked are set before us in type, it is declared concerning these last, that 'the enemy that sowed them is the Devil.' It appears therefore that our LORD was here delivering a prophecy of how the Church would appear in these latter days. And have not His words come true? Are not good and bad everywhere mixed together? do they not grow up side by side, sharing the same rain, and wind, and sunshine? Nay, cast your eyes over those assembled in Church on Sunday, and is there any way of distinguishing the wheat from the tares outwardly? GOD alone knoweth who are His.

The lesson supplied by the field is therefore *this*:—that the Church now presents the very appearance which Almighty GOD foresaw and foretold:—that the author of all the sin in the world is the Devil, who seeks to spoil the good work of GOD by sowing the seeds of vice everywhere:—that the righteous and the sinful are not two different kinds of beings; but, as tares are only a spurious kind of wheat, so the wicked are only depraved persons,—persons whom GOD willed to be holy. Lastly, that the great distinction between the good and the evil,—the wheat and the tares—is that the one are fruitful, while the other are barren. The wheat *bears fruit:* the tares have no corn in the ear. Let none therefore deceive themselves.

2. It will be remembered that the Servants came and asked the Householder how it happened that his field produced tares, since he had been careful to sow none but good seed in his field. What then may be gathered from this inquiry of the servants?

It teaches that GOD foresaw the surprise which men would feel at the sight of evil in the world. Holy Job felt it, when he asked, 'Wherefore do the wicked live, become old, yea, are mighty in power? Their seed is established in their sight, and their offspring before their eyes. Their houses are safe from fear, neither is the rod of GOD upon them.' He had seen wicked men prosper, and enjoy all worldly happiness, and could not understand the reason of it.—In like manner, the Psalmist says,—'I was envious when I saw the prosperity of the wicked; for they are not in trouble as other men are, neither are they plagued like other men. . . . . They increase in riches. Verily, I have cleansed my heart in vain!' And he adds,—' When I thought to know this it was too painful for me.'—The words of the Prophet Jeremiah are even more striking,—' Righteous art Thou, O LORD, when I plead with Thee, yet let me talk with Thee of Thy judgments: wherefore doth the way of the wicked prosper? Wherefore are all they happy, that deal very treacherously?' Thus, then, Job, David, and Jeremiah ask of GOD the same question which the Servants in the parable come and ask the Householder. They are perplexed at the sight of evil.—*We* also partake of the same perplexity, though we express ourselves in different ways. Some are heard to declare that Sin cannot be so very displeasing to the ALMIGHTY, or He would not suffer people to go on so long in sin. This is one way of expressing perplexity at the sight of Evil in the world,—at Tares growing among the Wheat.—Another way, is to wonder why GOD does not cut up the wicked root and branch, and to expect every day that He will do so; almost to lose patience because He does not.—Some there are who, from being perplexed, proceed to take the matter into their own hands. They say,—We will never be persuaded that the Church can contain so many wicked people. We must weed them out. We must belong to a Church, and frequent a place of worship, of our own; where none shall be seen but those who are in a state of grace. If we cannot gather up these tares, we must at least gather ourselves out from among them.

But they who thus speak quite forget the

THE FIFTH SUNDAY AFTER THE EPIPHANY.

parable of the Tares of the Field; and what the Householder said in reply to his impatient servants. If they are reminded of either, they are tempted to declare that the Field is *the World*, and not *the Church:* and therefore that the parable does not apply. But this is a mistake: for the Field was the World only till the sower sowed the seed of the Kingdom in it,—which seed is the Word of GOD. From that time, it became the Church. The visible Church is found to reach throughout the length and breadth of the land. You cannot leave one parish without getting into another. In other words, the spiritual territory of the SAVIOUR's Kingdom extends everywhere throughout the whole country. If therefore, in the parable, Tares came up mixed with the Wheat, this was a clear prophecy that wicked men would abound, and be seen mingled with the righteous, *in the Church.* — We do indeed read in Scripture of 'a glorious Church; not having spot, or wrinkle, or any such thing.' But *that* is the Church triumphant in Heaven, not the Church 'militant here in Earth.'

The inquiry of the Servants therefore, and the reply of the Householder, prove highly instructive; for they remind us that men are ever prone to wonder at the sight of evil within the Church, ever ready to take the matter in their own hands, in order to mend it. Whereas, there is no room for wonder,—since the thing was clearly foretold: no reason for interference,—since the Servants were not allowed to interfere.

3. And this brings us to the last head on which it was proposed to say a few words. The answer of the Householder to the inquiry,—'Wilt thou then that we go and gather them up?' was,—'Nay, lest while ye gather up the Tares, ye root up also the Wheat with them.' . . . It is as if the Great Householder were to say,—'I will not allow the wicked to be gathered out from among the good: first, because it is very hard to distinguish the one from the other, outwardly. There is danger of mistaking them; and so destroying the righteous *with* the wicked. That be far from Me! Secondly, as the roots of tares and wheat become entangled, so do good and bad persons become linked together; and it would often be *death* to the one to pluck the other away. A wicked Son is often bound by many a secret tie, strong as Love itself, to a Mother's heart. Husband and Wife again,—their very being is interwoven! Are they not one flesh? No: the wicked and the righteous must abide yet awhile!'

But he proceeds—'Let both grow together

until the harvest: and in the time of harvest I will say to the reapers, Gather ye together first the tares and bind them in bundles to burn them: but gather the wheat into my barn.'

These are solemn words, yet fully as plain as they are solemn. They set forth GOD's patience, and His lofty purpose. They reveal to us also the scheme of His government.... He lets men live on in Sin from day to day,—not because He is *indifferent;* but because He is *patient.* He sends them no outward token of His displeasure, but He is not therefore unobservant of them.... 'Let both grow together until the Harvest,' He says. Till then, we enjoy a share of the same blessings which befall our neighbours;—rain and dew, wind and sunshine,—we share them all alike. But let us never presume to think that this is any sign of GOD's favour. It is meant to move us to Repentance. The bow is bent, and the sword is drawn, and the pit yawns meanwhile, for the ungodly; and there will be an awful reckoning hereafter, 'in the time of Harvest,'—when the fruitful will be gathered into the Heavenly Barn, but the fruitless consigned to everlasting Burning!

The Sixth Sunday after the Epiphany.

LIKENESS TO GOD, THE CONDITION OF SEEING GOD.

1 St. John iii. 2, 3.

We know that, when He shall appear, we shall be like Him; for we shall see Him as He is. And every man that hath this hope in Him purifieth himself, even as He is pure.

Our Prayer Book contained no special service for the Sixth Sunday after the Epiphany until the last Review, which took place in 1662. The present Collect, Epistle, and Gospel were then introduced; and very instructive is it to find that *conformity to the Divine Purity* should be made the subject of that Collect; the great thought which the Services of the Day set before us. For 'who may abide the day of His Coming? and who shall stand when He appeareth[a]?' This last argument, with which Faith ever seeks to quicken Love, forms the Gospel for the Day: and thus has been gathered into a small compass

[a] Mal. iii. 2.

the sum of what we believe, as regards the future; and what we have to do, as regards the present.

It is impossible to be sufficiently grateful for the Church's earnestness in impressing her children with the great need of personal holiness. It is the way of Scripture itself to be thus for ever requiring at our hands holy acts and holy habits: but it has been the mistake of some of our brethren quite to overlook this part of the teaching of GOD's Word, and to lay undue stress on something else, which is the easier, and might perhaps be mistaken for the more spiritual course. Woe to those who in this way teach men to separate Evangelical Faith from Evangelical Obedience; and suffer any to imagine that the former may stand as a kind of substitute for the latter!

In the Gospel, on the contrary, nothing is known of a Faith which worketh not by Love. But, what it concerns us now far more to observe, the teaching of the Spirit is express that without conformity to the Divine Image,—or, in plainer language, (which we are however almost afraid to employ,) without becoming *like* GOD,—we shall not *see* GOD. This is indeed a matter of so much importance that it may well deserve our very special attention.

How many persons are there who, in their

thoughts about the World to come, speak as if it were a settled matter that a State of Rest awaits as many as lay down the burthen of the flesh, whatever their manner of life may have been. Even those who are better taught, are found to reason, or at least to act, as if they thought that a certain amount of sin is to be tolerated; provided the conduct be in the main virtuous, or, as it is called, *respectable*. But the very solemn tenor of the Gospel is far different. Its exhortations are all counsels of perfection. 'Be ye therefore merciful, as your Father also is merciful[b].' 'As He which hath called you is holy, so be ye holy in all manner of conversation[c].' 'Be ye therefore perfect, even as your Father which is in Heaven is perfect[d].'

It can surely scarce require explaining that when Holy Scripture thus speaks, it is not implied, nor indeed can be, that Man has it in his power to rival the Holiness of the Eternal GOD. The very thought were folly, bordering on blasphemy. GOD is unapproachable in His attributes, every one of which is a perfection: while Man's best endeavours are sinful. His very efforts after purity are impure in GOD's sight. His tears of repentance, (as some one has said,) require wash-

[b] St. Luke vi. 36.   [c] 1 St. Pet. i. 15.   [d] St. Matth. v. 48.

ing. The only likeness to GOD which man can display is therefore the likeness of the quality of his actions to the quality of the known actions of GOD; acts of Love, acts of Purity, acts of Peace. And there will be this further effort on the part of CHRIST's faithful soldier and servant,—namely, that he will not allow himself in any known breach of the Divine Law. He will strive to earn for himself the praise of Noah[e], of Abraham[f], and of the rest of GOD's chiefest Saints; and seek to be what Holy Scripture intends when it calls these men 'perfect.'

'Beloved,' (says the Disciple who was himself beloved,) 'now are we the sons of GOD; and it doth not appear what we shall be: but we know that when He shall appear, we shall be like Him, for we shall see Him as He is.' By which words, St. John seems to imply that some mysterious change is in store for these mortal bodies, by which we shall be fitted to stand in the presence of GOD, and to behold Him as He really is: for 'flesh and blood cannot inherit the Kingdom of GOD; neither doth corruption inherit incorruption.' Hence, 'as we have borne the image of the earthy,' so must we also 'bear the image of the heavenly[g]:' this vile body being fashioned

[e] Gen. vi. 9.   [f] Gen. xvii. 1.   [g] 1 Cor. xv. 49, 50.

like unto the glorious Body of CHRIST, 'according to the working whereby He is able even to subdue all things unto Himself [h].'—But as there must be this likeness to GOD hereafter, in order to the enjoyment of the vision of GOD, so also in this life must there be a constant endeavour to attain such a measure of likeness as the infirmity of the flesh permits. St. John lays this down in the very next verse: 'Every man,' (saith he,) 'that hath this hope in Him,' (that is in CHRIST,) 'purifieth himself, *even as He is pure.*'

Nor will any doubt that it is the truest love, the most tender compassion for our infirmities, which thus sets before us the very highest model of goodness to which our eyes can be directed; instead of suffering them to rest on any inferior object. It is even *more easy* to become followers of CHRIST, and to aim at perfection, than to tread in the uncertain footsteps of erring men, who are good only by fits and starts. And this is perhaps less faithfully remembered than it deserves to be. We do not require to be reminded that the Saints, under either covenant, are our patterns in the various Christian graces. But it may well be feared that the habitual looking to CHRIST *as our model,* is much lost sight of; although the

[h] Phil. iii. 21.

exhortation to do so, in Holy Scripture, is of such very frequent occurrence. Moreover, if any one will be at the pains to examine the Gospel with this view, he will be astonished to discover to what an extent the daily life and conversation of the REDEEMER is capable of being converted into an example. To take a single quality, of which we recognise on every side a surprising want, but of which we discover in Him amazing traces in almost every page of the Gospel, namely, *Forbearance.* Let any one consider how precious our LORD's example might become only in this one respect, and what blessed results would follow, if men would seriously apply themselves to the imitation of their great Example in respect of this single Christian grace.

While we thus speak, it is impossible to forget the kindred precept of our LORD, that men should take a lesson for their own imitation from the dealings of GOD with His creatures. Thus, He exhorts us to love our enemies, and to do good to them that hate us, that we may be the children of our Father which is in Heaven: 'for He maketh His sun to rise on the evil and on the good, and sendeth rain on the just and on the unjust[1].' How surprising a method is this,

[1] St. Matth. v. 44, 45.

of enforcing a sacred duty! Unaided by the Divine Guidance, how slow should we have been to discover that the sunshine and the shower, which fall alike on the just and the unjust, are intended to enforce the duty of being kind to the unthankful and the evil!

But the respect in which St. John in the passage before us, specially exhorts that we should conform ourselves to the Divine image, is the absolute and entire purity of His Nature. The beloved Disciple seems to imply that resemblance to the Holy One in this respect will be the very condition of our beholding Him hereafter. And in perfect conformity with this hint, is our LORD's declaration that the Blessedness of 'the pure in heart' will consist specially in *this*,—namely that '*they shall see GOD.*' A glorious promise truly! and one which may well prove a spur to holy living. Close akin to it is St. Paul's declaration that, without Holiness, '*no man shall see the LORD*[1].' Let us remember that Sight is that faculty which gives us the truest possible knowledge of natural objects: far more exact than can be attained by taste, or touch, or smell, or hearing. There are certain qualities indeed, (as colour,) with which nothing but Sight can

[1] Hebrews xii. 14.

make us acquainted. Transfer this thought to the Divine Nature; and then consider what it must be throughout the ages to be shut out from the knowledge of Him whose perfections we know, as yet, only by the hearing of the ear. O that, hereafter, the words of holy Job may rather be ours, —' I have heard of Thee by the hearing of the ear; but now, *mine eye seeth Thee*[k]:'—that in us might be fulfilled, in all its Divine fulness, the prophetic announcement,—' *Thine eyes shall see* the King in His beauty. *They shall behold* the Land that is very far off[l].'

[k] Job xlii. 5.   [l] Isaiah xxxiii. 17.

The Sunday called Septuagesima.

HEAVENLY PAYMENT.

St. Matth. xx. 9, 10.

And when they came that were hired about the eleventh hour, they received every man a penny. But when the first came, they supposed that they should have received more; and they likewise received every man a penny.

These words are taken out of the parable of the Labourers in the Vineyard,—which is one of the hardest of the parables, if not the very hardest of all. It may at least be taken for granted that the 'Labourers' denote Christian men and women. What 'early in the morning,' and 'about the eleventh hour,' may exactly mean, is perhaps doubtful; and the same must be said of 'the third,' 'the sixth,' and 'the ninth hour.' At the same time, it must be allowed that this is not a matter which concerns us much, since all the labourers received the same reward, whether they had been sent into the Vineyard late or early. To whichever of these five classes of men, we may find ourselves, by GOD's great mercy, in the last day belonging,—(I say 'by GOD's *great mercy*,' for all these men received *a reward*, and therefore it is among that blessed number that we pray GOD to give us *our* portion;) — to whichever class we may belong, we shall receive 'every man a penny.' Now, 'a penny' denotes about ninepence,—which was the wages of a day-labourer in a country where every thing is about twice as cheap as in England. This sum then, ('a penny,') stands for the eternal reward of the Christian labourer. 'Man goeth forth to his work, and to his labour, until the evening.' In the evening cometh the Master, and His reward is in His hand.

But here the question arises, (and it is one which affects us nearly, and is sure to present itself,)—Do all men, therefore, who go to Heaven enjoy equal happiness? Are there then no degrees of Glory in the future World? To some persons, it might seem so from this parable; since a penny is the reward of all alike. And a man might go on to argue that therefore one sin more or less cannot matter much; since, if Heaven after all is to be his lot, it will be as happy a place to him with that one additional sin to answer for, as it is to the greatest Saint in

Heaven.—There is no limit to the folly and wickedness of men. It is conceivable that this notion of Heaven being Heaven after all, a place of equal happiness to every one who treads its courts; it is conceivable, I say, that this notion might make men careless as to crime; mad enough to dream on of Heaven while they were hurrying along the path which leads to Hell.

On the other hand, think a moment of the many express declarations of a contrary kind which we meet with in the sacred Volume: as, that CHRIST shall render unto every man *according to his work:* that men shall give account for *every idle word they utter:* that he which soweth sparingly, *shall reap sparingly;* and he which soweth bountifully, *shall reap also bountifully:* that the servant who with ten talents had earned other ten, was set over *ten cities;* while he who with five talents had earned other five, was set over *five* cities. The teaching of one parable must be set against the teaching of another. If the parable of the Labourers in the Vineyard has led us to fancy that rewards in Heaven are equal, the parable of the Talents is enough to shew us our mistake, and to convince us of the contrary.

How then is the teaching of these two parables, in this respect, to be reconciled? How can there be different rewards, if 'a penny' is to be the hire of every one alike? How can there be different degrees of Happiness, different degrees of Glory, if the reward is one and the same? . . . . This shall now be explained in a few words; and it will be seen that some very important considerations arise out of the remarks we are about to offer.

Suppose that a Feast were proposed as the reward of a day's labour in the case of ten persons,—one of whom was too ill to be able to partake of the fare provided. Let us suppose that each one received at evening an equal portion of bread, and meat, and wine. These men will be all exactly in the position of the Labourers in the Vineyard; and yet, no one will say that the enjoyment of every one at the table will be the same. There will have been one Reward, yet different degrees of Happiness.

To take another humble illustration:—If the same summer ramble were enjoyed by a band of many brothers, one of whom was rather *deaf*, and another rather *blind;* the rest being in perfect health. *Who* sees not, that although the same cheerful sights and sounds would offer themselves to all the party, there would be one among them who would lose nearly one half of the pleasure;

and another, who would nearly lose the other half. —Thus there will again have been different degrees of Happiness, yet one and the same gift.

It is plain, then, that a reward may be at once the same, and different: the same, in itself; different, to the persons on whom it is bestowed: *quite* the same in itself; *altogether* different to those who ought to enjoy it. For it is evident that a thing is pleasant or not, as we are able to derive pleasure from it, or the contrary. In other words, the amount of every gratification depends upon ourselves. And in spiritual matters, this holds just as true as in temporal. Observe, for instance, the unwillingness of some men to come to Church: whereas the King of Israel said that a day in the Courts of the LORD was better than a thousand spent anywhere else. Here is a strange difference of opinion! David, slaking his thirst in the Waters of Life, appeasing his hunger with the Bread of Heaven,— while the heartless worshipper is only remarking on the length of the Service; wishing himself away; or distressing himself with thoughts of worldly anxiety!.... Imagine these two persons transplanted into Heaven. Set them down before the Throne of GOD. Let them hear the Angels cry aloud,— the Heavens, and all the powers therein,—the Cherubim and Seraphim continually crying Holy, Holy, Holy! Join them to the glorious company of the Apostles,—the goodly fellowship of the Prophets,—the noble army of Martyrs; let their lot be with those who are continually praising GOD. Both of these persons will *be* in Heaven; but which of the two will *feel* as if he were in Heaven? Surely not he who begrudged an hour a-week for his Master's praise! *He* surely will alone feel the blessedness of Heaven who longed for more opportunities of praising GOD, than ever he enjoyed here below: who rejoiced in the CREATOR's worship, and was very jealous for His honour and glory: who mourned over his own weakness, and smarted under Temptation, and groaned beneath the burthen of his sin! To him, pardoned and transfigured into his LORD's likeness, Heaven will be Heaven indeed; but not to the other.

We are therefore, perhaps, the authors of our own Eternal Happiness or Misery in a sense and to a degree, which we little suspect. Men are apt to speak of GOD as a severe Judge,—rewarding some, and condemning others, and having the fate of all men in His hand. But what if it shall appear hereafter that every man had his own fate *in his own hands*, and fixed his own eternal doom, for Joy or for Despair, by himself? Do but think, after all, that to be in Heaven is to enjoy the sight of GOD, as He is: and by whom shall this blessedness be enjoyed, except by 'the pure in heart?' *These* then are the persons who will enjoy supreme blessedness. 'The pure in heart' will 'see GOD.' The purest will enjoy the nearest and the clearest vision. What are acts of Sin, therefore, but a tarnishing and defiling of that mirror which ought to reflect the glories of the Most High?

To vary the figure:—As we bring vessels to the fountain when we would draw water thence, but the quantity of the water we carry away depends on the size of the vessel which we bring; so exactly is it in our approaches to the Fountain of all Goodness. If the capacity of our souls be small, how shall they be filled with the largeness of the Divine Love? He who mars his vessel, lessens the quantity of the treasure which he shall carry away: while those who have broken their vessels, must perforce return empty.

To conclude.—There need be no fear lest the discovery of our own responsibility should make us forgetful of GOD's free mercies in CHRIST. The more awful a sense we entertain of the largeness of the prize at stake, the more forcibly shall we feel ourselves drawn to Him for supplies of strength; the more frequently shall we feel ourselves compelled to implore His aid to enable us to resist our own sinful inclinations, and to obey the motions of His Holy Spirit. And if we have the strongest motive for dreading Sin, so surely have we the strongest motive supplied us for perseverance, constancy, and all godliness. Those who love GOD, will not only fear lest some one should take their crown: they will aim at a yet higher degree of blessedness in Heaven. Whatever GOD hates in them, they will learn to hate also; whatever GOD loves, they will prize and cherish,—as *that* which will draw them nearest to Him, and increase their bliss throughout the ages of Eternity.

The Sunday called Sexagesima.

THE PARABLE OF THE SOWER.

St. Luke viii. 5—8.

A sower went out to sow his seed: and as he sowed, some fell by the way-side; and it was trodden down, and the fowls of the air devoured it. And some fell upon a rock; and as soon as it was sprung up, it withered away, because it lacked moisture. And some fell among thorns; and the thorns sprang up with it, and choked it. And other fell on good ground, and sprang up, and bare fruit an hundredfold.

THREE things go to make up the present parable; THE SEED,—THE SOWER,—and THE SOIL; each of which will be found to supply a most important lesson. And first,—what do we learn from what is here said about THE SOIL?

1. We learn a thing which ought to make us very thoughtful and anxious; and set us, many a time, on a very strict examination, not only of our condition of heart, but of our whole manner of life: for it is found that the fate of the seed sown *depended altogether upon the soil on which it fell.* It was either trodden down before it had begun to grow; or it withered away as soon as it sprang up; or it was choked and yielded no

fruit after it was grown; or it bare an hundredfold;—as it fell by the way-side,—or on a rock,—or among thorns,—or into good ground. Here are three failures, and only one case of success. So that the chances are against us; and the chances are many; which make it a grave matter.

But the case becomes graver when the parable is explained; for our LORD says that, by 'the way-side,' He meant those persons who hear the Word indeed, but who take no pains to understand and take it in. They give little or no heed to it. They are hard as the beaten highway, and unfruitful. For, as seed which falls by the wayside is either devoured by birds, or trodden down by the heel of the passenger, so does it fare with GOD's Word in the case of these persons. Satan, knowing the life and vigour of the Word, knowing how sure it is to grow if it does but find a lodgment in the heart, comes immediately and snatches it away. But if he spares the seed, men's evil habits do his work just as effectually. Worldly thoughts, coming and going, in a heart which is exposed and unguarded as a highway, crush the life of GOD's Word with fatal certainty. Either way, nothing comes of it.—This then is a warning to the careless; to persons also who have indulged wandering thoughts and a dreamy habit of mind till they find it hard to fix their thoughts on things sacred, or indeed on any thing. It is a strong cry in the ears of all those who rise from the study of GOD's Word, or return from GOD's House, careless and unmoved. 'He that hath ears to hear, let him hear.'

The next case is that of the rock, which had a thin layer of earth over it. *Hard rock*, observe; not a stony soil, where wheat is found to grow very well,—because the roots find as much moisture as they require between the stones. No; our LORD speaks of the hard rock, covered over thinly with earth,—where the seed, as soon as it has sprung up, withers away for lack of moisture. And this, (He says,) is a figure of all those who when they hear, receive the Word with joy; but have *no root* in themselves; so they only believe for a while; and in time of trial, fall away. *They* are spoken of whose unsubdued natures afford no real lodgment for the Word. They have hard and unchastened hearts. Not that they *despise* Religion. On the contrary, they like it. Our LORD distinctly says that they receive the Word 'with joy.' And very remarkable is that saying: for how many have we known who will listen with attention when talked to about holy things; will even shed tears, and seem deeply moved; and at last go forth from Church with a glow of piety and joy; but who, underneath all this, carry a stubborn and untamed, an unbroken and unchastened spirit; one, in which nothing can strike root and grow: good feelings above, but shallow; while beneath, all is *rock*, with no *moisture* in it. 'He that hath ears to hear, let him hear!'

The next case is that of the seed which 'fell among thorns:' and this is a piteous one, for here there is no lack of earth. The soil is even good. But for that very reason, it bears thorns. The fate of the seed which falls in such a soil is that the thorns spring up with it, and choke it, and it yields no fruit.—And this, (our LORD says,) is the case of persons who, when they hear, go forth; and the cares, and riches, and pleasures of this life, and the lusts of other things entering in, choke the Word, and it becometh unfruitful. Let us beware then, lest through sloth, or covetousness, or the love of pleasure, we suffer thorns to spring up and choke *our* spiritual life. Verily, watchfulness is needed: for we are speaking of a soil in which the seed took root, sprang up, grew tall and strong; a heart, that is, in which the Word of GOD sinks deep, and seems to thrive. And this helps to delude men who are not watchful and wary; for they seem to themselves to be in as hopeful a way as those who have received the Word into an honest and good heart. They overlook the thorns, (worldly plans and worldly anxieties,) which surround them, and overtop the good seed, and threaten every day to choke it. Alas, how fast those thorns grow; and how they keep thickening about us! The business,—how it fills men's thoughts! Family cares, again! anxiety about children and relations; or, a far more selfish thing, anxiety about ourselves; hopes and fears as to our prospects in life. Then lastly, public business of whatever kind, with its many and increasing demands upon our time. But above all, ' the deceitfulness of riches' must be mentioned; for our LORD dwells especially upon *that*. These things thicken upon men as time goes on, and shut out the sun and air; draw away the nourishment which ought to sustain their spiritual life, and at last quite choke it. The end of the matter is that they become 'unfruitful.' They are full of good resolutions; but they never perform them. It is because the thorns are so strong, and so many. ' He that hath ears to hear, let him hear!'

This then is the lesson suggested by the soil into which the seed fell. To state it in the fewest words, there are three great obstacles to the fruitfulness of GOD's Word in the heart of

Man; against which, as he values the welfare of his immortal soul, he has need to watch and pray, constantly: namely, carelessness of heart,—hardness of heart,—and worldly distractions.—Of the rest of the parable we must speak more briefly. Let us now notice what THE SOWER teaches.

2. It is found then that though three parts of the seed perished, and only one part came to perfection, it was all sowed by one and the same hand. So then, it does not depend *on the Sower* whether the Word of GOD prospers in the heart of Man. It depends *on the heart of Man*, into which that seed is sown. This is a matter very much to be noticed. It is a humbling truth to preachers, indeed, who have any conceit of their own powers; and this is well, for none can think too meanly of themselves: but, at the same time, it is a tremendous warning to the people,—a stern rebuke to as many as lay the blame of their spiritual deadness, their unfruitfulness, to the minister of the parish in which they dwell. The blame of their lives rests in Time, and will rest throughout Eternity, with themselves, and themselves only. Not the mouth of the preacher, but the heart of him who listens, is in fault, as often as the words are caught away, withered as soon as grown, or choked before the time of fruit.

3. We conclude with some thoughts derived from THE SEED.—Now, it is plain that the strange thing in the growth of seeds is *this;* that though what is sown is *a seed*, what comes up is a very different thing,—namely, *a plant*. A grain of wheat, for example, becomes an ear of corn, growing upon a long bladed stalk: and so it fares with every other seed. In other words, seeds are sown in order to produce *a new life.*

Let it further be observed that the plant that comes up agrees with the seed sown: every plant brings forth fruit *after its kind*. This is a matter of great importance.—Lastly, it is to be noticed that there is *growth* in the plant which comes up: first, the blade,—then, the ear,—next, the full corn in the ear; and this, bearing a hundredfold as much as was sown into the earth. This also is a point to be carefully borne in mind.

Apply these remarks, then, to the sowing of GOD's Word, and see what follows. First, a new life must be the consequence. If the Word of GOD be indeed like seed, it must have this productive virtue in it, to bring forth the fruit of a new life: not only a new fashion of life outwardly, but a new nature, a new kind of life within; new thoughts, a new opinion of things, new delights, new actions.—Secondly, the acts seen must correspond with the nature of the Word sown. When 'the Word reveals GOD, His greatness and holiness, then it should beget pious fear and reverence, and study of conformity to Him. When it reveals His goodness and mercy, it should work love and confidence. When it holds up to our view CHRIST crucified, it should crucify the soul to the world, and the world to it. When it represents those rich things which are laid up for us, the blessed inheritance of the saints, then it should make all the lustre of this world vanish, and shew how poor it is; wean and call off the heart from it; and raise it to higher hopes and the prospect of a crown. And so it should be the seed of noble thoughts, and of a behaviour suitable to a Christian,—an immortal seed, as St. Peter calls it [a], springing up to no less than eternal life [b].'—It shall only be added, lastly, that if the Word of GOD be like seed, then must it bear fruit *gradually;* and *grow* in the heart, secretly, silently, slowly, but at the same time *certainly:* advancing daily nearer perfection; exchanging the blade for the ear, and the ear for the full corn in the ear; ripening with a slow and steady progress: bringing forth fruit an hundredfold, *with patience.*

[a] 1 St. Peter i. 23.   [b] Archbishop Leighton.

The Sunday called Quinquagesima,

or the next Sunday before Lent.

CHARITY, THE GREATEST OF VIRTUES.

---

1 Cor. xiii. 4—8.

Charity suffereth long, and is kind; Charity envieth not; Charity vaunteth not itself, is not puffed up, doth not behave itself unseemly, seeketh not her own, is not easily provoked, thinketh no evil; rejoiceth not in iniquity, but rejoiceth in the truth; beareth all things, believeth all things, hopeth all things, endureth all things. Charity never faileth.

On the next Sunday before the Season called Lent, which is the season of Conversion to God, (as will be found explained in the Sermon for Ash-Wednesday,) and indeed the season of religious *strictness* generally, the grace of Charity or Love is specially brought before us. It is thereby clearly implied that this most excellent gift is indispensably necessary to all who would attain or exhibit any other of the Christian graces. Self-denial is worthless without Love. Almsgiving is nothing without Love. And so, of all the rest.

The few words which have been already offered will have brought to mind the very remarkable chapter of St. Paul's first Epistle to the Corinthians which forms the Epistle for the Day, and from which the text is taken. A more carefully drawn portrait of any Christian grace is not to be found in the whole volume of the New Testament. The notes whereby it may be recognised, or its absence discovered, are so numerous and so exact, that there can be no possible mistake, if a very little attention be given to the matter. Moreover, when it is considered that Charity is declared to be the greatest of virtues; greater than Hope, greater even than Faith itself; no one who is at all desirous of pleasing GOD, and anxious for his own safety, can afford to overlook so very solemn and important a lesson. Let us therefore attend to this matter with some care.

And first we cannot help being struck by the very lofty place which the great Apostle assigns to Charity.—If any one were to come among us, and speak so eloquently that all paused to listen, while all who listened were enchanted; if the charm of his eloquence were such that tears flowed while he spoke, and men went away from his presence persuaded of the things he taught; we might be apt to think such an one a great favourite of Heaven, as well as a chosen instrument in GOD's hands. St. Paul however, speaking by the Spirit of God, expressly informs us that we might be mistaken in so doing. If this attractive speaker had not 'Charity,' he would be 'nothing.'

But we should be yet more certainly entrapped into a belief that we beheld a great and holy person, signally beloved of GOD, and destined certainly to occupy a high place in Heaven, if the person we have been already describing had the gift of prophecy, and understood all the mysteries of Religion. The treasures of Divine Wisdom, we are apt to think, cannot abide with any but the very good. We learn from GOD Himself, however, that they may exist where there is no Charity: and moreover, that if they *do* exist in one who has not Charity, that man is *nothing*.

A far severer trial would await us if we saw this person give proof of a most living Faith. What would be thought of one who could 'say unto this mountain, Remove hence to yonder place[a];' and straightway it should be seen to

---

[a] St. Matth. xvii. 20.

obey the command of the speaker, and roll from its everlasting seat? We should surely regard him as something more than human. We should certainly be bold to assume that he carried the Seal of the Eternal GOD on his forehead. And yet, the witness of the Spirit is express,—that this worker of miracles, if he were without Charity, would be as *nothing* in GOD's sight.

The crowning wonder yet remains. Watch this same speaker with the tongue of Angels,—this same mighty Prophet and deep Divine,—this same worker of miracles, who is possessed of 'all Faith,'—watch him as he retires from the scene of his preaching, of his display of sacred wisdom, of his acts of miraculous power; and behold him calmly making a sacrifice of all his earthly possessions, in order to benefit the poor, —to clothe the naked, and to feed the hungry. He is now himself a beggar. He has parted with 'all his goods;' and the objects of his bounty were the poor of the flock,—the Good Shepherd's 'little ones.' You *must* feel that this sight would completely silence suspicion and overcome doubt. We should be tempted, every one of us, to exclaim,—'This man is a real Saint!'

However: the plain *fact* is, that if I do all these things, 'and *have not Charity*, it profiteth me *nothing!*' This may appear strange; but the strangeness of the matter signifies nothing. It is *true*. There may be the gift of tongues, without the gift of Charity: the gift of prophecy,—the understanding of all mysteries, and the possession of all knowledge,—yet no Charity: Faith, that can move mountains,—yet no Charity: Almsgiving, (which is sometimes improperly *called* 'Charity,') —and yet Charity itself may be wanting. And, (which it concerns us most of all to notice,) if it *be* wanting, then, all the other wondrous gifts and graces are *nothing worth!* .... A more striking revelation concerning ourselves is perhaps hardly to be found in any page of Scripture.

What then is the nature of the gift concerning which such lofty things are told us? Verily, when we come to examine, our wonder increases. We expected something very magnificent, and everything we hear is something exceedingly lowly. We expected a proud flower, and we find nothing but a fragrant herb which creeps very near the ground. Let us go over St. Paul's description of Charity, feature by feature. It will not take us long, and we cannot possibly occupy ourselves more profitably.

First then,—'Charity suffereth long, and is kind.' Observe, therefore, that Charity does not do anything great: nay, it does not *do* anything at all. It *suffers*. It does not merely suffer, but it suffers *long*. Nor does it merely suffer long, but it is *kind* also.—Next, we learn that it is without envy. 'Charity envieth not.'—It follows that it 'vaunteth not itself; is not puffed up; doth not behave itself unseemly; seeketh not her own.' We may pause to point out that we are in the midst of a string of negatives; each of which demolishes, at a blow, a whole class of actions which disfigure the character. The boastful, the proud, the unseemly, the self-seeking,—all of these here meet with their reproof, and are reminded that Charity dwells with none of themselves.—Charity, once more, 'is not easily provoked:' and this is a feature of Charity which reminds us painfully how rarely Charity is met with in daily life; where, instead of unwillingness to take offence, we rather find people inventing causes of provocation where no offence was intended.—Again, she 'thinketh no evil.' O divine Charity, which 'thinketh no evil,' even while she dwells in the midst of a wicked world! It is because she 'rejoiceth not in iniquity, but rejoiceth in the Truth.' If we loved better whatever things are pure, and lovely, and of good report; if iniquity were a burden to our spirits, and a grief to our hearts; then, doubtless, we should be less prone to suspect its existence around us. Nay, we should 'think *no* evil' where evil was not proved to be.

Charity, lastly, 'beareth all things; believeth all things; hopeth all things; endureth all things.' And this lovely grace exhausts itself in no sudden act; but it becomes an abiding habit of the soul: 'Charity never faileth.'—Take notice then that *endurance* is again and again noted as its special work: nay, Faith and Hope themselves, are but two of its functions; and they are the only *acts* of Charity which St. Paul here enumerates at all.

This shall suffice on the subject of Charity, or Love. The few words which have been already offered should set us on a curious and somewhat anxious review of our own conduct. And truly, he must be a very holy person indeed who can examine the Apostle's picture, and not feel how very slender a likeness it presents of himself. Very certain are we that this page in the duty of a Christian man can never be too attentively studied; and that it is not by any means studied enough. The talk of what is called 'Society' is not the talk of Charity. The ways of 'the World' are not charitable ways. Public intercourse, and private friendship, are sadly marred by the absence of Charity. Charity is sometimes a stranger even in domestic circles; and the happiness of a whole household becomes embittered for years; it may be, for ever. Why is this? How does it happen that what GOD hath so admirably contrived for the happiness and well-being of His creatures, should become converted into a grief and vexation to them, as well as into an offence to Himself? It is because there is so little long-suffering in the world,—so little forbearance and kindness: so much envying; so many vaunting words and puffed-up ways; so much unseemly behaviour; so much self-seeking. It is because men and women are *so very easily provoked*, and are so prone *to think all evil* of one another. It is because there is so little inclination to cover faults; so much unbelief; so little hope. It is because there is so small a measure of *meek endurance* amongst mankind.

The First Day of Lent,

COMMONLY CALLED

Ash-Wednesday.

LENT, THE SEASON OF CONVERSION.

JOEL ii. 12.

Turn ye even to Me, saith the LORD, *with all your heart.*

EVERY season of the natural year, as it comes round, brings its special duties with it, and requires of the husbandman a change of occupation. The same thing holds true of the Christian Year. There is a season of preparation, and a season of joy; a season of self-denial, and a season of sorrow; a season of triumph, and a season of consolation. Every portion of it has its own peculiar complexion, and brings its own appropriate duty. If we must assign a special duty to the present season, we would speak of the forty days of Lent, which begin to-day, as *the season of conversion to* GOD.

The word 'Conversion,' thus applied, may

strike some persons as improper. But there is indeed nothing at all strange or wrong in this use of the word. 'Conversion' means 'Turning:' and when we speak of 'the season of Conversion,' we do but speak of the season when it is most of all fit that man should obey the summons of the prophet Joel,—'*Turn ye* even to Me, saith the LORD.' Sad indeed it is to think that language so plain should have become to that degree darkened, that 'Conversion' should stand for a process little short of miraculous; an effect to be produced altogether from without: whereas, in truth, it denotes a change taking place within us; a change wrought, not by the extraordinary, but by the ordinary influences of GOD's Holy Spirit; seen, not in any wondrous operation; attested, not by any remarkable outward sign:—but altogether brought about in secrecy and in silence; beginning and ending in the inner chamber of the heart of man.

Let us then consider together the nature and the duty of *Conversion to GOD.*—As already said, no outward signs are to be looked for. He who waits for any voice from Heaven, beyond that which we have this day heard; any call louder than that of the prophet Joel in the Epistle for Ash-Wednesday, will probably wait all his life long, in vain. There is a great risk that *he* will die at last, unawakened, who is mad enough to wait for a kind of summons which GOD has nowhere encouraged us to expect. Let us profit then by what we know of this matter, and be wise in time. *Conversion* is *Turning*. True enough it is that a man must *be* converted; but just as true is it that a man must *be* turned: 'Turn Thou us, and we shall be turned,' as it is written[a]. What is this however but saying what none deny; namely, that no one can come to GOD, except GOD first draw him? We know that 'we have no power of ourselves to help ourselves.' The inclination of the heart must come from Him. But then, this is only one part of the work of Conversion. The yielding to that blessed influence of GOD's Holy Spirit,—the turning ourselves to GOD, when GOD seeks so to turn us,—this must be done *by ourselves*. And this last part of the work, which is our own concern, is what we hold to be the special duty of this solemn season. Unless there be this readiness on our side, we may not expect that any good will follow. If there *be* this readiness, then let none doubt that GOD has already done His part; and that it rests with himself

[a] Jer. xxxi. 18: Lam. v. 21.

alone to be turned, or not.... All excuses, in short, for throwing the burthen of Man's repentance on the Father of Mercies, are a hollow deceit. They will not bear examination. They melt away like frost-work in sunshine, whether we test them by experience, or examine them by the light of God's Word.

The great work then which we have been describing, we hold to be the special work of the present season. The current of our thoughts and inclinations, the stream of our daily life, (to judge at least from one sad experience,) is certainly prone not to set heavenward. Either anxiety, or ambition; some worldly aim, or some family care; one or other of these is apt to clip the wings of the soul, and prevent it from soaring above this mortal scene. If there be no such influence at work, the very tendency of our nature, which is ever earthward, is a sufficient obstacle to that closer walk with God of which holy men tell, and which, in our wiser moments, we all think we desire. Now, the season which begins to-day has this peculiar claim on our gratitude, that it comes to us with a special call; inviting us to put earthly things away from us *now*, or at least to give them for awhile the second place,—reserving the first for 'the Kingdom of GOD, and His Righteousness.' We are invited, *now*, to apply our minds more than is our usual wont, to the things which concern our peace: to cultivate the spirit of Prayer, reviewing our practice in respect of this particular duty, and seeking to amend it: to examine our hearts, and to look closely into the habits of our daily life: to wean ourselves from whatever earthly thing has had too large a share of our affections,—in order thus to loosen the hold which Earth has upon us, and to give our spirits the opportunity of building their nest in Heaven. All these things seem included under the general head of Conversion, or the turning of the heart to GOD.

And it may further be supposed that this will be the work of the heart in secret. It will be begun by a sad review of our own state,—our own secret acts,—habits,—character: and this must, of necessity, be a work conducted privately. Then will come the steady contemplation of our Divine Master, and all His glorious promises, on the one side: on the other,—the World, the Flesh, and the Devil, with all their unholy allurements. Next, will come, (if so it may be,) a 'sense of the necessity and blessedness of solemnly choosing for ourselves, with all our hearts, the service of CHRIST our LORD[b].' Then will follow good resolutions; the firm and steady purpose to be more wary and watchful for the future; to be more on one's guard against temptation; to be more strict with oneself. Some good habits also will be commenced. And every stage of the blessed process we have been describing will be attended with fervent prayer. By this, no eloquent address or lengthy form of supplication, is meant. We do but mean a cry like that of the Blind man,—'LORD, that I might receive my sight[c]:' a cry like that of the Leper,—'If Thou wilt, Thou canst make me clean[d]:' a cry like that of the despised Publican,—'GOD, be merciful to me a sinner[e]!'

We request you also to observe the phrase in which the prophet Joel recommends the duty on which we have been enlarging. 'Turn ye even to Me, saith the LORD,—*with all your heart.*' It is a very special note of the Divine commands that they require this entire surrender of the affections. A heart 'not perfect' before GOD, is refused and rejected by Him. He will have *the whole heart,*—and accordingly, He calls Himself in a hundred places 'a *jealous* GOD.' Very

[b] Bishop of Oxford.
[c] St. Mark. x. 51.
[d] St. Matth. viii. 2.
[e] St. Luke xviii. 13.

merciful, surely, even in this requirement, as well as very just: for it is *easier*, far, to serve One whom we love entirely, than to render a wretched kind of half-service to him who has only a little piece of our affection ... GOD demands therefore such a free and full, such a hearty and unfeigned conversion of ourselves to Him: and He demands it specially *at this time.*

It does but remain that we implore every one who may have listened to what has been spoken, to accept it as an exhortation addressed to himself. The larger part of mankind need it but too plainly. Most of us have sunk into a deep slumber, and require to be awakened from it. The World has too many demands upon us. Every day brings with it too many duties which pertain to this life. Our hopes and fears, our cares and wishes, are all too many; and almost all of them have their beginning and their end in Time. We plant, and build, and heap up treasures, and lay plans, *not* for Eternity. We surely forget that here we have no abiding city; that four-score years are the outer boundary of the life allotted to man; that this fair Earth will be burnt up at the last, with all that it contains; and that *he* alone will stand immoveable in his lot, at the end of the days, who shall have turned himself to the LORD—with his whole heart.

Some plain practical hint has often been found of great service in enforcing a solemn duty. One easy precept of this kind shall now be offered. You will find it will much aid your obedience to the Divine Command which we have been considering, to commit to memory the Collect for Ash-Wednesday; and after learning it very exactly and faithfully, to repeat it, three times a day, throughout the forty days of Lent. The blessedness of this practice, and the help of it, will be discovered very soon by him who makes the trial in a humble spirit. It will assure the weak and doubting that the Author of their being hates nothing which His gracious Hands have made; but forgives the sins of all them that are penitent. It will at the same time remind all to implore Almighty GOD to create and make in them new and contrite hearts; to lament their sins, and acknowledge their wretchedness; and to seek of Him, the GOD of all Mercy, perfect remission and forgiveness, through JESUS CHRIST our LORD.

The First Sunday in Lent.

MAN SHALL NOT LIVE BY BREAD ALONE.

St. Matth. iv. 4.

He answered and said, It is written, Man shall not live by bread alone, but by every word that proceedeth out of the mouth of God.

The forty days of Lent, which Christian men observe in memory of the forty days during which our Lord fasted in the wilderness, begin on Ash-Wednesday. Those days of fasting were days of Temptation also: and, accordingly, the Temptation of Christ forms the subject of this Day's Gospel. We are about to invite your attention to that great event; and have chosen for our special meditation one portion of it, which will be found to suggest a train of thought suitable to the entire season, as well as to furnish help and guidance to us all.

Our Lord's Temptation, next to His Death and Passion, is the greatest event recorded of Him in the Gospel. The reason of this is evident. It was Messiah's first encounter with His great Enemy, Satan. Viewed aright, the scene so simply and briefly described in Scripture, is the most terrific which can be imagined, as well as the most sublime: for we cannot forget that it is none other than a contest, on the issue of which depended the Salvation of all Mankind. On the one side was the Eternal Son, made flesh; sinless indeed, yet compassed with all the infirmity of man's fallen nature: on the other, the chief of the fallen angels, Satan; that old Serpent, who in the beginning by deceiving our first parents had brought Death, and Sin, and Sorrow into the world. The Eternal Son, I say, stood on one side: the same who 'in the beginning' had created Man upright; and behold, all His works had been found to be 'very good;' while opposed to Him stood the Enemy who had marred and disfigured that good work, and brought in Ruin everywhere. Now, any interview between the Holy and Almighty One, and the Prince of the Evil Spirits, cannot but be brimful of awe and wonder.

But the interview described in the Gospel is far more wondrous than might be thought from any thing which has yet been said; as will at once appear from the following considerations:—

1st, There had been a prophecy, given in the beginning, that the Seed of the Woman should bruise the Serpent's head: that is, that One miraculously born of Woman, should at length appear, and destroy the Tempter by inflicting upon him a mortal injury.

And 2ndly, a voice from Heaven had just now proclaimed *Him* to be the SON of GOD, whom Satan now beheld standing before him:—'This is My Beloved Son, in whom I am well pleased.' A mere man He seemed: feeble, and famished too; and *not* beautiful as men reckon beauty. So that *doubt* mingles with *fear;* *surprise* is blended with hate, in the breast of Satan, as he approaches Him. At last, (with a kind voice and manner, doubtless; with every thing that could help to seduce and persuade,) the Enemy breaks silence with the words,—'If Thou *be* the SON of GOD, command that these stones be made bread!'

Concerning this Temptation, it must suffice to point out that yielding to it would have been sinful, under the circumstances; else, Satan would not have made use of it. Our SAVIOUR CHRIST, as very man, had been miraculously supported through His forty days of fasting: the last day had arrived, but was not yet ended: the Almighty Aid was already beginning to be sensibly withdrawn, and the pang of hunger had been awakened. Our LORD was conscious of His need; and Satan urged Him to gratify it in a manner different from what had been determined upon in the Divine Counsels. To comply would have been sinful.—Eve complied, and fell. Adam shared her guilt, and brought ruin upon mankind. What will *this* Mysterious Being do? If He complies, Satan is safe. If He refuses to comply, then has Satan found a formidable enemy. And what if He should prove to be indeed the SON of GOD,—as the Voice from Heaven had proclaimed at His Baptism? *Then* will Satan have found a dangerous Rival indeed! The long-promised Seed may have actually appeared at last who is destined to bruise his head: that is, effectually to destroy his power, and in the end to destroy *him!* . . . . It is time now to consider our LORD's reply to the infernal suggestion of the Evil One, which is contained in the words of the text.

But before we repeat the glorious words with which the Saviour of Mankind beat back His Adversary, and gave him his first death-blow, we shall do well to consider that, for any thing that appears to the contrary, He *might* have pursued a different course. For example, He might have simply said, Get thee hence Satan:—

or He might have been quite silent:—or He might have displayed some proof of His being Very God, and so scared the Evil One from His presence:—or again, He might have made him some lofty reply, the meaning of which would have been above us: words which might have silenced Satan indeed, but which men would for ever have wondered over, and desired to understand.—He took none of these courses, however; but is found to have used words which any feeble child of Adam, any one of ourselves, on being similarly tempted, may use with equal meaning, equal safety, equal success. He says nothing as to His being the Son of God, or not. He simply brings forward a text from the viiith of Deuteronomy, verses 2 and 3. The whole passage runs thus:—(Moses is speaking to the children of Israel.) 'Thou shalt remember all the way which the Lord thy God led thee these forty years in the Wilderness, to humble thee, and to prove thee, to know what was in thine heart, whether thou wouldest keep His commandments, or no. And He humbled thee, and suffered thee to hunger, and fed thee with manna, which thou knewest not, neither did thy fathers know; that He might make thee know *that Man doth not live by bread only, but by every word that proceedeth out of the mouth of the* LORD *doth Man live.*'

That Divine answer therefore, on our LORD's lips, seems, (as we humbly imagine,) to be to this effect:—'Thou hast tempted Me, these forty days, as thou didst tempt GOD's people Israel of old in the Wilderness for forty years. Thou biddest Me, now at length, distrust the power and providence of GOD. By His eternal Wisdom, by His Almighty Will, this painful fast hath been decreed: nor hath His heavenly aid been wanting hitherto to make it endurable by Me. So did it fare of old with GOD's chosen people. They lacked not Divine support in the howling waste: yet wast thou ever bent on inspiring them with impatience and distrust. In *their* extremity, indeed, GOD gave them bread from Heaven to eat: and thou wouldest have *Me*, in like manner, supply My own needs by spreading for Myself a table in the Wilderness. But mark the hollowness of thy proposal. It is written that the reason why GOD supplied the heavenly food called Manna, to His people of old, was, that they might know that Man shall not live by bread alone; but by every word that proceedeth out of the mouth of GOD. Learn then that His Word is My sup-

port: His Will, My joy: His Love, My life.'
.... Such seems to be the meaning of our
SAVIOUR's answer: words which baffled Satan,
and forced Him to assail our LORD with another
weapon, in a different way, and from a distinct
quarter.

You are entreated to take notice that this reply of the great Captain of our Salvation hath been bequeathed to *us,* His feeble and most faithless soldiers, as a precious legacy, as well as a most glorious pattern and example. Against Carnal Appetite, against the Lust of the Flesh, did Satan address his first Temptation when he assailed our LORD; and we may be well assured that he assailed the Holy One in *that* quarter because he knew it to be the quarter in which Human Nature is most vulnerable. It is a fearful thought for us all, but it is a truth against which we close our eyes at our peril. Nine out of ten are most open to assaults of a *fleshly* Nature. Here and there, worldly ambition,—here and there, spiritual presumption,—is the snare which beguiles a man and works his ruin: but it is far oftener gluttony or drunkenness, sloth or lust, which gives the Enemy an advantage over him; and, in the end, causes him to be dragged down to the very edge of the pit. Now, as already pointed out, the great Captain of our Salvation hath left us a weapon wherewith to repel such assaults, in the words of the text,—whereby He beat away the Tempter; disarmed him, and gave him a death-blow. On our lips (GOD be praised for it!) those words have exactly the same force which they had on *His*. They imply that Man hath a soul as well as a body: that the life of the body does indeed depend on its union to the soul, but the life of the *soul* depends on its union with GOD: that bread is indeed the support of man's lower nature, yet not of his higher; as it is written,—'Man shall not live by bread *alone*.' The spiritual meat is to do the will of GOD. And while Man continues to be such as he is, so long will it be the true answer to all fleshly solicitations, solemnly to profess that a man's life consisteth not in the things which he possesseth; that he has loftier needs than aught on Earth can supply; that his meat is to do GOD's Will; that his life is to lean upon GOD: for that in Him, and through Him, and by Him, he lives, and moves, and hath his very being.

The Second Sunday in Lent.

THE WOMAN OF CANAAN.

St. Matthew xv. 21—22.

Jesus *went thence, and departed into the coasts of Tyre and Sidon. And, behold, a woman of Canaan came out of the same coasts, and cried unto Him, saying, Have mercy on me, O* Lord, *Thou Son of David; my daughter is grievously vexed with a devil.*

Very striking is the statement which awaits us on the threshold of this wondrous history; for St. Matthew is telling about *a woman of Canaan;* one, therefore, who was descended from that accursed race which, for their great and heavy sins, God had so repeatedly commanded the Israelites to destroy. But, as we remember, they destroyed them not all, but put them to tribute instead. Accordingly, some few kept on dwelling in the old place;—through the days of Joshua, of the Judges, of the Kings, —there they still were, living on! The Royal House had passed away: the latter days had set in: Messiah Himself had at last appeared; and lo, the Canaanite is found to be still in the land! When JESUS 'departed into the coasts of Tyre and Sidon,' (the very spot where it is said in the Book of Genesis that the Canaanites had their border,) 'behold, a woman of Canaan came out of the same coasts, and cried unto Him, saying, Have mercy on me, O LORD, Thou Son of David; my daughter is grievously vexed with a devil.'

The strangeness of the history begins at once to strike us; for we read,—'But He answered her not a word. And His disciples came and besought Him, saying, Send her away; for she crieth after us.'

What they meant was, 'Pray grant her her petition!' 'Satisfy her, and send her away!' This appears from our LORD's reply. But how loudly must this poor creature have repeated her passionate prayer, 'Have mercy upon me, O LORD, Thou Son of David!' for the Apostles to have come to their Divine Master with such a request. They had probably tried, in vain, to silence her themselves. They had discovered that the woman was *determined* to obtain her petition.

Our LORD's reply is wonderful. 'He answered and said, I am not sent but unto the lost sheep of the house of Israel.' A beautiful saying, truly: at least as beautiful as it is stern. 'The lost sheep!' The Good Shepherd is therefore in pursuit of 'the people of His pasture and the sheep of His Hand,' even now; and though '*other* sheep He has, which are not of this fold : *them* also must He bring, and they shall hear His voice; and one flock shall there be, and one Shepherd;' yet must He *first* fulfil His ancient Covenant; first, make the offer of Salvation to the seed of Abraham. After *that*, He will send His chosen vessels to the Gentiles.

'Then came she and worshipped Him, saying, LORD, help me!'—an entreaty which called forth that famous reply, and rejoinder. 'But He answered and said, It is not meet to take the children's bread, and to cast it to dogs. And she said, Truth, LORD : yet the dogs eat of the crumbs which fall from their masters' table:' or, as her words may be more exactly rendered,—' Even so, LORD, *for*,' (not ' yet,' but '*for*,') 'the dogs eat of the crumbs which fall from their masters' table.' And the meaning is,—' Even so, LORD : be it as Thou sayest. Let the Jews be the children : let *us* be the dogs. I take Thee at Thy word, and gratefully accept my place in the picture which Thyself hast drawn : for the dogs, look you, eat of the crumbs which fall from their masters' table : and I ask no more!'

Now this is indeed a marvellous history. A man had need to be careless indeed not to be amazed when he reads it: or, if the extent of the woman of Canaan's boldness never struck him, he must have a strange mind indeed if he does not kindle when he has the matter thus brought before him. Notice how persevering and earnest she has been! She followed CHRIST in the way, and He spurned her; but she cried to Him the more. He endeavoured to escape her, but she pursued Him. St. Mark says that He hid in a house[a], but she found Him out. She renewed her prayer; but He repulses her, and calls her a *dog*. She kissses the Hand that smites her, and wrestles with Him whom she knows to be a GOD of Mercy, a GOD of Love, (the Father of Mercies, and GOD of all Comfort, as St. Paul speaks[b];) wrestles with Him, and turns His argument against Himself; proves that, by His own shewing, He is bound to grant her petition; and wins a victory, even when she seems to have experienced a defeat! *'I will not let Thee go,'* (she seems to say,) *'except Thou bless me[c].'*

O marvel of marvels! The Canaanite is still in the land, and it is a Canaanite who speaks thus! A Gentile,—a heathen,—an alien from the Com-

---

[a] St. Mark vii. 24. [b] 2 Cor. i. 3. [c] Gen. xxxii. 26.

monwealth of Israel,—an outcast,—a very *dog*,—can wrestle with GOD, and prevail! .... This woman had the spirit of the patriarch Jacob, and she renewed his deed. 'Yea, he had power over the Angel,' (saith the prophet Hosea,) 'and prevailed. He wept, and made supplication before Him [d].' So did Jacob at Penuel, and so did *she*. They wrestled with the same Divine Being, and they used the same means, and they met with the same success: for, in Jacob's case, it is added,—'And He blessed him there:' in her's,—'JESUS answered and said unto her, O woman, great is thy faith. Be it unto thee even as thou wilt!'... Be sure therefore that 'her daughter was made whole from that very hour:' for *that* was the thing which she 'willed;' the one thing which had brought her to CHRIST!

Such is the marvellous history recorded in this day's Gospel; and which is doubtless set before us as a great example of *prevailing prayer*. The intention of the Church thereby, it is not hard to discover; for if Lent be the season of Conversion to GOD, the season when we call specially to mind our LORD's Temptation, and after His glorious example, as well as by His Almighty aid, seek to gain the mastery over Satan, by

[d] Hos. xxii. 4.

resisting our own corrupt affections and lusts,—it must be of the highest importance to us to be reminded, now, of the true method of obtaining from GOD that assistance without which we can do nothing. Of Fasting, as a help to self-discipline, we have nowhere spoken particularly; but the Epistle and Gospel for Ash-Wednesday, as all will remember, recommend the exercise. We may observe, in passing, that Fasting is *a means*, not *an end;* and though 'Self-denial' during Lent is doubtless incumbent on every one, without exception, yet 'Fasting,' in some few cases, may be even improper. Not so Prayer. It is the one weapon without which no soldier of the Cross can hope to prevail. A certain kind of possession 'goeth not out,' we are informed, except ' by Prayer *and Fasting*ᵉ.' Without '*Prayer,*' however, let us be well assured that *no* kind goeth out.

Let us then briefly gather up the lessons on the subject of Prayer which are taught us by the History of the woman of Canaan.

1. The value and efficacy of 'Intercession,'—the prayer, that is, which one person makes for another,—is here strikingly shewn: but we will not dwell upon that view of the subject now. We

---
ᵉ St. Matth. xvii. 21.

will notice what is taught us concerning Prayer in general.

2. And certainly, before all things, we learn that it ought to be earnest, and persevering. We are shewn the effect of earnestness, or rather of *importunity*, (if need be,) in our addresses to the Throne of Grace. . . . The parable of the Unjust Judge was delivered by our LORD to this end; namely, to shew 'that men ought always to pray, and not to faint[f].' The miracle which we have been considering was surely wrought with the selfsame view, and for the selfsame purpose! . . . . 'Ask, and it shall be given you. Seek, and ye shall find. Knock, and it shall be opened unto you.' So runs the promise. But take notice that if 'asking' will not suffice, there must be a 'seeking' by more painful means for that mercy which yet it is promised that we shall assuredly 'find.' If 'seeking' avails not, then must we 'knock.' And what if we shall have to knock often, and loud, and long? 'I say unto you, Though He will not rise and give him, because He is his friend, yet because of his *importunity* He will rise and give him as many as he needeth[g].'

3. Lastly,—we are reminded that our Prayers will perhaps not be answered immediately: that

[f] St. Luke xviii. 2.   [g] St. Luke xi. 8.

God will perhaps seem as if He heard not. Let us observe, however, *why* it was that our Saviour made Himself strange to this woman; and even seemed, (to those, at least, who behold the outside of things alone,) exceedingly severe. It was only because He knew *the strength of her Faith*. Was it not *His* gift? and to whom men have committed much, of him do they not ask the more? He yearned towards her with Love unspeakable; but, (like Joseph among his brethren,) 'He made Himself strange, and spake roughly.' He designed her greater blessedness thereby. 'Open thy mouth *wide*, and I will *fill* it,'—as it is said in the Psalms. By making her heart dilate with the more longing, He was able to fill it the fuller with Himself. He tried her Faith, only because He knew that she had the Faith to try. And if we never experienced anything of the kind, in our own persons, we shall do well to believe that it is only because we are as yet but babes in Faith: and that Christ deals with us so gently, only because He knows that we are so weak.

The Third Sunday in Lent.

THE RELAPSED DEMONIAC.

St. Luke xi. 24—26.

When the unclean Spirit is gone out of a man, he walketh through dry places, seeking rest; and finding none, he saith, I will return unto my house whence I came out. And when he cometh, he findeth it swept and garnished. Then goeth he, and taketh to him seven other spirits more wicked than himself; and they enter in, and dwell there: and the last state of that man is worse than the first.

INASMUCH as Prayer and Fasting are two great instruments, under the Divine Blessing, for enabling us to overcome those suggestions to evil with which the Enemy of souls is for ever plying our fallen nature; a great example of the efficacy of either, is made the subject of the Gospels for the first two Sundays in Lent. The warning which is brought under our notice today completes the lesson. In the words of the text is declared the condition of a soul from which the Evil Spirit has been expelled; namely, its liability to renewed assaults, and those of a more violent kind than ever.—Let us give to this matter a little close attention; and endeavour, by God's blessing, to derive from the amazing revelation thus made to us, some useful hints for our own guidance.

Above all things, it is obvious to remark that the doctrine here so plainly delivered, is one which, if it had not been made a matter of express revelation, we could never have discovered for ourselves. Other statements of Holy Scripture we feel that we might, by patience and observation, have attained to; but *this* one, certainly never. Sundry considerations arise out of it, every one of which is entitled to distinct notice:—

And first, the *reality* of the agency of evil Spirits is not only pressed upon our notice, but even forced upon our acceptance; for our Lord's account of what happens when 'the unclean Spirit is gone out of a man' is altogether without meaning, unless His words are taken in their plain, literal sense. We will not now argue the question; or pretend to explain what is so much above us as *the manner* in which spiritual natures are permitted to influence us for evil. While we freely admit, on the one hand, that there is reason to believe that the Power of Satan hath been effectually broken; that the Stronger than the Strong hath once for all overcome him,—taken from him all his armour wherein he trusted,—and divided his spoils; yet are we forced, on the other hand, to maintain that the Empire of Satan, although broken, continues to exist in the World,—if only because of the many passages of Scripture which describe it as being yet in operation. Thus, when St. Paul urges Christians to put on 'the whole armour of GOD,' it will be remembered that the very ground of his injunction is the Spiritual warfare in which Christian men are continually engaged. 'For we wrestle not against flesh and blood,. but against Principalities, against Powers, against the Rulers of the darkness of this world, against spiritual wickedness in high places[a].'

We are at liberty therefore to consider the case which is here set before us, as the history of what may happen in the case of an individual Christian. It proved to be '*also*' the history of that generation which 'crucified the LORD of Glory,' as our SAVIOUR Himself foretold; but the proper fulfilment of His words, He declared to be personal, private, and particular. 'When the unclean Spirit is gone out of *a man*, he

[a] Eph. vi. 12.

walketh through dry places, seeking rest, and finding none.' In such striking terms is the *restlessness* of the fallen Angel described, on finding himself forcibly ejected from the Temple of the Human Body. His usual opportunities of working evil are suddenly cut off, and he is straightway rendered miserable. He is banished into 'dry places,'—that is, 'the barren wilds of Heathenism, on which the dews of Grace have not descended, and where there are no shoots of Divine planting to corrupt, and destroy.' Here he 'walketh, seeking rest, but finding none.' It now becomes all his object, therefore, to regain his former habitation,—'*my House,*' as he presumes still to call it, though indeed it is *his* no longer. He comes, accordingly, to take a survey of the scene of former defilement, and to ascertain its condition: 'and when he cometh, he findeth it swept and garnished;' cleansed and adorned by that HOLY SPIRIT to whose powerful interference he owed his own recent expulsion. Some deep craft, or some bold assault, will assuredly be required to enable him to re-enter; and the better to be enabled to pursue either course, he 'goeth and taketh to him seven other spirits *more wicked than himself.*'—Consider how circumstantially all this is related! What a lifting up of the veil from the unseen World is here! What a picture is thus discovered to us of malice and deliberate design! What a history of what takes place 'when the unclean Spirit is *gone out of a man!*'

We would next remark that the 'going out' here spoken of can mean nothing else than a violent *expulsion;* such as takes place when One, stronger than 'the Strong Man armed,' has come upon him, and overcome him, and spoiled his goods. The time of Baptism may be pointed out as the occasion when such an expulsion takes place; but we would not limit and restrain our LORD's words to that particular occasion. We would rather cling dutifully to His wondrous saying; and observe that what we have been recounting in detail, takes place '*when* the unclean Spirit is gone out of a man,'—whenever, through GOD's great Mercy and Power, *that* may be. The thing rather to be observed is, that, according to the case supposed, the banded Spirits succeed in effecting their deadly purpose. 'They enter in, and dwell there.' 'And,' (it is added with fearful emphasis,)— 'the last state of that man is worse than the first!'

Here then is a picture of departure from grace

given, of relapse into a yet worse than the original state of impurity, which it concerns us all to contemplate with serious anxiety, and godly fear. Our danger is set before us in lively colours, and the source of it is clearly stated; namely, 'the crafts and assaults' of the Enemy with whom we have to do. The mind is here suffered to rest on no second causes. Nothing is said of the natural results of sinful actions: of the unhinging of character: of men's proneness to fall a second time: of the influence of acts in promoting a deadly habit. Two *Persons* are set before us besides ourselves:—(1) GOD, by whose power, (clearly implied, though not expressed,) the unclean Spirit goeth out of a man; and (2) that unclean Spirit himself;—walking about restless under expulsion, and eagerly plotting a return to his house whence he came out. From such a view of the matter, delivered to us by CHRIST Himself, we surely turn away at our peril! For any doubt as to our LORD's meaning, there is no room whatever. Let us then gather what must, at all times, be our plain duty; but what, at this season of Lent, we seemed called upon to make the object of our especial care.

The 'House' into which the banded Spirits effected their return must have been found by them in an unguarded state when they came to assault it; or they would assuredly have found it impossible to effect their purpose. Take notice that they looked for resistance. Only *one* unclean spirit had been expelled; but *eight*, (and seven were '*more wicked*' than the other,) were employed to recover the lost habitation. They 'entered in,'—perhaps by surprise; perhaps by violence. We are not told how. What is certain, they did not meet with the resistance they expected. The 'good man' cannot have been 'watching[b].' There must have been a want of vigilance and Prayer. He had forgotten to 'watch and pray,' or this terrible result could never have been effected.

A terrible result, truly! inasmuch as the last state of him who so relapses into Sin, ' is *worse* than the first.' 'For if, after they have escaped the pollutions of the World through the knowledge of the LORD and SAVIOUR JESUS CHRIST, they are again entangled therein, and overcome, the latter end is worse with them than the beginning. For it had been better for them not to have known the way of Righteousness, than, after they have known it, to turn from the holy commandment delivered unto them[c].' ... And

[b] St. Matth. xxiv. 43.   [c] 2 St. Pet. ii. 20. 21.

this is the end of the matter: it is the threat, as it were, which follows the warning; the penalty which attends the violation of the Divine Law! 'Wherefore, let him that thinketh he standeth, take heed lest he fall[d]!' Every advance in Holiness does but provoke the Enemy's malice; every successful effort to expel the plague of our own heart[e], is but a challenge to the Adversary to come on. Our truest strength is to *know* ourselves weak. Our best confidence is to cherish godly fear. He is our only Hope, who hath promised to be our 'refuge and fortress[f];' but who, in the meanwhile, commands that our habit shall be Watchfulness: our weapon, Prayer.

[d] 1 Cor. x. 12.   [e] 1 Kings viii. 38.   [f] Ps. xci. 2.

The Fourth Sunday in Lent.

THE FEEDING OF THE FIVE THOUSAND WHEN THE PASSOVER WAS NIGH.

St. John vi. 4—6.

And the Passover, a feast of the Jews, was nigh. When Jesus *then lifted up His eyes, and saw a great company come unto Him, He saith unto Philip, Whence shall we buy bread, that these may eat? And this He said to prove him: for He Himself knew what He would do.*

These words will be recognised as forming part of this day's Gospel. They are found in a very striking narrative, namely, the miraculous feeding of the Five Thousand. St. John relates that our Saviour had crossed the Sea of Galilee: that a great multitude 'followed Him, because they saw His miracles which He did on them that were diseased;' and that, having gone up into a mountain, He 'sat there with His Disciples.' It was evening. 'When Jesus then lifted up His eyes, and saw a great company come unto Him, He saith unto Philip, Whence shall we buy bread, that these may eat? And this He said to prove him: for He Himself knew what He would do.'

Our LORD addressed these words to *Philip*, because He desired to arouse that Disciple to a sense of His Divinity. 'Have I been so long time with you, and yet hast thou not known Me, Philip^a?' were His words, a year after, to the same favoured follower. Philip remarked that as much bread as two hundred pence would buy,—(all their store of money, probably,)—would not suffice to feed so great a multitude. Our LORD inquired how many loaves the Disciples had. A little boy, it was answered, had five barley loaves and two small fishes. The command was given to make the men sit down. They did so, on the green grass, in parties of a hundred and of fifty. Our LORD then lifted up His eyes to Heaven, gave thanks, and brake. To each of the Twelve, He then delivered a portion; and lo, it was found that the Creator's Hands had endued that Bread with unheard-of power of growth! those fishes, with mysterious power to increase and multiply! The Apostles brake, and gave away; but the fragment that remained was not less than it was before. A fresh piece had grown where there had been a

[a] St. John xiv. 9.

piece removed: and thus, as they went about from company to company, they discovered to their amazement that Creative Power had impressed upon those wondrous morsels the faculty of self-production and endless increase. All did eat, and all were filled; and, O wonder! there remained in the end more than had been in the beginning. Every Apostle filled his basket with the fragments that abounded; so that twelve baskets-full were taken up. 'Then these men, when they had seen the miracle that JESUS did, said, This is of a truth that Prophet that should come into the World!' They meant to say that our SAVIOUR must surely be, (as He surely *was*,) the Prophet whom Moses had foretold as hereafter to be raised up like unto himself[b]. Moses had fed the people in the Wilderness: CHRIST had done the like. He was, 'of a truth, that Prophet that should come into the World!'

And now, what is the teaching of this wondrous incident?—It sets forth, beyond a doubt, and in the most lively manner, the benefits of the great Sacrifice which CHRIST Himself was to offer shortly upon the Cross. This becomes clearer, when it is stated that on three out of

[b] Deut. xviii. 15.

the four Passover seasons comprehended by our LORD's Ministry, He went up to Jerusalem: namely, on the first, the second, and the fourth. *At the third* Passover season, however, He went *not* up to Jerusalem, at all: but instead, He wrought the Miracle of feeding the five thousand. It was to call our attention to this circumstance that St. John introduces those few words,—'The Passover, a feast of the Jews, was nigh.' He leaves us to infer that the mighty wonder he was proceeding to relate, had some mysterious connexion with that Festival. And dull of heart must he be who reads the vith chapter of St. John's Gospel without perceiving what that connexion is.

Slow of understanding, and dull of heart, must he be who sees not that the True Bread was He who came down from Heaven,—even the Son of Man Himself. 'My flesh,' (He says,) 'is meat indeed.' 'Except ye eat the flesh of the Son of Man, and drink His blood, ye have no life in you.' And how is CHRIST's Body to be given, taken, and eaten, except after a spiritual and heavenly manner in the Blessed Sacrament of His most precious Body and Blood? .... He gave the typical Bread to the *Disciples*, and made *them* distribute to the multitude; as if to teach that it is by the hands of His unworthy servants, His appointed ministers, that He is pleased to convey His choicest blessings,—yea, that He communicates *Himself* to His people. For this our life is none other than a journey through a wilderness; and what do *we*, but faint for want of food by the way?

From Mid-Lent Sunday, then, our eyes are guided to look forward to the Passion of our LORD, and to His victory over Death: while the benefits which result to ourselves therefrom are set forth in this great Miracle,—which may be regarded as a Parable in action. Let us beware how *we* incur the reproach of the Disciples, as yet untaught to 'see the wondrous things of GOD's Law.' *We*, at least, will not, after our LORD's express warning, be 'slow to apprehend that in this, and the other miraculous feeding, something more than common bread was denoted by the food imparted, and the baskets that remained^c.'

The thing is soon told: but the lesson is one which should fill our hearts, and deeply impress our minds; should be calmly pondered over; remembered often, and considered long. With unusual solemnity has the HOLY SPIRIT com-

^c St. Matth. xvi. 8 to 12; St. Mark viii. 17 to 21.

mended it to our notice. It is the only one of all our LORD's Miracles,—indeed it is the only event before the Passion,—which all the four Evangelists conspire in recording; and they agree in relating it with singular fulness and detail. It is moreover made by the Church the subject of the Gospel for two Sundays in the year[d]. How appropriate it is to the present season, will be felt at once; for the Christian Passover, a Feast of the Israel of GOD, is now drawing very nigh; and beyond a doubt, we require reminding of the mysterious import of that Festival: beyond a doubt, we stand in need of whatever may rouse us from that sluggish indifference into which our souls are for ever sinking. Night and day, winter and summer, storm and sunshine,—these are for ever succeeding each other in a silent, settled order; and we forget that we live on the confines of two Worlds,—that there is only one step betwixt us and death;—that, pass a few short years, and we shall be gathered into the unseen World; but that, in the meantime, Holy Seasons and Festival-days come to rouse us. Advent and Christmas, Epiphany and Lent, Easter and Whitsuntide,—each brings its warn-

---

[d] Divested of its preface, it recurs as the Gospel for the twenty-fifth Sunday after Trinity.

ing; each comes with a message to us from the other World: a strong cry to awaken, or a call to rejoice in CHRIST; an invitation to behold His miracles of mercy, or to sympathize in His miracles of suffering; a summons to rise with Him from death, or to receive and entertain the Blessed Comforter, which is the HOLY GHOST... Such is the Sacred Year: such is the intention of the Church in her services. To-day, she sounds a note of preparation. She reminds us expressly, that the Passover is nigh. Yes, it wants three weeks to Easter!

We shall *then*, one and all, (as many of us, that is, as have received the sacred rite of Confirmation,)—all of us will then desire to be partakers of the sacred Feast which derives all its *reality* from the great sacrifice of Good Friday, and which was set forth in type by the miraculous event we have been now considering. May the same Almighty One who both gave Himself to be a sacrifice for our sins, and spread a Table for the five thousand in the wilderness,—may *He* touch our souls with a lively sense of their great and urgent need, as well as supply it. . . . Not from habit, nor yet through shame; not because others come, nor for any other unworthy reason, let *us* be induced to give a lifeless attendance at the Holy Table of our LORD! No; but first, because we have repented of our past sins, are steadfastly purposed to lead a new life, and are in charity with all mankind: and next, because we desire a closer walk with GOD, and know that there can be no surer way than this of attaining to so great a blessedness. Lastly, because we call to mind the glorious things which are told us of this blessed participation, in the case of as many as receive the Sacrament worthily; and because we earnestly desire, above all things, to know the comfort of them by actual experience.

The Fifth Sunday in Lent.

THE ONENESS OF OUR LIFE.

St. John viii. 51.

Verily, verily, I say unto you, If a man keep My saying he shall never see Death.

The Gospels for the three first Sundays in Lent seem to glance backward, as if in the direction of Ash-Wednesday: those for the three last Sundays look forward to the Sacrifice of Christ; or rather, to the Divinity of Him who suffered. The words before us will guide us to a profitable train of meditation, if we seek to follow out the hint they contain that our existence, in Time and in Eternity, is *one;* and thus, succeed in persuading ourselves that it is a dream and a delusion to suppose that a life,—begun, continued, and ended sinfully in this World,—can be followed by a life of Happiness in the next.

Now, there seems to lie at the root of this matter one mistaken notion in particular, which we should by all means seek to remove from our minds: namely, the inveterate notion that Death itself will work a wondrous *change* in us; so that the unfitness for Heaven, we lived and died in, will be purged away, even by the very process of Death itself.—For, will Death work *any change in us at all?* It would seem *not*. Resurrection will work a wondrous change, doubtless: but no change, (that we are aware,) passes upon the soul by Death. There will be the separation of soul and body; but no change effected in the moral *condition* of the soul; except that it will be compelled to put away its dreams and delusions, and to see itself as it *is*. Nay, will even Resurrection itself work the kind of change expected? We cannot think it. For the only question is,—Will it convey new dispositions, and impart new habits, and make the sinful man a Saint? Impossible! It will introduce us to another sphere of life and action; and there will therefore be given to us the needful faculty of exercising that new mode of being; but neither Reason nor Revelation warrant us in supposing that Death will work any change whatever in our tempers or dispositions. There will be a gift of new and wondrous powers: of this, Scripture leaves us in no doubt; nor indeed, Nature either. But will not those ennobled powers be a blessing only in the case of those whom GOD accepts?

He who reads the Gospel with care will find

scattered up and down, secret hints or open sayings which all look one way; and can in no other manner be explained than by the great truth we are seeking to explain; namely, that our Life is *one*, in Time and in Eternity; a continued state; changed indeed as to the manner of its being,—as a corn of wheat becomes changed after it has been sown in the Earth; yet the same, also, throughout all its increase, by virtue of a law impressed upon it by GOD. Our Life is one; a continuous, uninterrupted state. 'He that liveth and believeth in Me,' (said our SAVIOUR to one of His Saints,) 'shall never die[a].' He spoke, doubtless, (as He speaks in the text,) of 'the Second Death[b]:' but His Divine words convey a lively image of sameness, not change; of continuance, not interruption. And so, on another occasion :—'This is Life Eternal, to know Thee, the only true GOD, and JESUS CHRIST whom Thou hast sent[c].' Observe how it is thereby implied that *Life Eternal* begins in *Time;* that the Life which now *is*, is the beginning of the Life *to come.*—So also the beloved Disciple :—' We know that we have passed from Death unto Life because we love the brethren.' He who could so write, regarded Death with

[a] St. John xi. 26.   [b] Rev. ii. 11: xx. 6.   [c] St. John xvii. 3.

very different eyes from ourselves[d]. There was to him 'no more Death.' The end of his mortal Life would be but a 'failing,' (as our LORD speaks;) ' When ye *fail*,' He says[e]; not, ' When ye *die:*' for the death of the righteous is but a failing,—as when a strong man faints at the end of a long race. It is but a closing of the eyes to the things of Time, in order to open them on the things of Eternity. And, in the case of St. John himself, his Death was announced to him by his LORD under, if possible, a yet milder figure. 'I will that he tarry—*till I come*[f].' He was not to *die*, but he was to *wait*. *He* was not to *go;* but *CHRIST* was to *come!*

Let us think of Death, then, less in its accidents, and more in its true essential nature. It is the name we give to the moment at which we pass out of this visible World into the World which is invisible: but our consciousness is not for a single moment suspended; nor are we, previous to Resurrection, at all changed. As we would be eternally, therefore, so must we die; and as we would die, so must we live. Our Life is one.

This may be admitted generally, in words; but it is not believed to any practical purpose,

---

[d] 1 St. John iii. 14.   [e] St. Luke xvi. 9.   [f] St. John xxi. 22.

or the course of this World would perforce be very different from what it is found actually to be. There is a dream and a delusion somewhere. The disobedient, and uncharitable, and impure, and unjust, persuade themselves that they shall not be unjust and impure, uncharitable and disobedient, for ever. They talk of sins pardoned, and offences blotted out; of the SAVIOUR's mercies, and the efficacy of CHRIST's Death: but they talk all to no purpose if they forget that Repentance must open the door to Pardon; and that the merits of the REDEEMER's Cross and Passion must be applied, by Faith, to the needs of each single soul. No! as we would *die,* so must we *live:* as we would be *hereafter,* so must we be *now.* Our Life is one.—There must be hearty endeavours to serve GOD, however imperfectly, in Time; and there will be hearty endeavours, crowned with perfect success, in Eternity. The 'pound' must gain us five or ten by earthly trading, as Servants; and then, as many cities will be committed to our heavenly rule, as Kings. Our Life is one.—Every act of Sin, every dallying with Temptation, is a part of eternal Misery: every striving after Holiness, every reaching out of the soul to GOD, is a part of eternal Joy. Our Life is one.—Not *one* in

Time, and *one* in Eternity, but *one altogether*. Not one Life till Death, and another Life, (as the Life of Angels,) after; but one long, continuous, uninterrupted, human Life; woven, (so to express oneself,) all out of the same piece. *Such* a life, that the soul might go away into the unseen World for four days, (as did the soul of Lazarus,)—and come back again to Earth,—and again depart;—and yet the Life, to all intents and purposes, be *all one Life*.

Such remarks seem worth making; not only because they are true, and perhaps not common; and further, because they may help us to get rid of the indefinite notion we all seem secretly to entertain concerning a blessed futurity in store, however impure and unworthy the previous life: but also, because some useful considerations are found to grow out of them.

For it will follow from what we have been saying, that Life is to be regarded as a preparation for Eternity: that we are acquiring *here* the habits we shall need *there;* training ourselves *now*, for the graces we shall want to use *then*. And this thought will prove a great consolation to the sick and suffering soul; for it will remind him that he is learning patience; sowing in tears that he may reap in joy. The poor Brother will find comfort, if a very heavy and bitter portion is his; for he will be reminded that he is being trained for the possession of good things hereafter. The life of self-denial will lengthen out into a long avenue of Love; and the pure in thought, in word, in deed, will discover in the end that they have been brightening a mirror wherein will be reflected the image of the Eternal! 'Blessed are the pure in heart,' (it is written,) 'for they shall *see* GOD!'

Let this thought, then, sustain all men in their several callings; abide with each in his separate walk of Life. Let Learning and Science indulge a glorious hope of their own future rewards. Yea, let every social, every domestic virtue, rejoice in the thought that it is, in its nature, imperishable; that its destiny, like the soul which harbours it, is eternal: that here below, it is but a seed; or at best, a leafy stem: the blossom, (of unimagined beauty,) the fruit, (of unsuspected sweetness,) being reserved for the climate of the skies. *There*, doubtless, not only does a high reward await, but undreamed-of opportunities also are doubtless there prepared, for as many as have cultivated any single Christian grace, and sought to bring it to perfection. Nay, more,—the humblest Christian who ponders over the Word of

Life, and closes the volume for the hundredth time with a sigh that he yet understands so little,—let *him* be sure that his reward will come at last, and that GOD will open his eyes in the latter days, that so he may see the wondrous things of GOD's Law. Let him be well persuaded that he will find none of his labour lost, none of his painstaking superfluous; but that he will see the clearer *then*, exactly in proportion to his striving for more Light *now*.

Nay, we may boldly carry our speculations further yet; and persuade ourselves that the services of the Sanctuary,— the Psalms and Prayers which we go to Church to join in,—are eternal things.; the beginnings of an everlasting service. They are patterns, (the SPIRIT expressly informs us,) of things in Heaven: and the Saints of GOD will doubtless in Heaven prolong the note of praise begun on Earth; fulfil in some higher sense their daily service; keep, after a yet loftier fashion, their Christian Feasts; and discover that, of a truth, however sublimed and ennobled, their Life in Time and Eternity has been indeed but one: the righteous, righteous still; the holy, holy still! changed—only in respect of brightness: differing—only in their degrees of glory!

The Sunday next before Easter.

THE TIME OF VISITATION.

St. Luke xix. 44.

Thou knewest not the time of thy visitation.

So spake our Saviour, addressing Jerusalem, when His Ministry was drawing very near its close; and the fate of the City was sealed for ever. It was as on this day that He entered His capital in lowly triumph. 'And when He was come near, He beheld the City, and wept over it, saying, If thou hadst known, even thou, at least in this thy day, the things which belong unto thy peace! but now they are hid from thine eyes. For the days shall come upon thee, that thine enemies shall cast a trench about thee, and compass thee round, and keep thee in on every side, and shall lay thee even with the ground, and thy children within thee; and they shall not leave in thee one stone upon another; because thou knewest not the time of thy visitation[a].'

[a] St. Luke xix. 41 to 44.

Now, in all this, you are requested to notice only one thing; namely, that although the visitation of Messiah had been long foretold, and long expected, yet, when it actually occurred, it took men by surprise. The time and the manner of Messiah's Coming had been declared: some of the most minute points in His history had been described beforehand; and the reality corresponded strictly with the prophecy. And yet, men did not *know* that reality when they *beheld* it. The misfortune of Jerusalem was that she '*knew not the time of her visitation.*' *This* it was which made the Saviour of the World pause for a moment on the brow of the hill which overlooks the City, and give vent to the sorrow of His human heart in a flood of sacred tears.

How did it happen, then, that Jerusalem,—in other words, that the Jewish people,—did not know the Day of their visitation?

It was because the prophecies relating to Christ, although they were fulfilled strictly, and to the very letter,—were yet not fulfilled *in the way the Jews expected*. I believe this may be said of them all. For example:—it had been foretold to David by Nathan the prophet, 'When thy days be fulfilled, and thou shalt sleep with thy fathers, I will set up thy seed after thee,

THE TIME OF VISITATION.

and I will establish His Kingdom. He shall build an house for My Name; and I will stablish the throne of His Kingdom for ever.' From this, it had been rightly inferred that the SAVIOUR was to be born of the royal line of David: but men were not prepared to find the prophecy fulfilled at a time when that House had fallen into deep decay, and extreme poverty. And so, the Infant, wrapped in swaddling clothes by His poor Mother, and laid in a manger, escaped notice: although He was the twenty-eighth in lineal descent from David. CHRIST had come to visit His people: but He came in so unexpected a manner, that they knew not the time of their visitation.

The place of our LORD's Birth had, in like manner, been distinctly foretold by the prophet Micah: yet, inasmuch as He was born in a manger, the circumstance was overlooked entirely. A blazing star had brought Wise Men from the East to inquire for the King of the Jews; so that all Jerusalem was troubled. The old prophecy was thereupon referred to and quoted: all men were therefore reminded. But it mattered not. It was all of no avail. Jerusalem looked for a powerful King, and a temporal SAVIOUR:—so that when the King of King came to visit her, because He came 'in great humility,'—she knew not the time of her visitation.

Yet once more. CHRIST's Entry into Jerusalem had been distinctly foretold. 'Shout, O daughter of Jerusalem; behold thy King cometh unto thee ... lowly, and riding upon an ass.' He came, as Zechariah had promised. Moreover, when He was come into Jerusalem, some were found to ask, 'Who is this?' And the multitude said in reply, 'This is JESUS, the prophet of Nazareth of Galilee.' But the most learned of the nation had made up their minds that the 'King' spoken of by Zechariah would be like the kings of this world: and it is plain that the multitude gave no further heed to the simple pageant which entered their gates. So simple was it, so far removed from what she had imagined, that Jerusalem *knew* not,—even when she *beheld*,—the time of her visitation.

To us, however, all these may perhaps seem clear cases of fulfilled prophecy. We will turn from these events, therefore, which the Jews *ought* to have understood and recognised when they saw them; and invite your attention to another set of events, which, it must be confessed, are darker, and seem to lie deeper; so that they might easily, (we think,) have been overlooked.

And these are coincidences which it concerns *us* especially, to take notice of; as we will presently explain.

Our LORD had been often spoken of in prophecy as 'the Branch:' in the xith of Isaiah for instance; where it is written, — 'There shall come forth a Rod out of the stem of Jesse, and a *Branch* shall grow out of his roots.' And this was fulfilled (St. Matthew says) when He went to live at Nazareth, and was called 'a Nazarene.' (For *Nasir* means a *Branch* in Hebrew.) It must be admitted that this was a strange,—and, as one might say, improbable,—fulfilment of prophecy.

Again. It had been said by the prophet Hosea,—"I called My Son out of Egypt.' And this was fulfilled, we read, when, at the death of Herod, the Holy Babe was carried up out of Egypt by command of an Angel of the LORD. This also is so remarkable, that even when the fulfilment is exhibited side by side with the prophecy, it requires not a little sacred learning to see what the Evangelist means.

Again. Isaiah had foretold that a great Light would be seen in the latter days by the people who dwelt on the confines of Zabulon and Naphtali: that, to them, Light would spring up. And this came to pass (St. Matthew says) when our LORD went to live at Capernaum. *That* city certainly does stand on the very spot which the prophet named: but consider how improbable it must have seemed to carnal eyes, that a forlorn Stranger, a poor persecuted Man, flying from Nazareth, (where the people would have killed Him if they could!)—that *He* should be the Great Light which was to make glorious the land of Zabulon and the land of Naphtali!

Examples might be multiplied to a great extent; but these will suffice. They are quite broad enough to build some remarks upon,—remarks which the Holy Season on which we this day enter make very opportune as well as important.

We declare, then, that it is our solemn conviction that one great reason why, in the Gospel, we are shewn Jerusalem not knowing the time of *her* visitation, is in order that *we* at least may be made aware of *ours*. *Her* misery is set before us, in order that *we* may escape the like fate. And that we *have* seasons of visitation: that special trial is made of ourselves at special seasons, we do not think it necessary to stop to prove. Indeed, all men are very ready to confess it. All are aware that, every now and then, the Arm of GOD finds them out; and that the touch of a Hand which was pierced for their sins, comes far nearer home to them than they care to admit. The great office however of the seasons of the Sacred Year seems to be *this*,—that they admit us to all the privileges, (and alas! to all the perils,) of GOD's ancient people. And thus it happens that our SAVIOUR CHRIST visits *us* in great humility at Christmas; manifests Himself, in power, to *our* eyes throughout Epiphany; invites *us* to sympathy in His sufferings during Lent; as to-day approaches *us* in lowly triumph; and as on Good Friday, is 'evidently set forth, crucified' *among ourselves* [b]. This may not be very evident, at first. It may seem to be only a way of talking,—not a reality; but we are persuaded that the truth of the remark will be discovered and admitted, in proportion as men attend to the teaching of the Prayer-Book, and seek to realize in practice the great truths of our Holy Faith.

You are requested, at least, to take notice that the reason why Jerusalem knew not the time of her visitation was because the manner in which her LORD came to her was so very different from what she had expected. This was the only reason. And shall we not profit by her miserable fate? When Holy-Week next comes round,

[b] Galat. iii. 1.

what if any one of ourselves should have gone to our rest? and what if, in reply to our secret thought that we received but little warning, it should be told us,—'CHRIST came *to thee* last Holy-Week. In the affecting services of those very solemn days, He came *to thee*. Thou wert reminded of thy short-comings: of many a sin unrepented of; many an evil habit unbroken: many a temptation unresisted. The end of those who lead careless lives was also set before thee. Many a holy thought was put into thine heart. Thou wert even prevailed upon to form many a godly resolution. Yea, by lips unworthy indeed, yet faithful in this matter, the notion was distinctly brought home to thee that *this* might be *thy last* opportunity. For a brief space, thou wert even brought to realize the thought that as CHRIST came suddenly to Jerusalem, even so, at that very season, He was passing, unsuspected, very nigh to *thee*'... And should such solemn words, my friends, be addressed to any of ourselves hereafter, GOD of His Mercy grant that it may not be added, — 'But thou, in spite of all, *knewest not the time of thy visitation.*'

Monday before Easter.

THE BLIND AND THE LAME.

St. Matthew xxi. 14.

And the blind and the lame came to Him in the Temple, and He healed them.

The recorded events of Monday in Holy Week are few indeed, but full of solemn interest: the Cursing of the barren Fig-tree; the Driving of the buyers and sellers out of the Temple; and the cluster of miracles referred to, rather than described, in the text. In the profound conviction that, at such a moment, nothing which was done was trifling; and that, where so little is recorded, the few incidents which find distinct notice must be regarded as of unusual moment, as well as of most solemn meaning; we have selected for remark St. Matthew's brief statement, that 'the blind and the lame came to Him in the Temple, and He healed them.' We cannot think that we shall thereby have lighted on ground which will prove either barren in edification, or unproductive of delight.

And first, it is obvious to point out how much it is the manner of the inspired writers to throw out sublime statements concerning Almighty GOD, or descriptive of His works; not only without any attempt to set off such statements to advantage, and to call attention to them, but even with marked simplicity and disregard of effect. Thus, a whole cluster of miracles is here despatched in one short verse of Scripture; and as, in Nature, we separate with the telescope star from star, and proceed to make observations on the several bodies which before presented to the eye the appearance of a single shining mass, so is it reserved for the eye of Faith to discover the surprising fulness, as well as the mysterious design, not to say the marvellous beauty, of a statement like the present, which at first sight seems descriptive of a single act of Mercy.

Of the many 'wonderful things[a],' therefore, which our SAVIOUR performed on the present occasion, the Evangelist St. Matthew notices only the miracles of healing performed on *the Blind* and *the Lame;* and it demands but little acquaintance with Holy Scripture to be aware that either of these two forms of bodily ailment is the common, as well as the obvious emblem of

[a] St. Matth. xxi. 15.

a corresponding moral defect. Thus, it was the declared purpose of our SAVIOUR's Coming into the world, 'to open the blind eyes, to bring out the prisoners from the prison, and them that sit in darkness out of the prison-house[b].' And when we further find Him spoken of as 'a Light to lighten the Gentiles,'—'a great Light' that was to spring up 'to as many as sat in the region and shadow of Death[c],'—do we not feel that the language of the Evangelical Prophet is so plainly figurative, that we are even surprised at finding our LORD engaged so frequently in the *literal* act of restoring sight to the blind? As a matter of fact, more of our SAVIOUR's miracles are recorded as having been wrought on blindness than on any other form of human infirmity: and we can but admit that all such acts were symbolical of the great purpose of His Coming,—namely, to inform and enlighten the consciences of men, and to enable them *to see*. 'Open Thou mine eyes,' (exclaims the Psalmist,) 'that I may see the wondrous things of Thy Law[d]!' The language of Nature offers the most convenient vehicle for expressing the strong desires of the children of Grace.

What, in like manner, mean those many an-

[b] Is. xlii. 7.   [c] Is. ix. 2.   [d] Ps. cxix. 18.

nouncements of what should befal 'the Lame' in the days of Messiah, but that strength should then be given to faithful men to '*run* in the way of GOD's commandments?' 'Then shall the lame man leap as an hart, and the tongue of the dumb sing,' (says the Evangelical prophet;) 'for in the wilderness shall waters break out, and streams in the desert^e.' He gives as the reason, the plentiful supplies of grace which should then be shed abroad. And can we read the Gospels without being struck with the frequency of this class of cures also? 'Go and shew John again those things which ye do hear and see,' said our SAVIOUR to the two messengers of the Baptist: 'the blind receive their sight, *and the lame walk*^f.' And when great multitudes came to CHRIST as He sat upon the mountain, the two first classes of persons which are named, are the '*lame*' and the 'blind^g.'

A subject is thus set before us in which we find our place without difficulty. We are reminded of our own great spiritual infirmities; of our need of *His* Almighty aid who poured the light of Day on sightless eyes, and gave those ancle-bones strength which before were powerless in Israel. For surely, the life of many of

^e Is. xxxv. 6.   ^f St. Matth. xi. 4, 5.   ^g St. Matth. xv. 30.

us,—our own life in too many respects,—is the life of the blind. We grope our way, in self-reliance, and we often lose it. We stumble and fall. We feel after, and we find not: we reach forth, and we grasp not.—We read GOD's Holy Word, yet we see nothing, or very little, of the many wonders which it contains. The veil is upon our hearts while we read. — We look abroad on the miracles of Love which surround our dwelling; we look within, on the mystery of Divine Goodness in which we live and move and have our being; yet we recognise little or nothing of the Hand of GOD either within us or without us. Our state may be almost described in the language which the beloved Disciple applied to his unbelieving countrymen:—'But though He had done so many miracles before them, yet they believed not on Him: that the saying of Esaias the prophet might be fulfilled .... They have blinded their eyes, and hardened their heart; that they should not see with their eyes, nor understand with their heart, and be converted, and I should heal them[h].'

Who again does not see in the helplessness of the Lame a lively type of his own condition; which, so far from 'running in the way of GOD's

---

[h] Such is the correct translation of St. John xii. 40.

commandments,' knows not how to '*walk* with GOD' for a single hour? What means our reluctance to begin whatever we know to be holy; or to persevere in those right courses which, by GOD's grace, we have already begun? Whence the sluggishness of our spiritual life: our slow advance, our irregular endeavours, our carelessness about reaching the goal and winning the prize? How is it, again, that the hour of Prayer is not impatiently expected; and that Prayer itself is regarded as a task, rather than a recreation? While engaged in Prayer, why do the thoughts wander, and the desires of our hearts seldom keep with the words of our lips? Whence is all this, but because we are '*lame* as well as blind;' and need healing as much, aye, a thousand times more, than those suffering ones who, as on this day, came to the SAVIOUR of the World 'in the Temple, and He healed them?'

The common words of Holy Scripture, doubtless, were meant to be our instructors. It cannot be in vain that we are told concerning Enoch and Noah that they '*walked* with GOD[1];' and, concerning Enoch, that we are told nothing else. To 'walk with GOD' is precisely what 'the lame' cannot do: and it is not hard to perceive how,

[1] Gen. v. 24: vi. 9.

in that short sentence, may be summed up the whole of a good man's life. He '*walks humbly*' with his GOD. He is content to keep pace with his Guide: (for ' can two walk together except they be agreed[k]?') and he is content to advance by '*walking*' only. There is progress therefore, but it is slow: his advance is slow, but it is constant. There is no halting by the way. He was 'lame' at first; but lo, he hath been 'healed' of his infirmity!

They 'came to Him *in the Temple,* and He healed them.' Of so short a text, let us not miss a single word; neither let us doubt that, in so brief a record, every word is full of heavenly meaning. Blind indeed must we be to miss the intimation thus conveyed, that it is to the House of GOD that we must repair if we would be healed by Him: the implied assurance that *in* the House of GOD we may reasonably expect that the Holy One will still manifest His miracles of Mercy; still shew Himself a GOD of Power. Thither let us carry, as often as we may, (especially at this holy season,) our infirmities; *there* let us fervently implore their removal. When, at the end of the Litany, we cry, 'O Son of David, have mercy upon us,'—shall we forget that

[k] Amos iii. 3.

we are using the language of the two blind men who followed CHRIST into the house[1]; as well as the cry of the other two blind men at Jericho[m]? and, remembering this, shall our faith so little resemble theirs, that the effect in *us* shall not be what it was in *them?* For we read that JESUS had compassion on them, and touched their eyes, and immediately *their eyes received sight;* and—'*they followed Him*[n]' '*in the way*[o],' 'glorifying GOD[p].'

[1] St. Matth. ix. 27.   [m] St. Matth. xx. 30.   [n] St. Matth. xx. 34.   [o] St. Mark x. 52.   [p] St. Luke xviii. 43.

Tuesday before Easter.

NOTHING LITTLE IN GOD'S SIGHT.

St. Luke xxi. 2.

He saw also a certain poor widow.

The history of Tuesday is fuller, than of any other day in Holy Week. First comes the walk of the Twelve Apostles and their Lord from Bethany, at early morning; when they remarked how the fig-tree which had been cursed twenty-four hours before, stood blighted and blasted in the spot where yesterday morning it had looked so fair and flourishing. Repairing, as usual, to the Temple, the Saviour is encountered by many enemies; who doubtless foresaw that His intention was, throughout this week to present Himself daily in the Sanctuary of God: but He put them to silence with a question respecting the Baptism of John; and then delivered the Parables of the Two Sons, and of the Vineyard let out to Husbandmen. In consequence of these discourses, (the prophetic character of which they at once perceived,) our LORD's enemies sought to lay hands on Him; but were deterred through fear of the populace. Next, the parable of the King's Son was added: after which, the Pharisees and the Herodians proved Him with a question respecting the payment of tribute. The Sadducees next assailed our LORD, and were quickly confounded out of their own Books; whereupon the Scribes assailed our SAVIOUR with an inquiry respecting the Law. But after our LORD's reply, we hear that none durst ask Him any more questions. In turn, *He* also put one question,—which the Pharisees were not able to answer: whereby He silenced them for ever. This done, He denounced eight woes upon the Pharisees and Sadducees; ending with that passionate lament for Jerusalem, —'How often would I have gathered thy children together, even as a hen gathereth her chickens under her wings; and ye would not!'... 'And JESUS sat over against the Treasury;' 'and He looked up, and saw the rich men casting their gifts into the Treasury. And He saw also *a certain poor widow casting in thither two mites.*'

He rose, and left the Temple with His Disciples; prophesying its destruction, as He lingered for a moment on its threshold. Then, taking His seat on the Mount of Olives,—the Temple spread out before Him, and all the beautiful buildings of Jerusalem full in view,—in reply to the earnest questionings of Peter, and James, and John, and Andrew, He spake of 'when these things should be;' and of 'what should be the sign of His Coming, and of the end of the World:'—in Heaven, the sun darkened; and the moon forgetting to give her light; and the stars falling, like fruits from the tree: on Earth, distress of nations with perplexity, the sea and the waves roaring; men's hearts failing them for fear, and for looking after those things which are coming on the Earth. Lastly, the Coming of the Son of Man in Glory, and all His Holy Angels with Him!

The Parables of the wise and foolish Virgins, and of the Talents, followed; and our LORD described how the just and the wicked shall be dealt with in the last day:—after which, it being night, He 'went out, and abode in the Mount of Olives.'

Now, the one circumstance in all this wondrous and varied narrative to which we wish to call attention, is, that amid all these mighty discourses and amazing prophecies; amid all the weariness of His Human Body, and the anguish of His Human Soul; amid griefs unrevealed, and bitterness of spirit unutterable; the LORD of

Heaven and Earth was at leisure to sit down and watch the ways of one of the very humblest of His creatures. 'He saw also—a certain poor widow.'.... After His eight withering woes denounced upon the Scribes and Pharisees, which must have goaded them to madness, (for they were at once the proudest and the most powerful of the people;) after *this*, and just *before* He entered upon that far-sighted prophecy which glanced onward, from the coming destruction of the City to the very end of the World,—blending the near, and the far future, so wondrously; and shewing that the Blessed Speaker's eye was filled with images of magnificence and grandeur unspeakable,—the destinies of the whole Human Race, and the consummation of all things:— (the moment is well worth observing; for it was the brief moment which separated the SAVIOUR's discourse concerning the things of Time and of Eternity,—the little halting-place between His leave-taking of His enemies, and His anticipation of the ruin which was to be wrought upon them; first, by His avenging armies; next, by His legions of Angels:)—it was at that particular instant, we repeat, and therefore while His heart must have been occupied in the way we have been describing,—that our LORD, seating

Himself over against the Treasury, (that is, the alms-chests which were destined to receive the offerings of the people,) looked up, and beheld how they cast money into the Treasury. And many that were rich cast in much. And there came a poor woman; and (as St. Luke remarks,) 'He *saw* her!'... He saw before Him the destruction of the Temple, and the Fall of Jerusalem, and the wreck of Nature, and the crash of Worlds, and the setting up of the great white Throne, and the gathering together of all the Tribes of the Earth: all this He saw. But 'He saw also—*a certain poor widow.*' And she threw in two mites, which make a farthing.... He had the leisure, had the inclination, had the sovereign will, to scrutinize the act, and to weigh it in a heavenly balance, and to pronounce upon it,—calmly, and at length,—as if Life and Death hung upon the issue. He called unto Him His Disciples, and saith unto them,—'Verily, I say unto you that this poor widow hath cast in more than they all. For all *they* did cast in of their abundance: but she, of her want, did cast in all she had; even all her living!'

These gracious words on the lips of our SAVIOUR awaken in us a deep sense of wonder and admiration; they remind us of all we have ever heard or read concerning 'the widow's mite.' But we cannot now afford space for any reflections on the transaction itself. No: we desire to fill our minds with the single thought of GOD's watchful and observing eye; which nothing is so little as to escape; nothing is so trifling as not to interest and engage. The Psalmist has expressed this in a single verse of the cxiii[th] Psalm,—'Who is like unto the LORD our GOD, that hath His dwelling so high; and yet humbleth Himself to behold the things that are in Heaven and Earth?'

Strange as it may appear, we have great need to fill our minds with this thought; and to convince ourselves of its truth and constancy. It is hard to realize the notion of a Providence which *really* takes note of the fall of a sparrow, and numbers the very hairs of our head. We all profess to believe it; but it may well be suspected that there are few indeed who truly entertain the notion of such perfect Knowledge, such watchful Love, as we are describing. It is not difficult to embrace the conviction that a mighty Empire is the object of GOD's care; because to us, a great Empire seems a great thing: but, that the fortune of the meanest person within that realm, in all its minutest details, should be equally the subject of His concern,—*this* seems hardly credible. So again, we find no difficulty in believing that the more considerable events in our own lives are duly noted in the Book of GOD's remembrance, because they are, *to us*, all in all: but the various petty chances which day by day befal us; the many minute acts which go to form a habit, and which together make up a character,—these, because they seem to ourselves so very petty, we are inclined to believe may be by GOD altogether unheeded. Thus we make ourselves the standard of all things; and even judge of GOD's eternal Attributes by the measure of our own imperfections.

Surely, we shall do well at this time to try to banish from our minds so serious a mistake: serious, because this habit of regarding some things as *little* with GOD, lies at the root of all Sin; and occasions that practical Infidelity of which men are guilty as often as they speak as if they were overlooked by His Providence; uncared for, and as it were forsaken by Him: their trials unmeasured, their tears unnoted, their inward bitterness a secret to GOD as well as to man. Let it be ours to remember that we have to do with One who doth indeed measure the waters in the hollow of His Hand, and mete out

Heaven with the span, and comprehend the dust of the Earth in a measure, and weigh the mountains in scales and the hills in a balance;—yet, who feedeth His flock like a shepherd; and gathereth the lambs with His arm [a].

[a] Is. xl. 11, 12.

Wednesday before Easter.

SIN A HARDENER OF THE HEART.

St. Matthew xxvi. 14—16.

One of the Twelve, called Judas Iscariot, went unto the chief priests, and said unto them, What will ye give me, and I will deliver Him unto you? And they covenanted with him for thirty pieces of silver. And from that time he sought opportunity to betray Him.

The exact history of Wednesday in Holy Week is, it must be confessed, somewhat doubtful. What at least is certain,—Judas, as on this day, made his wicked compact with the chief priests to betray his Lord to them, for money: and truly, so astonishing a transaction, so black and revolting a crime, may well have the thoughts of a whole day to itself. The event of to-day has been felt in fact by the Church from the earliest period to be so tremendous, that all the Wednesdays in the year derive from the Wednesday in Holy Week a character of solemnity second only to that which the sacrifice of our Lord's Death on Good-Friday, has imparted to all the other Fridays in the year.

On reviewing the sacred record of the transaction thus brought under our notice, how many thoughts force themselves upon us! How unlovely seem our gains! and how unblessed a thing, until GOD hath blessed it, seems the pursuit of gain!—How subtle, also, must the snare be which could lure an Apostle into the betrayal of the innocent blood; and *that* blood, the blood of Him who came into the World to save the World!—Then further, how unavailing do the loftiest opportunities, the most precious privileges, prove to be, in and by themselves, to promote our chiefest good!—The several trains of thought, thus suggested, we may follow out with advantage for ourselves in private. It is proposed now to derive another lesson from the crime of Judas; which may indeed be regarded as the very mystery of iniquity, and as containing within itself the whole history of sin.

Above all things, probably, we are here struck with the deadening, hardening effect of sin upon the heart. Else, surely, the words of CHRIST would have melted Judas, many a time, into sorrow, — wrought in him repentance, — awakened in him some natural touch of pity. It was *his Friend* whom he was about to betray,—*his Benefactor* whom he was about to injure so irreparably: the One who had walked with him, and always in meekness and love, for three years and upwards. For a miserable sum of money, he was about to work the ruin of One who had displayed so many a time in his presence Almighty Power; yea, who had conferred on himself the gift of working miracles. He was going to deliver into the hands of men, thirsting, (as he was well aware,) for nothing less than the blood of their victim, the Holy Being who had gone about doing good to all,—curing diseases,—relieving want,—preaching the Gospel,—for the space of three years. He would have to look upon that sacred forehead bruised with stones; those lips, silenced for ever; those hands, powerless; those limbs, stark and cold. Never more, if he effected his accursed purpose,—never more by the hill-side, could they take their simple meal together; sweetened by *His* solemn converse; made a holy thing by *His* blessing! . . . Never more by the Lake, or upon its grey waters, or along its further coast, would they be found,—those twelve Disciples and their LORD; the words of eternal Life flowing the while from His lips, 'sweeter than honey or the honeycomb.' . . . . . Never more in the Garden would they rest at evening, together; seeing *Him* engaged in mysterious prayer, while *they* watched, and prayed yonder! ... Meantime what was to be the Traitor's compensation for all he was to lose? What was to be his miserable solace for beholding bloody violence done to the person of CHRIST; cruelty and ferocity, and in the end Death itself? It is hard to believe that 'thirty pieces of silver' was 'the goodly price that He was prized at[a]:' that for 'thirty pieces of silver' Judas was content to lose his soul.

We shall miss the benefit of this warning, we shall indeed, if we suffer our minds to dwell simply upon this latter circumstance; or indeed, to *dwell* upon it *at all*. We do not for an instant suppose that any one present, that we ourselves, could be induced to commit a monstrous crime for a paltry sum of money. GOD grant that none of us may ever become in any degree the slaves of the special lust which proved the undoing of Judas. No. If we desire to profit by the warning of the Gospel, the warning of this Day's history, we shall notice rather the hardening, deadening effects of sin,—*any* kind of sin, *every* form of sin,—upon the heart. It has often been remarked, (and, it would seem, with great truth,) that *cruelty* and *lust* com-

[a] Zech. xi. 13.

monly go together. They appear widely severed. Softness and Indulgence,—the yielding to appetite and inclination,—this whole class of crimes, it might be thought, would shrink from violence and cruelty; from bloodshed, and the like. But it is not so. Sensual appetite is found to harden the heart quite as much, more perhaps, than covetousness itself. Potiphar's wife was content that Joseph should dwell in prison. Doubtless, she would have endured his death likewise, undisturbed.—Herodias wanted to *see* the bleeding head of John Baptist, in a dish. She desired to feast her impure eyes on the lifeless features of him whose stern rebukes had alone interfered with her guilty pleasures.—Consider again, how David's shameful love for Bathsheba could make him plan Uriah's death: not only take the little ewe-lamb from the poor man, but even become the murderer of him to whom it belonged!

Indeed, that the general tendency of Sin, of whatever kind, is to harden the heart, to darken the conscience, to blind the inner eye,—there can be no doubt. Still, one would not have thought that it could so deaden the natural instincts of humanity as, in the case of Judas, it is found to have done. Let us take the warning, humbly, each one of us, to ourselves. Our LORD pleaded with Judas most tenderly, but it availed not. If the warnings, secret and open, which the Traitor received at the lips of CHRIST from first to last, are added up, those at the close of the Gospel history especially, we shall be surprised at their frequency, their earnestness, their particularity. But it was all in vain. He was like the deaf adder which stoppeth her ears, and refuseth to hear the voice of the charmer, charm he never so wisely. The fact is thus adverted to only to shew that beyond a certain point the very pleadings of Divine Love, the strivings of GOD's Indwelling Spirit,—grieved, yet still indwelling,—may be, must be, in vain.

And it is worth our observing, in connexion with this subject, that the Divinity of CHRIST's person cannot have been so apparent a matter, as, in our devotion towards our REDEEMER and our GOD, we are sometimes apt to imagine. There must have been a very thick mantle spread over His GODHEAD. The Glory of His Deity must have been curtained close; so very close, that scarcely a ray,—if even so much as a ray,—could ever break through, and meet the eyes of men. Everything in the Gospel helps to shew this. He spoke like a Galilean. No one is ever said to have been struck by His aspect. His voice did not, by any means, always persuade. His speech was cavilled at. Men asked Him to depart out of their coasts. Towards the close of His Ministry,—as every day's Gospel reminds us, till our hearts sicken at the dismal tale,— soldiers could strike Him with their fists, and smite Him with their open palms; blindfold Him; force a thorny crown into His temples; scourge Him; spit upon Him; torture His parched lips with gall; crucify Him; thrust a spear into His lifeless side. Now, we know what *might* have been, had He willed. Once only He appeared to three of His Disciples in the nearest approach to His proper glory which their mortal eyes could bear to look upon, and live; and next day, when He descended the Holy Mount, the multitude 'came running to Him.' But this was only for a moment. It soon passed away. In His person then, and doubtless in many other respects also, our LORD's Divinity was not very apparent,—*could* not have been *very* apparent,— while He was upon earth, or men would not have rejected Him; His own nation would not have crucified Him; Judas would not have betrayed Him for thirty pieces of silver.—To a few, the Divinity of His sayings, was doubtless known:

by some few, in His person He was *seen* to be 'fairer than the children of men.' Yea, the blind eyes could behold Him; the deaf ears were enraptured by His voice. And this brings us back exactly to what we desire to enforce; namely, that it depends on the heart of man, whether CHRIST shall be recognised or not: whether, (like Judas,) we shall discern Him nowhere,— neither in His Word nor in His sacraments; or whether it shall seem to us that He beautifies our lives with His abiding presence, and encircles us with countless tokens of His enduring Love. It is Sin that hardens the heart, and darkens the inner eye; whereas, 'Blessed are the pure in heart,' (it is written;) 'for they shall see GOD!'

Thursday before Easter.

LONG-SUFFERING AND FORBEARANCE.

Hebrews xii. 3, 4.

Consider Him that endured such contradiction of sinners against Himself, lest ye be wearied and faint in your minds. Ye have not yet resisted unto blood.

Our Saviour's Betrayal took place as yesterday: as to-day, was His last Supper: as to-morrow, His Crucifixion: as on Saturday, His rest in the grave: as on Easter-day, His Resurrection. Thus, each day, from yesterday, has one great event to itself, which makes it unlike every other day in the year: and each day, from yesterday, has proper lessons appointed for it. But the history of to-day and to-morrow have this peculiar feature; that they run into one another, in one continuous stream. When the Paschal Lamb, and whatever else was required for the Paschal Supper, was ready, and the evening had come, our SAVIOUR, with His twelve Apostles, sat down in that guest-chamber which had been so mysteriously prepared for their reception; and, from that moment forward, there is no break, no interruption, in the narrative, till to-morrow evening, when the SAVIOUR's lifeless Body is conveyed to the tomb. If we must draw the line somewhere, and consider that the events of Thursday end about midnight, it will be found that the chief events of the day,—or rather, of the evening,—were, the washing of the Disciples' feet; the Institution of the LORD's Supper; the long and heavenly discourse of the Holy JESUS, which followed after Judas had withdrawn; the repeated prediction of St. Peter's denials; the Agony in the garden; and the treachery of Judas. CHRIST is then brought before Annas, and before Caiaphas; whose servants spit upon Him, blindfold, buffet, smite, and mock Him. Such is the piteous sight presented to as many of us as have the leisure or the inclination, (and surely neither should be wanting!) to follow up our LORD's history throughout Thursday in Holy Week, with care.

But we must fix our attention on some one thing, in this long and varied narrative: and if we are wise we shall make choice of what may prove of practical *use* to us. Of this kind, seems to be the merciful and patient treatment which the traitor Judas met with at the hands of his LORD. He appears to have received checks and warnings without number, before he fell hopelessly. Thus, throughout a very long space of time, our SAVIOUR's patience with him,—His long-suffering and forbearance,—becomes in a very singular manner our example.

As far back as the first sending forth of the Twelve Apostles, by two-and-two, it is worth observing that the companion of this cold, selfish man was Simon Zelotes; whose very name implies that he was a zealous, earnest, warm-hearted one. Such a companion must surely have been, in itself, at once a help and a check! Take notice also that our SAVIOUR, in the Charge which He delivered to the Twelve, before He sent them forth, makes very plain reference to the sin which proved the ruin of Judas; warning all the Apostles against it in a very marked and peculiar manner. Now, we all know, that when some fault of our own is spoken of in our presence, we always take the words of the speaker to ourselves,—although nothing may have been less in the speaker's thoughts than to say any thing personal. Our SAVIOUR, however, 'unto whom all hearts be open, all desires known, and from whom no secrets are hid,'—when He said, 'Provide neither silver, nor gold, nor brass in your purses;' 'Freely ye have received, freely give,'—must have *meant* that Judas should take to himself a full measure of the caution!

Then, as the time drew nearer, these warnings grow at once more solemn, and more frequent. At first, they are general; by degrees, they grow particular; at last, they are spoken to Judas himself. The Betrayal, which was to take place at Jerusalem, is at first darkly hinted at; but the warning is again and again repeated,—for the last time, to the Twelve Apostles apart, while they were going to keep the last Passover at Jerusalem.—Judas received his next check in the house of Simon the Leper.—Presently, (as on the evening of to-day,) they sat down to eat the Passover. Judas beheld his Divine Master kneel down to wash his feet; and heard Him say, on rising from His lowly task, 'Ye are clean; but *not all* of you!' Then, 'I speak not *of you all*. I know whom I have chosen.'—By and by, our SAVIOUR was 'troubled in Spirit,' and said, 'Verily, verily, I say unto you, that *one of you shall betray Me!*'—Then came the Institution of the LORD's Supper; and Judas received from his Divine Master's Hands, the Sacrament of His Body and Blood: surely, in itself, a most affecting circumstance; a pledge of something more than friendship! more even than a legacy of love! Thus had he been reproved, checked, warned, times without number: two or three times in the course of a single hour. A moment is still given, one final opportunity, for recollection and repentance; but in vain. JESUS then gives him the sop; yet so secretly and silently was even *this* done, that, though eleven others were sitting at the table, (and every eye had by this time grown anxious and attentive,) not *one* person present, except Judas, knew what it meant... Then came the Betrayal: and even then, our LORD addressed him as, 'Friend;' asking him on what business he had come? ... Now, if the *recorded* warnings of Judas are so many, what must the unknown reality have been! Do but think of the looks and words of kindness; the benefits conferred; the example of poverty and self-denial set him; the unearthly discourses; the heavenly counsels! .... Nay, look back to the very beginning of our LORD's ministry; and notice, in the Sermon on the Mount, the large space devoted to a warning against Covetousness. Consider whether the mystery of Iniquity, revealed at last, is not pointed out from the very first: whether Judas was not solemnly warned against the particular sin which in the end proved his ruin, even from the first day that he was drawn to his Divine Master's side!

The picture of our SAVIOUR's long-suffering and forbearance, thus presented to our notice, will be complete, when to every active endeavour on His part to reclaim Judas from ruin, we add the recollection of the keen suffering which the mere presence of such an one as Judas must have daily occasioned Him; and the patience with which that sorrow was submitted to by our LORD. How exceeding great must have been the grief, where the meal had to be daily partaken of with one who would some day rise from eating His bread to betray Him into the hands of His enemies! where the hollow unreality had to be daily endured, and the gross hypocrisy witnessed, — of one whose prayers, whose preaching, whose professions, were all, from first to last, *a lie;* and would all, in the end, turn to the greater condemnation of one who might have become one of GOD's chiefest Saints! . . . . Throughout the Gospels we nevertheless meet with no one speech of bitterness addressed to Judas: no single reproach of his ingratitude: no word, to the very last, but of the tenderest Love. And is it possible to take notice of such things, and yet to overlook their personal teaching?

It cannot be! And yet it is strange indeed to notice how little impression this Divine example of long-suffering and forbearance seems to have made on the Christian World at large. Each one seems to think himself at perfect liberty to resent a neighbour's ingratitude: while misplaced confidence, and good offices ill requited, —*these* are deemed a fair occasion for bitter complaint; a valid ground for laying claim to the sympathy of every other member of the Christian community. It is forgotten how fruitful a source of disappointment is misplaced confidence; and therefore, how often the fault of unrequited kindness is, in truth, all our own: how paltry, at best, are the benefits which we are ourselves able to confer on another: and how grossly ungrateful to the GOD which hath fed us all our life long unto this day, we have already, in countless ways and on countless occasions, shewn ourselves to be. All this we forget. *We* are wronged, it may be; but *He* was *betrayed!* *We* are injured; but *He* was *slain!* *We* made the man our friend; but *He* made of Judas *an Apostle!* *We* are sinful; but *He* was perfectly holy, just, and good! Why then must it be added that while no reproach was ever found on *His* lips, yet angry vindictive expressions are ever so rife on *ours?* Why will we not 'consider Him that endured such contradiction of sinners against Himself;' that so we may escape the shame of proving easily wearied and faint in our minds? we, who have not yet resisted,—nor, it may be, ever shall resist,—as our LORD and SAVIOUR did, 'unto blood.'

Good-Friday.

CHRIST CRUCIFIED.

St. John xix. 30.

He said, It is finished: and He bowed His head, and gave up the Ghost.

This day is so entirely unlike every other day in the year, so past all telling solemn, that silence seems the only fitting occupation for us, as often as it comes round. It is the anniversary of more than a Parent's death, (which seems impossible;) for it is our Saviour, who, as on this day, died for us. Add the circumstances of His death, and the burthen of grief becomes truly appalling. It is not only true that He died *in order to save us;* but it was *our sins* which made it needful that He should die. Nor was it any common death that He died; but a cruel, murderous death; the prolonged torture of the Cross, sharpened by every indignity which malice could devise, or Love submit to.

Nor have we yet said all: for this Saviour

and Benefactor, this crucified REDEEMER, was very GOD as well as very Man. This is a stupendous thought, and one which we cannot completely master; but which we must nevertheless accept, and, in our degree, seek to realize. In truth it took more than man could offer to redeem the souls of men ; so that man must have ' let that alone for ever[a].' None but GOD, taking Man's nature, could have availed to redeem Mankind. And in speaking of the human sufferings of CHRIST, His GODhead must be clearly kept in view; if for no other reason, at least for *this*, that we may thereby form the truer notion, (incomplete indeed, yet truer,) of those very human sufferings. For a perverse spirit might be found to reason thus : ' Many before, and since, have undergone Crucifixion. CHRIST, therefore, did but suffer that which thousands besides had suffered.' He who can so wickedly argue, overlooks every circumstance of unequalled injustice, shame, and torture. But, (what is far more to the purpose,) he forgets that He who suffered was very GOD as well as very Man. We say not, of course, that GOD suffered the bitter death of the Cross. Heaven forbid that we should so speak! for GOD can suffer *nothing*. But we *do*

[a] Ps. xlix. 8.

say that the Godhead was, in a mysterious way, joined to the Manhood, in the one person of CHRIST: that, in one single person, there were two distinct natures,—the human and the Divine. And it is quite certain that the effect of this miraculous union must have been to render immensely more acute every pang, whether of mind or of Body. As the sword which has been sharpened, and then made hot by fire, will not only cut, but burn also, so must the frame of Him who was GOD as well as Man have had *powers of suffering*, (if the phrase be allowable,) of which we can really have no conception. No wonder that a venerable sister Church, in her Liturgy, besides praying to the SAVIOUR 'by His Agony and bloody sweat, by His Cross and Passion,'—adds a prayer by His '*unknown sufferings*,' likewise: for, of a truth, the unknown agonies through which our SAVIOUR's Soul and Body passed, were such as no man knoweth; nor indeed *can* know.

'Is it nothing to you that pass by? Behold and see if there be any sorrow like unto My sorrow[b]!' So spake Jeremiah, prophetically, in the person of CHRIST. And, as we have said, before such a spectacle of sorrow, to sit down in

[b] Lamentations i. 12.

silence seems our only becoming course,—especially for men of impure lips, as we are; and guilty too,—aye, guilty of the very sins which brought about all this grief.... But our part is to say somewhat. Instead of turning away from the Cross therefore, let us strive to fix our eyes upon it; and to fill our hearts with the piteous sight which we there behold.

The History of Thursday in Holy-Week flows on, in one continuous stream, through the night, into the morning of Good-Friday. Indeed, it meets with no interruption until the limbs of the Holy One are laid, as on this evening, in the rich man's tomb. And such a history of grief and pain submitted to,—of injury and insult inflicted, —*who* has ever met with elsewhere? In the Garden, last night, did He not water the Earth with His tears; while 'His sweat was, as it were, great drops of blood falling down to the ground?' was not His mysterious necessity so great, that one of His own created Angels was seen, from Heaven, 'strengthening Him?'—Then came the kiss of Judas, bringing its pang of exceeding bitterness; second, it may be, to none. And then, we behold the SAVIOUR, meek and unresisting, though more than twelve legions of Angels were longing for the signal to come forth in bright array, and terribly to avenge His cause. —Next, we behold Him dragged first before Annas; then, bound, and conveyed to the palace of Caiaphas; then, hurried through the insults of a mock trial, and charged with blasphemy. Next came the three denials of Simon Peter,— sharper each, it may be, than the very thorns which pierced His temples: and thus, in mockery and insult, — scourged, blindfolded, buffeted, stricken, spitted on,—were consumed the hours of that hideous night and morning. Nothing was wanting that the malice of the Devil could suggest; assailing the Son of Man, now, through every avenue of Pain, as, in the Wilderness, he had assailed Him through every avenue of Pleasure. And how was all this endured? *So* endured, that Pilate himself relented; and again and again sought to release his victim. But the voices of the High-priests prevailed; and, at six o'clock in the morning, after a night of ceaseless violence and torment, the Holy JESUS was formally delivered up to the will of His infuriated enemies.

At the end of three hours, we behold our SAVIOUR, hard by the City-gate, fainting beneath the burthen of His Cross. Some compassionate soul offers Him a draught of wine and myrrh, to lull

His pain, but He puts it from Him. He will drink of His FATHER's Cup, and of none other, to-day!.... And then, they nail His Hands and His feet to the Cross, between two malefactors; thus adding foul insult to terrible crime,—of which we may understand somewhat from the very silence of Scripture. 'FATHER, forgive them, for they know not what they do!'

And what can be imagined more awful than the spectacle which we finally behold? The SAVIOUR's Life ebbing away, slowly; as, drop by drop, the sweat from His temples, and the blood from His Hands, trickles down to the Earth; and this, amid the blasphemy of the beholders, the mockery of His enemies, and the reviling voices of the malefactors who shared His fate, but not His pains. Meantime, His disciples stand afar off; and presently, (most mysterious thing of all!) He will be brought very low by the sense of desertion, even of GOD the FATHER Himself!... The very Sun goes out, at so awful a sight, and suffers portentous eclipse by the space of three hours. Doubtless the air grew silent also: and men heard His cry of agony, as He thirsted; and as He complained of desertion; no less than His promise of mercy to the repentant malefactor. They heard Him declare also that the Work which He had come into the World to do, was 'finished;' and 'FATHER,' (they heard Him cry,) 'into Thy Hands I commend My Spirit.' . . . After which, the Disciple who alone watched Him, saw Him bow His head, and expire!

What wonder that at such a spectacle the Earth is felt to quake, and the rocks are seen to yawn asunder? Well may the Veil of the Temple be rent in twain, from the top to the bottom; and the graves be opened; and the very sheeted dead be roused from their deep sleep to walk the Earth again! What? Shall the CREATOR undergo such amazing dishonour, and created Nature, the work of His fingers, the offspring of His Will,—shall *it* endure no pang of mysterious sympathy? In truth, we wonder not that the Heavens put on black, and that Earth felt the pang to her inmost centre. If the stones well nigh found voices and cried out when He entered Jerusalem, as on Sunday last,—what must have been her portentous anguish, as on this day?

And to all that has gone before, we will not seek to add anything: as indeed nothing can be added. Nor will we offer one practical hint, or attempt to make a single application of the History of Good-Friday to ourselves. It concerns us *wholly :* and if so amazing an anniversary can come and go, and yet avail not to awaken in our hearts either Fear or Love, Hope or Anxiety,— truly must those hearts have grown past feeling; and we ourselves be as trees 'twice dead, withered away.'

Easter Eben.

CHRISTIAN SORROW A PRELUDE TO CHRISTIAN JOY.

Psalm cxxvi. 5.

They that sow in tears shall reap in joy.

A FEW verses of St. Matthew's Gospel contain the sum of what has been revealed concerning the history of to-day; which, in truth, is not so much the history of our LORD, as of His enemies. He, laid in the rich man's tomb, rests on the seventh day from the work of Redemption, as, in the beginning, He rested on the same day from the work of Creation. All now is peace and repose with *Him*. The terrible violence of yesterday has exhausted itself: malice has done its worst. It can, after all, do no more than take away life; and though torture may prolong the process, the end of all must be the death of the victim. So did it fare in the case of the SAVIOUR of Mankind: who, 'very Man,' was crucified, dead, and buried, as yesterday; and, as to-day, rested in the grave. His human body rested; but His human soul 'descended into Hell,' (as the unseen dwelling-place of departed souls is sometimes called in Scripture;) and there He 'preached unto the spirits in safe keeping[a].' Of this amazing transaction we know indeed wondrous little; doubtless, because it concerns us not to know more. Enough however has been revealed to convince us that no part of our destiny as men was left untried by Him. He, therefore, that walks 'through the valley of the shadow of Death' is able henceforward to comfort himself with the thought,—'I will fear no evil, for *Thou* art with me!' Thou didst tread this pathway first; and, by so doing, didst rob Death of its sting, and the grave of its terrors.

The history of to-day, then, as far as it is recorded, is less the history of our LORD than of His enemies. 'The chief priests and Pharisees came together unto Pilate, saying, Sir, we remember that that deceiver said, while He was yet alive, After three days I will rise again. Command therefore that the sepulchre be made sure until the third day, lest His disciples come

[a] 1 St. Peter iii. 19.

by night, and steal Him away, and say unto the people, He is risen from the dead: so the last error shall be worse than the first. Pilate said unto them, Ye have a watch: go your way, make it as sure as ye can. So they went, and made the sepulchre sure, sealing the stone, and setting a watch[b].' .... Let us turn from these to that little band among the living in whom we feel far greater interest,—the Disciples and friends of the Crucified. *Their* history supplies us with many comfortable thoughts; of which one, which lies on the very surface, will suffice for our present purpose.

The words of the text will have shewn that we are about to allude to the joy which was in store for the Disciples, in this, the hour of their greatest despondency, and even despair. It is hard indeed to imagine disappointment more complete, despair more hopeless, than theirs. They knew *whom* they had trusted. He had proved Himself in countless ways, and on countless occasions, to be 'very GOD.' Openly had He declared Himself to be 'the MESSIAH, the Prince.' And *what* more deeply interwoven, as well with their religious faith as with their national pride, than that MESSIAH was to restore

[b] St. Matth. xxvii. 62 to 66.

the kingdom to Israel? A *crucified* SAVIOUR! A *despised* King! A REDEEMER who should prove an easy victim to the first band of enemies who conspired to take away His life! It is easy to perceive how entirely all this must have perplexed their notions, as well as destroyed their hopes. And the point we have to notice, is, that when their hopes were at the very lowest ebb, (if indeed they had not become utterly extinct;) and when their notions had been in the completest manner outraged; even *then* it was that those hopes were destined to receive a fulfilment beyond any thing which the disciples could ask or think; while the notions they had formed were about to be as entirely exceeded, as they had before been threatened with disappointment.

'Man's extremity,' it has been said, 'is GOD's opportunity;' and many a time are we reminded in Holy Scripture that so it is indeed. It was not till the water was spent in the bottle, and the child had been cast under one of the shrubs, and the sorrow-stricken mother had gone and sat her down over against him a good way off, (for she said, Let me not see the death of the child;) not until she had lifted up her voice and wept, in the depth of her agony and the fulness of her despair; that an Angel's voice was heard asking her, 'What aileth thee, Hagar[c]?'

It was not until the altar had been built, and the wood laid in order, and Isaac bound, and laid on the altar upon the wood; not until Abraham had stretched forth his hand, and taken the knife to slay his son; that the Angel of the LORD called unto him out of Heaven, and said, 'Lay not thine hand upon the lad.' And, 'By Myself have I sworn, saith the LORD, for because thou hast done this thing, and hast not withheld thy son, thine only son: that in blessing I will bless thee, and in multiplying I will multiply thy seed as the stars of the Heaven[d].'

So again, at Cana's feast, it was not until the want of wine had made itself *felt*, that the mighty supply was produced which banished the very memory of the threatened need.—The history of the Storm on the Lake supplies another example of the same method of GOD's Providence: and our LORD's walking on the Water, again, with another.—These are all examples of one and the same law, as it seems: a law written very clearly in the history of what befalls our own bodies; in the case of which, decay and sickness,

[c] Gen. xxi. 17. [d] Gen. xxii. 16, 17.

Death itself, and the utter dissolution of all that was comely, is the indispensable prelude to future glory. It doth not indeed yet appear what we shall be; but that we shall be like to the angels, we know; yea, and like unto *Him:* 'for we shall see Him as He is.' Moreover, from the degradation of complete decay, we are expressly informed that the change to this 'exceeding weight of glory' will be effected 'in a moment, in the twinkling of an eye.' So that, here again, a transition is made from the lowest pitch of what it is shocking to contemplate, to the very loftiest point of our future destiny.—Shall we fail to discern, in all this, a precious earnest that blessings are ever nearest at hand when they seem to be furthest withdrawn? that we are never so close to what we long for, as when the last ray of hope has faded quite away?... CHRIST waited till Lazarus had lain four days in the grave, ere He would proceed in the direction of him whose sickness had been duly announced to Him many days before. And yet, He knew how ardently the sisters were longing for His presence; knew the extremity to which His friend was reduced. At the end of those four days, however, He went indeed, and wrought wondrously.

Shall not these examples be our lessons, and make us wise to eternal Life? Shall they not remind us that the moment of greatest humiliation commonly precedes the moment of greatest glory? Let us only have faith in GOD; and we shall ever find His Love, manifesting itself in power, the nearest to us *then,* when it seems to heed us least. Let us only have faith in GOD. And even if it should be 'expedient' for us that the thing we love best should be taken away; and though He seem therein to slay us; shall we not, like righteous Job, '*trust* in Him,' even *then?*

Yes, we will seek to walk by Faith, not by sight, in this matter; and to cherish the lesson of Easter Even, long after the season of Easter has passed away. Obedience shall be our rule, and Christian Hope our portion: and we will be content to sow now in tears, sure that thus we shall in the end reap in joy. 'Heaviness,' it is written, 'may endure for a night, but joy cometh in the morning.' Do not those words seem as if they had been written to describe the first Easter Even, and the first Easter Day? It is, however, the privilege of Christian men to know that the words of the SPIRIT belong to every age, and every Season. And doubtless, the promise is an abiding one, that he that now goeth on his way weeping, and beareth forth good seed,— shall come again with joy, and bring his sheaves with him!

Easter-Day.

THE EASTER ANTHEM.

1 Corinthians v. 7.

CHRIST our Passover.

THESE words will be at once recognised as the beginning of the New Song which we sing on this day, (like the redeemed in Heaven[a],) in praise of the Victory of THE LAMB. Very divine is that song, which all the Churches have been this day using instead of the Psalm, 'O come, let us sing unto the LORD!' It reminds us of this day's great mystery in a very lovely manner: for, by simply bringing together the language of either Covenant, it explains, without explanation, the hidden meaning of the last Jewish Passover, by the open meaning of the first Christian Easter.

Our business shall be on this occasion, without attempting to set forth in detail the glorious doctrines which Easter-Day brings to light, rather to avail ourselves of the hint which the Church supplies in her Easter services; and first, to

[a] Revelation v. 9.

notice how the words of our Easter anthem invite us to connect the most important of the ancient types with its fulfilment.

How dark, then, to the eyes of GOD's ancient people must this, their most solemn Festival, have been! A male Lamb, without blemish; to be eaten with bitter herbs; and with unleavened bread: the blood of this Lamb to be sprinkled on the lintel, and the two side-posts of the door: the Lamb itself to be sacrificed, and eaten in the evening; a sheaf of the first-fruits of the wheat-harvest to be waved before the LORD on the morrow after the Sabbath:—how dark was all this! yet how clear was it all made when CHRIST our Passover was sacrificed for us!

For He who is so often called 'the Lamb of GOD,' pure and spotless, gave Himself in a figure on this Thursday; and, in reality, 'was brought as a lamb to the slaughter[b]' on the Friday of the first Holy-Week. In bitterness of soul was the symbol of His sacrifice given: in far greater bitterness was the great sacrifice of Himself perfected: and this was what the 'bitter herbs' had foreshewn. In wondrous sincerity, and most perfect truth, in deepest and sincerest love, on the part of Him whose lips knew no guile,—was

[b] Is. liii.

the whole mystery transacted: and this was what was meant by the 'unleavened bread' of which all who ate the Passover must partake. By the precious blood of this Paschal Lamb we are preserved from the Destroyer; and led out from the bondage of Sin and Death into the Heavenly Canaan,—the promised Land of CHRIST's Kingdom: and this was what the sprinkled blood had foreshewn. CHRIST ate His Passover in the evening: in the evening, 'CHRIST our Passover was sacrificed for us.' And when He rose as on this glorious day, was He not 'the first-fruits of them that slept?' the beginning of that harvest which He longs to gather into His Heavenly garner? The corn of wheat had fallen into the ground and died, as on Good-Friday. It was destined hereafter to bear much fruit [c]. 'But every man in his own order: CHRIST the first-fruits: afterward, they that are CHRIST's at His Coming [d].' ... Enough has been said to recal the hidden teaching of the early wheat-sheaf. The Priest lifted it up before the LORD on the morrow after the Sabbath. And what was *that* but a lively image of Him whom GOD raised up as on this day,—'the first-fruit of them that slept?'

It is surely not too much to say that when

[c] St. John xii. 24.   [d] 1 Cor. xv. 23.

CHRIST, who is our Life, rose upon the World, He lighted up the obscure places of the Old Testament, as the rising of the Sun lights up the obscure places of the Earth. Misty and dark, unlovely and indistinct,—aye, *unseen*, until the Sun is up,—how beautiful and bright becomes every object afterwards! A veil seems lifted off the face of things: and lo, the heart rejoices; it cannot *but* rejoice. Shall this hold true in Nature, and not hold true in Grace? It cannot surely be! The view of types departing, and shadows fleeing away; dark sayings brightened into beauty, and actions, apparently trivial, shewn to be brimful of mysterious meaning: *this* should surely fill with rapture every Christian heart; waken thoughts of deep delight; call out words of glowing praise; and send forth to acts of Love, and dutiful obedience.

As if to make it impossible that we should miss the teaching of the Old Testament in this behalf, the first Lessons for the Day are those chapters of the Book of Exodus in which the institution of the Passover is mentioned, and the Israelites' deliverance from Egypt described. For 'as on that day Israel saw the great work which the LORD did upon Egypt, so on this day we see the great conquest over Hell and Death finished, by CHRIST's triumphant Resurrection from the dead[e].' And how conformable it must be to the mind of the SPIRIT that we should thus dwell on type and antitype, would be sufficiently proved, (if any could be found to doubt it,) by the remarkable language of the Evangelist St. Luke, when he relates the subject of the heavenly conversation between Moses and Elijah and the Incarnate WORD upon the Mount of the Transfiguration. They spake (he says) '*of His Exodus*, which He should fulfil at Jerusalem.' O marvellous revelation! The Exodus of Israel from Egypt was therefore '*fulfilled*,' when ' CHRIST our Passover' was sacrificed for us! It was deemed a fit subject for the Discourse of the SAVIOUR of the World, and two of His greatest Saints in bliss. Shall it not be deemed, on Easter-Day, the worthiest of all subjects of meditation for ourselves?

The Proper Psalms for the Day all conspire to swell the note of Praise. 'Thou art My SON,' (it is said,) ' this Day have I begotten Thee[g]!' ' Set up Thyself, O GOD, above the heavens,' (we exclaim,) ' and Thy Glory above all the Earth[h].' For the blessings which Easter brings, ' I will

[e] Bp. Sparrow.
[f] St. Luke ix. 31.
[g] Ps. ii. 7.
[h] Ps. lvii. 12.

give thanks unto the LORD with my whole heart[l].'
.... Now indeed 'the LORD is high above all heathen, and His Glory above the Heavens[k]!' If 'when Israel came out of Egypt[l],' the Church of CHRIST rejoiced exceedingly, what should be her strain of rejoicing *now!* 'This is the Day which the LORD hath made. We will rejoice and be glad in it[m]!'

For impossible is it to join in the services of Easter-Day without a sense of relief; as when one awakes from some terrible dream, or a threatened danger has been averted. It is impossible to hear those calm words of Triumph,—'CHRIST being raised from the dead, dieth no more: Death hath no more dominion over Him;' without deep emotion: *deep* in proportion to the sympathy with which we have followed Him through the History of His sufferings and Death. The very simplicity of the announcement, and the calm tone of Divine certainty which it breathes, are more congenial to the soul than any elaborate statement could have been: for we feel that the wonder is altogether above us and beyond us. It is the most important announcement which human language was ever employed to convey: a truth far too sublime and too tremendous for

[l] Ps. cxi. 1.   [k] Ps. cxiii. 4.   [l] Ps. cxiv. 1.   [m] Ps. cxviii. 24.

words to attempt to garnish, or even to pretend to explain.

But the chief solace which the tidings of our SAVIOUR's Resurrection procure to a Christian heart arises from the secret certainty that *His* Victory over Death is a pledge that *we* also shall pass through that shadowy valley unharmed: that *His* glorious Resurrection is a precious earnest of our own. This, also, is glanced at in our Easter Anthem: 'For since by Man came Death,' (it is said,) 'by Man came also the Resurrection of the Dead. For as in Adam all die, even so in CHRIST shall all be made alive.'

And thus, in a few deep words, the history of our Redemption is set before us. By Nature, we are in Adam: by Grace, we are in CHRIST. He is the beginning of the New Creation. Baptized into Him, we are declared to be 'members of His Body, of His Flesh, and of His Bones[n].' And thus we are born again: not only made partakers of a new Nature, but born into a new World; invested with new powers; introduced to new hopes. Where our Head hath gone before, there it is our joy to know that we, the members, shall assuredly follow; provided we do but '*abide* in Him[o],' and prove 'faithful unto Death[p].'

[n] Ephes. v. 30.   [o] St. John xv. 4.   [p] Rev. ii. 10.

And this is the point at which the Collect for Easter-Day takes up the thoughts which Easter-Day is calculated to inspire: grafting the fruits of Holiness on a living Faith; seeking to turn the theory of Religion into practice; faithfully reminding us that if we *know* these things, happy are we if we *do* them, likewise. This, in truth, is eminently the office of our Book of Common Prayer,—namely, to endeavour to give a practical turn to every commemoration; to engraft a living act on every saving Doctrine. Nowhere more remarkably than on Easter-Day does this appear: for no sooner have we acknowledged the mercy of Almighty GOD, who through His Only-begotten Son, JESUS CHRIST, hath overcome Death, and opened to us the gate of Everlasting Life, than we humbly beseech Him that as, by His special Grace preventing us, He doth put into our minds good desires, so, by His continual help, we may bring the same to good effect; through JESUS CHRIST our LORD.

Monday in Easter-Week.

BELIEVING WITHOUT SEEING.—(Part I.)

St. John xx. 29.

Jesus *saith unto him, Thomas, because thou hast seen Me, thou hast believed: blessed are they that have not seen, and yet have believed.*

The occasion on which these words wer' spoken, we all remember. On the evening of Easter-Day, the Ten Apostles being gathered together, (with closed doors, however, 'for fear of the Jews,') our Blessed Saviour,—who about eighteen hours before had risen from death, and had already appeared to Mary Magdalene, to the company of women, to Simon Peter, and to the two disciples going to Emmaus,—suddenly stood in the midst of them, and spoke words of Peace. Let us hear the account of an eye-witness, and more than an eye-witness, of all that followed. 'But Thomas, one of the Twelve, called Didymus, was not with them when Jesus came. The other disciples therefore said unto him, We have seen the Lord. But he said unto them, Except I shall see in His hands the print of the nails, and put my finger into the print of the nails, and thrust my hand into His side, I will not believe. And after eight days again His Disciples were within, and Thomas with them: then came JESUS, the doors being shut, and stood in the midst, and said, Peace be unto you. Then saith He to Thomas, Reach hither thy finger, and behold My hands;. and reach hither thy hand, and thrust it into My side: and be not faithless, but believing. And Thomas answered and said unto Him, My LORD and my GOD. JESUS saith unto him, Thomas, because thou hast seen Me, thou hast believed: blessed are they that have not seen, and yet have believed[a].'

And now that all the facts of the case have been set before us, let us seek to draw a lesson from it for our personal comfort, edification, and guidance. Not that we purpose to prate about the 'unbelief' of one who spread the Faith to the remotest corners of the earth: not that we are about to sit in judgment on that great Saint and Apostle St. Thomas, whose name is written on one of the foundations of the heavenly Jerusalem. No. We have already spoken about *his* very striking share in the transactions of the

[a] St. John xx. 24—29.

first Easter[b]. It shall be our part to-day to look nearer home. The words of our SAVIOUR CHRIST which form the text, are words addressed in a very remarkable manner to ourselves. *We* are the persons He had in view when He pronounced those words. This is much to be noted. He was standing amid men who *had* seen, men who *were seeing*, when He said,—'Blessed are they that have *not* seen!' To us, therefore, who were then afar off; to us and to our children, were these words spoken; and by applying ourselves to the task of discovering what message they convey, we shall be, as it seems, acting most dutifully towards their Blessed Author.

The first thing, then, which strikes a thoughtful man on reading this history, is the lovingkindness of Almighty GOD displayed[c] towards *us*, therein. It might seem to some persons that the first Christians,—those disciples of our SAVIOUR who lived in the days of the Gospel,—enjoyed an undue amount of blessedness. They beheld the REDEEMER. They listened to the voice of His Words. They handled Him, and dwelt in His very presence. He went in and out among them. We,—separated by well nigh

[b] In the sermon for St. Thomas' Day.

two thousand years,—depending for our knowledge of CHRIST on four short Histories, (the Gospels,)—living amid divisions and strife,—with so much to perplex, so much to mislead us;—how different a fate is ours from theirs! What wonder if our faith burn low? What wonder if the flame is dim? . . . The inquiry of Esau we are prone to take to ourselves, as well as to make his passionate prayer our own; for we think we have been unfairly dealt with. 'Hast thou but one blessing, my Father? Bless me, even me also, O my Father[c]!' Those, our brethren, were blessed abundantly. Because they came before us, they obtained the blessing. Hath GOD reserved no blessing, then, for us?

The answer to this question is to be found in a hundred places of the Gospel. For example: we have the solemn assurance that though we may no longer minister to our Divine LORD, in person, yet, inasmuch as we do it unto one of the least of His little ones, we do it unto *Him*[d].

Again: 'Touch Me not,' (it is said;) '*for* I am not yet ascended unto My FATHER[e].' The meaning must be, When I *am* ascended, then ye *shall* touch Me. . . . . Again: 'Lo, I am with you always, even unto the end of the World[f].' . . .

[c] Gen. xxvii. 38.   [e] St. John x. 17.
[d] St. Matth. xxv. 40.   [f] St. Matth. xxviii. 20.

Again: 'If a man love Me, he will keep My words. And My FATHER will love him; and we will come unto him, and make our abode with him[g].'... Again: 'Because thou hast seen Me, thou hast believed: blessed are they that have not seen, and yet have believed.'

These passages of Scripture, then, assure us of *our* Blessedness: assure us that a mighty blessing has been reserved for *us* by the Father of mercies. They should set us on realizing our privileges also. They should make us very inquiring, very anxious, as to *how* these things can be?—But the last text is the strongest; and, as it were, sums up and contains all the others. So that, in all that follows, we shall derive our remarks from its implied teaching. And the great thing we have to notice is, that a special blessing is here pronounced on all those who *believe* without having *seen;* in a word, on *Faith* without *Sight.* Herein, if we do but 'stir up your pure minds by way of remembrance[h],' we shall be discharging a very useful office; but how much will it concern those who are led, by what is spoken, to think seriously of this most solemn matter for the first time!

Now, when the earliest martyr, St. Stephen,

[g] St. John xiv. 23.   [h] 2 Tim. i. 6.

looking up stedfastly into Heaven, saw the Glory of GOD, and JESUS standing on the Right Hand of GOD,—he might well rejoice, and feel strong.

But, 'Blessed are they that have not seen, and yet have believed.' Blessed, (in other words,) is he who, when persecuted for Righteousness' sake, can look up; and without *seeing* any thing, can *believe* that he has the self-same Advocate with the FATHER,—JESUS CHRIST the Righteous.

And to put this matter into the very plainest form :—our SAVIOUR and our GOD pronounces as many of us '*blessed,*' as have the heart to trust Him entirely with our cause amid any kind of trial which may arise from the persecution and unkindness of our fellow-men. As for persecution in the shape in which it befel St. Stephen and St. Paul; St. James and St. John; in a word, the early Christians generally; it is not to be expected now. We need not look for it; nor consider how we should act under it. No. But persecution changes its shape at different times. It comes upon us occasionally in so strange a guise, that it seems hardly fair to call it by the same name of persecution. Call it however by whatever name you will; and we mean it to include every form of misrepresentation, or undeserved unkindness; all returns of evil for good;

all ill-natured things said of one; distorted and untrue accounts of one's character, actions, sayings, temper, purpose, meaning. All these things may be summed up under one common head; and we say of them all, that the act which our LORD pronounces 'blessed,' is the act of him who *believes* without *seeing* that he has an Advocate with the FATHER: *believes* that GOD will take his cause in hand, and make his innocence and his righteousness, in the end, ' as clear as the light, and his just dealing as the noon-day:' *believes* all this, we repeat, yet *sees nothing!*

So much, then, for Faith under Persecution. It will be well worth our while to pursue this subject a little further; and to consider the office of Faith without Sight under other circumstances also. But this must, perforce, be reserved for a separate occasion. Let us not dismiss the subject, however, until we have briefly reminded ourselves of the special matter with reference to which these words of our LORD were spoken: namely, a belief in the truth of His Resurrection.

And here, the office of a real and living Faith is forced upon us. We are constrained to remember that a barren assent to a form of words, a mere reciting of the Creeds of the Church, is a thing quite apart from such a Faith as GOD approves and requires. To believe in the Incarnate WORD crucified, dead, and buried, and on the third day, risen from Death, is rather to embrace this living Doctrine with that entire acceptance which transforms it into a living principle of action. It should become our great, although our secret joy, at this season, to say to ourselves, (as the Apostles said one to another,) 'The LORD is risen indeed.' And then, as risen ourselves with CHRIST, to 'seek those things which are above, where CHRIST sitteth on the Right Hand of GOD[1].' That the first believers should thus have acted, is easily accounted for. The limbs which they had seen hanging lifeless on the bitter Cross, and consigned to the grave, they beheld moving before them, endued with new life. They beheld, and they handled, and they adored. It is a sight which these bodily eyes will assuredly behold hereafter[k]; but not now. We may believe it indeed; believe it as entirely as if we had seen it with our eyes: but we may not yet actually see it. 'Blessed are they' (it is written,) 'who have not seen, and yet have believed!'

[1] Coloss. iii. 1.   [k] Rev. i. 7.

Tuesday in Easter-Week.

BELIEVING WITHOUT SEEING.—(Part II.)

St. John xx. 29.

Jesus saith unto him, Thomas, because thou hast seen Me, thou hast believed: blessed are they that have not seen, and yet have believed.

In the sermon for Monday in Easter-Week, we remarked upon the gracious manner in which the apparent superiority of advantages enjoyed by the Apostles, and first believers, over ourselves, has been compensated for by our Lord. And, wherein those persons were more highly favoured than we are, it was suggested that the promise which we enjoy of blessedness in believing without having seen, becomes in itself a most precious inheritance, and one which is altogether our own. We also spoke of Faith under Persecution, and of Faith in our Lord's Resurrection from Death. Let us pursue this line of thought, and take notice how fruitful it is in edification. And first,—what of Faith in Prayer?

Now, it is plain that when Daniel beheld the man Gabriel fly swiftly, and felt his touch about the time of the evening oblation,—he had sufficient reason to believe, or rather to *see* that his prayer had been heard. . . . . When Cornelius received the message of the Angel, assuring him that his prayers and his alms had come up as a memorial before GOD,—he believed, of course, that GOD had heard his prayer. He could not *but* believe it, because he *saw*.

But our SAVIOUR pronounces that man blessed who, without seeing, yet believes: the man who, in his necessity, cries earnestly to GOD, and casts all his burthen upon Him. Is some matter too difficult? Then, let it be brought before One with whom nothing is impossible. Is some want too severe? Then, bring it under the notice of One who hath promised that His yoke shall be found easy, and His burthen light. Is some doubt too harassing? some anxiety too perplexing? some sorrow too grievous? The man is '*blessed*' who looks for no Angel to relieve him from his distress: nay, far more than *that;* who looks for nothing but the sense of support which the HOLY SPIRIT is certain to bestow; and, leaning his whole weight on that strong stay, lives on contented; can even look up and smile; can be calm and cheerful. And why? Because he can *believe*, though he cannot *see*, that all things are working together for good: that GOD is even now, in some mysterious and most marvellous way, contriving his blessedness; his blessedness in the very matter of his prayer. He cannot *see* any thing; but he can *believe* all things. Very blessed is he therefore; for 'Blessed are they that have not seen, and yet have believed.'

So again, in respect of the ministration of the holy Angels to the sons of men:—what wonder if Abraham believed? or Jacob? or Joshua? They could not *help* believing. They *saw* Angels; —talked,—reasoned,—wrestled with them. They heard the sound of their voices, or experienced some sensible mark of their Love or their Power. The same is true of David and of Daniel, of the Twelve Apostles, and of so many more.

But it is *our* Blessedness to believe *without* seeing. Do any water their pillow with bitter, yet virtuous tears? They know that Angels bend above their heads; sorrow with them, and for them. Does loneliness sink on the spirit like a weight? No one, surely, is alone! The Angels of GOD unseen bear us company. Do any tremble for the fate of the absent child, or parent? the husband, while away, for the wife of his bosom? the friend for the friend?

No need to tremble! All may be sure that Angels encamp about those whom GOD loves; go with them, guard them, sustain them, watch over them sleeping and waking. 'Are they not all ministering spirits, sent forth to minister for them who shall be heirs of Salvation?'

Once more: when Balaam heard the dumb ass speak, and saw the Angel with a drawn sword standing in the way to slay him,—what wonder if he believed that an accident (as men speak) is sometimes sent to protect us from danger, or it may be from Death? He *saw* the danger: he *saw* his escape. He had been convinced, as no one probably ever was before or after, that the obstinacy of a dumb animal may be an instrument in GOD's Hand to awaken self-recollection; to cause a change of purpose. In short, because he *saw*, he *believed*.

But how 'blessed are they that have not seen, and yet have believed!' Little checks; little hindrances thrown in the way; the reproof of dumb creatures, (as one may describe the matter;) the obstinacy of things without life:—all these become instruments of blessedness to those who are not as Balaam was. Blessed, surely, are they who are not wholly insensible to such guidance; who have never seen weapons of Death in angelic hands, but have been willing to believe that so it might be; and have desisted accordingly,—desisted, (of course we mean,) *only* when the voice of Conscience spoke loud and clear, and warned them not to persist in what they were doing a moment ago. To all such, Almighty GOD says,—'I will guide thee with Mine eye. Be ye not like to horse and mule, which have no understanding: whose mouths must be held with bit and bridle^a.' .... In all such guidance, how blessed are they, who, not having *seen,* yet have *believed.*

Only one example more. When Sarah's maid espied the fountain of water, and the widow of Zarephath saw the barrel of meal visibly filled from day to day:—when ravens brought Elijah meat, and manna was seen on the ground in the days of Israel's wanderings:—when water was made wine, visibly; and five loaves grew into food for as many thousands:—how easy *then* was the office of Faith in GOD'S care for the bodily wants of His children! The multitudes,— the disciples,—prophets,—widows,—bondsmen; —they saw, they *saw* the bountiful Hand of the CREATOR, employed in behalf of His creatures. There was no effort of Faith here: Faith in GOD'S

^a Ps. xxxii. 9, 10.

care for the very least of His creatures, was swallowed up in a joyous certainty. They *saw* it, and they *believed* it: believed, *because* they saw.

But,—for the last time,—*they* are pronounced 'blessed,' who, though they *see* nothing, yet can believe *all things!* It is a blessed thing to look to GOD day by day for one's supply of food, of clothing, in a childlike spirit, which *knows* that the Father of Mercies will not withhold any thing that is good from His children. It is a blessed thing, we mean, when wants arise and make themselves *felt*, to learn to say secretly,—This shall not distress me. I will mention it calmly in my prayers. The Enemy shall have no advantage of me in *this* matter: for, at the very worst, a few years will span my earthly needs; and I shall gather up all my wants into a marvellous small compass in the end; and the grief will have been long forgotten, when it shall be said over these lifeless limbs, 'Earth to earth, ashes to ashes, dust to dust.' . . In the mean season, I will not distress myself, from a yet higher consideration,—namely, that it would argue a distrust of GOD's good Providence to do so. He fed five thousand on the mountain side with five barley loaves and two small fishes; and what were *they* among so many? He fed four thousand, very shortly after, out of an equally scanty store: and, after one of these bounteous miracles, seven baskets full of fragments were gathered up; after the other, twelve! .... And if He wrought so then, shall He not sometimes work so now? Nay, what saith He? 'Take no thought for your life,' (that is, no anxious, distressing thought,) 'what ye shall eat, or what ye shall drink; nor yet for your body, what ye shall put on. Is not the life more than meat, and the body than raiment? Behold the fowls of the air: for they sow not, neither do they reap, nor gather into barns; yet your heavenly FATHER feedeth them. Are ye not much better than they?' Presently, He adds,—' And why take ye thought for raiment? Consider the lilies of the field, how they grow; they toil not, neither do they spin: and yet I say unto you, that even Solomon in all his glory was not arrayed like one of these. Wherefore, if GOD so clothe the grass of the field, which to-day is, and to-morrow is cast into the oven, shall He not much more clothe you, O ye of little faith? .... But seek ye first the Kingdom of GOD, and His Righteousness; and all these things shall be added unto you[b].' *Here* then is the

---

[b] St. Matth. vi. 25—33.

gracious promise! Here is the ground of our hope; yea, of our confidence! They of old time knew something of this matter; for, as says the Psalmist,—'I have been young, and now am old; yet have I not seen the righteous forsaken, nor his seed begging bread[c].' But *we* know far more: as it is written;—'Blessed be the GOD and FATHER of our LORD JESUS CHRIST, which according to His abundant mercy hath begotten us again unto a lively hope by the Resurrection of JESUS CHRIST from the dead, to an inheritance incorruptible, and undefiled, and that fadeth not away, reserved in Heaven for you, who are kept by the power of GOD through faith unto salvation ready to be revealed in the last time.... That the trial of your faith, being much more precious than of gold that perisheth, though it be tried with fire, might be found unto praise and honour and glory at the appearing of JESUS CHRIST: whom having not seen, ye love; in whom, though now ye see Him not, yet believing, ye rejoice with joy unspeakable and full of glory: receiving the end of your faith, even the salvation of your souls[d].'

[c] Ps. xxxvii. 25.   [d] 1 St. Peter i. 3—9.

The First Sunday after Easter.

THE VICTORY THAT OVERCOMETH THE WORLD.

1 St. John v. 4.

This is the victory that overcometh the World, even our Faith.

MANY are the hints given us in the Bible that the days of our life are days of warfare. We are spoken of as soldiers, repeatedly: our spiritual armour is described again and again. In the text, we hear of an enemy to be resisted, and a victory to be won. True indeed it is that words of Peace were ever on the SAVIOUR's lips; as on this day, for example, when He came to the forlorn band of Disciples at evening, and stood among them. True it also is that His peace,—'which passeth all understanding,'—is intended evermore to keep our hearts and minds in the knowledge and love of GOD. Yet is it certain that we have enemies who can disturb that peace; and would take it away from us altogether, if they might. Such an enemy is this present World, as most of us are aware already; and *all* will know it for themselves in time. The text conveys a precious word of promise, or rather, it reveals a blessed and most important secret; namely *this*, that our Faith as Christians *overcometh the World.*—Let us inquire briefly then into the nature of the Faith here spoken of, and of which such wonderful things are declared; and take notice of the method of operation whereby it can be said to overcome the World. First however we should perhaps state briefly what we understand by 'the World.'

Now GOD did not make the World evil, but good; and even now, when Sin hath done its worst, the World we inhabit retains much of Goodness and of Beauty. If a ruin, it is, at least, a very beautiful ruin. And yet, this very beauty is a seduction and a snare: for it makes us love unduly the pleasures which the World supplies; and covet unduly the honours which are the World's, not GOD's. It makes us also desire unduly possessions which are of the earth, earthy; and regret unduly every privation, every sorrow, which is sent to wean us from this present life,—to weaken the hold which the World has upon us, and *we* upon the World . . . By 'the

World,' then,—which our Faith is said to overcome,—we understand whatever things of earthly growth have a tendency to interfere with spiritual progress; to impair the heavenly mind; to enslave the heart and affections; to disturb our confidence in GOD, our belief in His perfect wisdom, goodness, and love; to make life, and health, and ease, and affluence seem the greatest of goods; privations of whatever kind,—sickness, suffering, death,—as the greatest of calamities. No Christian man, of course, can live in so extremely unchristian a frame as this: but in proportion as he feels the tendency of the World to affect him in the manner we have been describing, he is made conscious of the Blessedness of that Faith which overcometh the World.

What then *is* the 'Faith' of which the beloved Disciple speaks? Is it that strong principle of confidence in God which so many claim to themselves? We sometimes hear Faith spoken of as opposed to Works; and *so* spoken of, as to convince us that men know not of what they speak. Is it a strong feeling of *belief*, then; a mere act or habit of the heart or mind, which St. John here refers to? Certainly not. He has not, in fact, left us in any doubt as to his meaning: for, after saying,—'This is the victory that overcometh the World, even our Faith;' he immediately adds, —' Who is he that overcometh the World, but he that believeth *that* JESUS *is the* SON *of* GOD?'.. When St. John says, therefore, that '*our Faith*' overcometh the World, his words amount to this, — that our Christian confidence in the great truth *that* JESUS CHRIST *is come in the flesh*, is the secret of our strength, as Christian men. In other words, he asserts the divine efficacy of the great doctrine of our LORD's Incarnation; declaring that as many as have embraced that momentous truth, and realized it also in their lives, are in possession of a secret which will enable them to overcome the World. 'This is the victory that overcometh the World, even our Faith. Who is he that overcometh the World, but he that believeth that JESUS is the SON of GOD?'

It remains to consider the method whereby a belief in what may be truly called 'the pillar and ground of the truth,'—(namely, that JESUS CHRIST, the 'only Son, our LORD, was conceived by the HOLY GHOST, born of the Virgin Mary, suffered under Pontius Pilate, was crucified, dead, and buried; descended into Hell; the third day rose again from the dead, ascended into Heaven, and sitteth on the Right Hand of God the FATHER ALMIGHTY, from whence He shall come to judge the quick and the dead;') how the belief and entire acceptance of this article avails to 'the victory that overcometh the World.' In other words, wherein lies the secret power of the doctrine of our LORD's Incarnation. By what means shall it avail to the overcoming of the World?

And truly the lessons of the recent Holy Season are too fresh in our memories that we should be at any loss for a practical answer to this question. We have witnessed the building in of the key-stone of the arch,—the laying again the corner stone of the entire structure,—by the sacred solemnities of—Good-Friday and Easter-Day. All are fully conscious that a suffering REDEEMER was presented to their minds throughout Lent; especially towards its close: and further, that on Easter-Day His exaltation and glory was the Church's sole subject of rejoicing. We make no doubt that these tremendous scenes supply the reason for the choice of this particular Epistle to be read in the Churches on this particular day: for we are persuaded that the sight of the Humiliation and Glory of the Son of Man hath wrought in all a livelier faith in Him who is the object of our Hope, and of our worship. Our Faith hath been made very strong; and though we go forth at once into the world of sense, and though its manifold seductions assail us with renewed violence, on every side,—yet are we made sensible that something hath been given us whereby effectually to resist and withstand them, if we will. The image of Him who was so recently set forth crucified before us; His empty sepulchre, and the glorious message brought to us by Angels, that He is risen; are things too recently in our thoughts to have yet faded away; and we feel, we *feel* their power. Calamity, indignity, and wrong; unkindness, ingratitude, desertion; sickness, and suffering, and death;—these things have been met and overcome by the Captain of our Salvation. We have been brought into a wondrous nearness with Him; made one in a great mystery: and we cannot but feel that we are not only called upon to tread in His blessed footsteps of suffering, but are endued with strength and power to do so likewise. 'In the world ye shall have tribulation,' He said before He suffered, to His Disciples and to us, and to as many as are yet afar off: 'but be of good cheer, *I have overcome the World.*' What avails the victory; wherein lay the force of that consolation; if we are, in no way, made one with Him?

We need not perhaps speak more particularly

of that Faith in a crucified and risen LORD which avails·to the overcoming of the World; for our hearts will now supply all that need be added. Besides inspiring a mighty consolation and confidence, the Doctrine of our LORD's Incarnation supplies us with strength to conquer, and gives us the victory as well: for how worthless become the bribes for which some have been content to sell their souls! and how barren seem the joys in which some are content to waste their lives! How hollow seems the world's friendship, and how unreal the world's honours; and present prosperity,—how little is it to be trusted! and apparent success,—how little is it to be taken as an index of what shall be abiding! Consider the history of our LORD's Passion; and see Pilate, wise in his own conceit, prudent doubtless in the estimation of all! See him and Herod becoming friends in the betrayal of the Just One! and the chief priests accomplishing their wicked purpose! and Judas selling his soul for money!

How blessed, on the other hand, seem the afflictions which make us like to Him! and how high the privilege to be invited to set our feet in any of His footmarks! Nay, hath not death itself lost its terrors? Death, the worst threat which *the World* knows; the greatest terror which *our Flesh* can contemplate, or *the Devil* contrive, for shaking the soul from her stedfastness;—surely, He hath disarmed Death, and the shadowy valley which lies beyond, and the doubts which, but for *Him*, must have so darkened the soul of the dying man; He hath robbed them all of their terrors by dying and rising again! Not only hath *He* overcome the World; but our Faith in Him giveth *us* the victory likewise!

The rest must be left to the private experience of every believer. Many will have wonderful things to relate about this matter, which we will not attempt to predict particularly. But assuredly if there be such things to Christian hearts as support in hours of deepest affliction, and songs in the very darkest night; consolations which sustain the failing spirit, even when all consolation seemed gone; and hopes which come up and blossom even on the very grave of Hope:—trace these back to their beginnings, and you will find that the great Doctrine of 'the WORD made flesh' is the strong root out of which they all derive the secret of their growth: that verily '*this* is the victory that overcometh the World,—even *our Faith*.'

The Second Sunday after Easter.

THE SHEEP KNOWN AND KNOWING.

St. John x. 14.

I am the Good Shepherd; and know My sheep, and am known of Mine.

WE are here reminded, first, of the intimate knowledge which CHRIST possesses concerning every one of ourselves. He knows us as a shepherd knows his sheep. We may think ourselves overlooked and forgotten, sometimes; but we may be assured,—this very saying assures us,—that it is not so. As 'He telleth the number of the stars, and calleth them all by their names,' so doth He know *us*, every one! 'I am the Good Shepherd, and *know* My sheep.'

But far more than that is implied by these words of our SAVIOUR; for, proceeding as He does from the statement, 'I know My sheep,' to that other statement, 'and am known of Mine,'—He reminds us, further, that the knowledge of which He speaks is a knowledge not all on one side; but a mutual knowledge: *one*, shared by the two persons between whom it subsists. And this opens a solemn view of the subject. Let us, however, carefully guard against *one* mistake; and then, offer the few words which present themselves on so lofty a matter.

You have heard of the Doctrine of *Predestination:* by which is sometimes understood merely GOD's fixed decree concerning every one of ourselves; whether as heirs of Heaven, or of Hell: and it might be thought that reference is here made to the certain knowledge possessed by GOD in this behalf:—'I know My sheep.' But this doctrine, in the case of curious and carnal persons, has naturally given rise to presumptuous views of their own acceptance with GOD,—their own certainty of entering into rest. The belief in such absolute Predestination, in a word, on GOD's part, has given rise to an equally unscriptural desire of absolute assurance on the part of Man. And it might, unhappily, be assumed by some, that when to the declaration, 'I know My sheep,' our LORD adds the declaration, '*and am known of Mine*,'—He speaks of this necessary and certain knowledge on Man's part. The whole saying would therefore amount to little else than a declaration that, between GOD and His elect, there exists a secret certainty,—on the one side, of intended Mercy; on the other, of coming Happiness. Small comfort this, for the desponding and the doubtful; for those who think most meanly of themselves! for as many as are ready, at all times, after a review of their own weakness, and their own sin, to cry out, 'O wretched man that I am!'

But the words, whatever meanings they may wrap up and contain besides, do not certainly look chiefly in the direction just alluded to. The remark seems worth making, (indeed the present place of Scripture reminds us of it,) that close beside many of the deeper and more mysterious revelations of the SPIRIT, is found a key or clue to their meaning. Thus, the words before us are guarded by the very words which immediately follow. The entire sentence would run thus: 'I know My sheep, and am known of Mine,—*even as the* FATHER *knoweth Me, and I know the* FATHER.' It does not, indeed, stand exactly so, in the English; but it seems to be exactly to such a purpose that our LORD spoke. And you perceive, at once, how this latter part of the sentence explains, or at least helps to fix the meaning of, the former part. CHRIST knows His sheep, and, in return, is known of them,—*as the* FATHER *knoweth the* SON, *and* in return, *is known of Him.*

So, the question arises, What are we told of the nearness of connexion or relationship between the FATHER and the SON? And the answer is ready; namely, that they are *One;* not by confusion of Persons, indeed, but by unity of Substance. They are so united as to be *One;* and by virtue of this mysterious union, (which is shared by no other who is not GOD,) our LORD is able to declare that 'no man knoweth the SON, but the FATHER; neither knoweth any man the FATHER, save the SON[a].'

With this thought in our minds, if we approach the text, we shall obtain some insight into its meaning. 'I know My sheep, and am known of Mine,' will therefore imply the sweet and sacred,—of course, the very *secret,*—intercourse of the soul with GOD. Observe the order of the words, for doubtless they indicate the order of the operation also. 'I know My sheep:' *that* must be the first step. The beginning of knowledge must be on GOD's side: and Man's will follow,—'I am known of Mine.'

On the side of GOD, *therefore,* there will be the secret strivings of His Grace in the heart; the blessed influences of His SPIRIT upon our own Spirit . . . To be known of GOD is not only

[a] St. Matth. xi. 27.

to be observed, and taken knowledge of, by Him,—as when man makes acquaintance with a stranger, or may be said to know his fellow-man. It is, in some such way to be known by Him, as *He* is known by the FATHER:—*to be made one* with Him, therefore; and, by virtue of such union, to be blessed with Heavenly influence. *This* is the portion of His 'sheep'! The Good Shepherd does more than search them out, and know them. He does more than know their down-sitting and their up-rising; as well as so observe them, that there is not a word in their tongue but He knoweth it altogether. He directs their path, and guides their steps, and keeps their foot from falling. Moreover, He supplies good words; *so* opening their lips, that their mouth shall ever shew forth His praise. Thus far then, concerning the declaration,—' I know My sheep.'

On the side of Man, it must be implied by the words which follow, — (' and am known of Mine,')—that there is a deep and mysterious Communion between GOD and Man, of which Man is directly conscious. And here we would speak humbly; lest it should be thought that we lay claim to privileges which we enjoy not; and draw from an experience which we possess not.

But holy men are here our teachers; and they tell us wonderful things concerning this intercourse of the soul with its REDEEMER. Thus, speaking of the Sacrament of the LORD's Supper; or rather, of the high spiritual delights which spring from that most sacred participation of CHRIST's Body and Blood; one says, — 'The very letter of the Word of CHRIST giveth plain security that these mysteries do, as nails, fasten us to His very Cross: that by them we draw out, as touching efficacy, force, and virtue, even the blood of His gored side. In the wounds of our REDEEMER, we there dip our tongues. We are dyed red both within and without. Our Hunger is satisfied, and our Thirst for ever quenched. They are things wonderful which he feeleth; great which he seeth, and unheard of which he uttereth, whose soul is possessed of this Paschal Lamb, and made joyful in the strength of this new wine!' . . . How shall we find a more striking indication that our SAVIOUR CHRIST not only knows His sheep, but, in return, *is known of them?*—The words are Hooker's.

Hither, then, are to be referred all those sweet heavenward yearnings, those blessed stirrings of the heart, which good men discourse of so familiarly; only, doubtless, because they experience them so largely: *that* confidence in a SAVIOUR who never yet failed those who truly trusted in Him: *that* certainty that love, somehow, was concealed in the bitterest cup:—*that* cheerful Hope which is the very rod and staff of dying men:—every display of Faith, in short, which faithful hearts exhibit; no less than those daily strivings to keep the thought of Him immediately before the inner eye; making *Him* the object, the secret object, of every act, of every hour, of every day:—all these, we repeat, are signs of that deep and mysterious communion to which we allude; and which we suppose our Blessed LORD to have intended, when He said,—'I know My sheep, *and am known of Mine.*'

Many are the places of Holy Scripture where this Divine experience is more or less clearly alluded to: but St. John it is who tells us most; and who puts his information into the most precious, because the most practical shape. Great is the danger lest men should be misled by Enthusiasm, or by Blindness,—by Spiritual Pride, or by any other snare of the Enemy,—into a mistaken view of their own state; deluded into the notion that they are themselves of the number of those who know CHRIST, as well as are known of Him. The beloved Disciple, therefore, has left more than one solemn caution on this subject. 'He that *loveth not*, knoweth not GOD,' he says: 'for GOD is Love[b].' 'Hereby we do *know* that we know Him,' he says again. And *what* is the ground of that certainty? the sign by which we may *know* that we *know* Him? 'Hereby we do know that we know Him, *if we keep His Commandments*. He that saith, I know Him, and keepeth not His Commandments, is a liar, and the Truth is not in him. But whoso keepeth His Word, in him verily is the Love of GOD perfected. Hereby *know* we that we are *in Him*[c].'

'*In* Him:' that expression surely reveals all! *In* the World, but not *of* it: *so* in the World, that we may yet truly be said to be *in* CHRIST! All those expressions in Holy Scripture which allude to the Life which is '*hid with* CHRIST *in* GOD,' these surely remind us of the true nature of that Heavenly knowledge which the text *declares* without *describing*: . . . To each one of us may GOD grant a large measure of it, for JESUS CHRIST's sake!

[b] 1 St. John iv. 8.   [c] 1 St. John ii. 3.

The Third Sunday after Easter.

THE SORROW OF GOD'S SAINTS.

St. John xvi. 20.

Ye shall weep and lament, but the World shall rejoice: and ye shall be sorrowful, but your sorrow shall be turned into joy.

THOSE who read their Prayer-Book with attention will have observed that this is the first of four successive Sundays which take their gospel from the xvith chapter of St. John. They will have been struck with the care and skill displayed in so distributing the several parts of the chapter in question, that each successive Sunday shall have what is most appropriate to it. All, however, agree in *one* respect: namely, that they look forward; and contain allusions more or less distinct to the great outpouring of the SPIRIT which took place at Whitsuntide.

It may be well to advert briefly to the words preceding the text in the gospel for the Day. JESUS said to His Disciples, 'A little while, and ye shall not see Me: and again, a little while, and ye shall see Me, because I go to the FATHER. Then said some of His disciples among themselves, What is this that He saith unto us, A little while, and ye shall not see Me: and again, a little while, and ye shall see Me: and, Because I go to the FATHER? They said therefore, What is this that He saith, A little while? we cannot tell what He saith^a.' Now the best explanation of these words, is to be obtained by connecting them with the great mystery of Pentecost. The place, in short, seems to mean this: 'A little while and ye shall not see Me,'—for I am to die to-morrow: 'and again, a little while and ye shall see Me, because I go to the FATHER,'—and will then pour out upon you that unspeakable gift whereby ye shall see Me indeed.

'Now JESUS knew that they were desirous to ask Him, and said unto them, Do ye enquire among yourselves of that I said, A little while, and ye shall not see Me: and again, a little while, and ye shall see Me? Verily, verily, I say unto you, That ye shall weep and lament, but the World shall rejoice: and ye shall be sorrowful, but your Sorrow shall be turned into Joy[b].' Those are the words of the text.

We wish you to observe concerning them that

[a] St. John xvi 16—18.   [b] St. John xvi. 19, 20.

they do not contain a direct reply to the difficulty and doubt of the Disciples. The particular question they wished to ask is not answered: but our LORD gives them a general assurance of Blessedness in store for them. He promises them Sorrow now, but Joy afterwards. 'Ye shall be sorrowful; but your Sorrow shall be turned into Joy.' He also contrasts the state of the World, (that is, *of the wicked*,) with theirs. ' Verily, verily, I say unto you:' (the solemn words of Him who was the Truth itself!) ' ye shall weep and lament, while the World shall rejoice. Yea, ye shall be sorrowful: but *your* Sorrow shall be turned into *Joy:*' while the World's Joy, (it is clearly implied,) shall be turned into Sorrow.—Let us briefly dwell on these two solemn aspects of our SAVIOUR's words.

The contrast of the present state and future prospects of the wicked, with the present state and future prospects of the just, is strikingly set forth in this brief statement. It is given only in general terms. The children of this World are declared to rejoice; to be rejoicing, while the children of GOD weep and lament. Such words are of course addressed to understanding ears. It is not meant, (how *can* it be meant?) that tears shall all day long flow down the cheeks of the pure and good; while rejoicing is to be the perpetual portion of fools. So far is this from being the case, that a day passed with these two opposite characters would doubtless discover that something far better deserving the name of Joy, abides with the virtuous: something far more like Sorrow with the wicked. Peace and Content,—a quiet Confidence,—sometimes a holy Joy,—would at least be found to dwell with those who are striving to walk in the way of God's commandments. On the contrary, disappointment and self-reproach,—gloom, and it may be even tears,—would be found in the case of the disobedient, the self-willed, the unholy. But, for all that, what our Lord says is known to be strictly true; is found to be so every day. Sorrow, in some shape; trials, (that is,) and much that flesh and blood shrinks from, are constantly found to be the portion of the children of God. So that the Apostle was able to say,—' Yea, and all that will live godly in Christ Jesus shall suffer persecution.' The very submission of one's own will in all things to the Will of the Most High, is in itself, at first, a sorrow. Privations, —losses,—bereavements,—many a dispensation sent by God in Love, not in Anger,—make up the fulfilment of the prophecy,—' Ye shall be sorrowful.' . . . On the other hand, *that* temper, and those habits, and those desires, which know nothing of restraint, self-denial, or mortification, —are all implied by the general term, 'Rejoicing.' The World 'rejoiceth,' (or rather, seemeth to rejoice,) because it knows nothing of CHRIST's yoke: the children of GOD are sorrowful, (or rather, to outward appearance seem so,) because they seek to submit themselves; to make a sacrifice of their own will, in all things.

But the point we have to notice is, that it is clearly implied by our LORD that *real* Sorrow is in 'store, as the abiding portion of the wicked: that theirs is only a *short-lived* rejoicing. It would be well for all to bear this ever in mind: for very attractive, certainly, are the pleasures of Sin. It is useless to deny that the Enemy of souls seeks to beguile us with most seductive snares. Yet surely, the thought that bitterness will be the end of the matter, should be enough to check those who are most greedily bent on the gratification of a sinful desire. Thus, the drunkard is warned that the liquor he loves, 'biteth *at the last* like a serpent.' The fornicator is warned against the strange woman who flattereth with her lips, that '*her end* is bitter as wormwood: sharp as a two-edged sword.' To the covetous, our LORD addressed the question, 'What shall it profit a man, if he shall gain the whole World, and *lose his own soul?*'—'*The end* of those things is *Death*,' as St. Paul declares. Such pleasures, such rejoicing, turneth into Sorrow at the last.

But the very reverse is the prospect of the children of GOD. 'Ye shall be sorrowful; but your Sorrow shall be turned into Joy.' Let us cherish the certainty that these words belong to GOD's faithful children for ever. They contain a perpetual prophecy, and a perpetual promise. A perpetual prophecy:—'Ye shall be sorrowful.' For what is that but to say in other words,— 'If any man will come after Me, let him deny himself, and take up his cross, and follow Me?' —The same thing which is elsewhere conveyed thus,—'In the World ye shall have tribulation.' But the promise (blessed be GOD!) is perpetual also: 'Your Sorrow shall be turned into Joy.' And this is what strengthens the wavering spirit, and supports the feeble knees, and cheers the drooping heart. It hath ever been thus. 'Our light affliction which is but for a moment,' (says the great Apostle,) 'worketh for us a far more exceeding and eternal weight of glory: while we look not at the things which are seen, but *at the things which are not seen:* for the things which are seen are temporal; but the things which are not seen are *eternal.*'

How, in any particular instance, godly Sorrow shall be turned into Joy, we know not; nor what is the nature of that far more exceeding and eternal weight of glory which affliction is intended to work for the children of GOD. We do but know that He is faithful who promised; and that He will assuredly bring it to pass. It may be, that to have done lowly offices of Love upon Earth; to have tended the sick, to have taught the ignorant, to have protected the weak, to have upheld the fainting; these acts and the like of these, done through life at the cost of much privation, and no little self-denial, *may* prove a training necessary to be gone through by those who are to be ministering Angels hereafter; whose glorious privilege it will be to stand before GOD; whose glorious office it will be to receive His orders, and execute His will, in far parts of the Earth, in remote worlds: aye, and why not to minister to those who bear their name, or share their blood, or owned their friendship, and are yet in the flesh?—It may be, again, that as many as laboured most to keep themselves from any thing that might defile, will find their surpassing Bliss in being thereby enabled to receive into themselves a truer image of the Eternal GOD. They were 'sorrowful;' for they sought to cultivate that particular Christian grace which perhaps demands the largest sacrifices: but immense will be the reward.—In like manner, those who have striven most to live a life of Righteousness,—who have hungered after it, and felt the grief and pain of every hindrance which kept them back,—*these* persons will from that very circumstance be capable hereafter of being filled the fuller.—In some such ways, then, will the Sorrow of GOD's Saints be hereafter turned into Joy.

And what remains but to impress ourselves deeply with the greatness of the reward, the largeness of the Joy, thus set before us; and to seek to regard every pang of the threatened Sorrow as a previous pledge and reward of the promised Joy?

The Fourth Sunday after Easter.

OUR BODIES, TEMPLES OF THE HOLY GHOST.

1 Corinthians vi. 19.

What? know ye not that your body is the Temple of the Holy Ghost which is in you, which ye have of God, and ye are not your own?

To ask a question in this manner, is the strongest way of making an assertion. The Apostle declares it as no new truth, but appeals to it as something received and allowed by all, that the bodies of baptized persons are *Temples of the* Holy Ghost. And this declaration of his we shall do well to consider at this season. The services of the sanctuary guide our thoughts in the direction of the text; for Whitsuntide, which is now fast approaching, is the season when we call to mind God's great gift to the Church; the gift, namely, of His Indwelling Spirit;—and there is perhaps no one doctrine which conduces more to personal holiness,—no one truth which grows more readily into a constraining motive for purity of life,—than this which the text contains. It states (1st) that the HOLY GHOST *dwells within us; resides in our very Bodies:* and (2ndly) declares it to be a truth, known and received of all men, that our bodies are *Temples*. On either of these two heads a few words shall be offered on this occasion.

1. Now, it is certain that every one of us, at Holy Baptism, received this marvellous gift of the HOLY SPIRIT. To explain how His personal inhabitation takes place, is manifestly above us. Let it content us to know that it is He who moves us to holy actions; puts into our minds high and holy thoughts; gives us effectual repentance for sins committed; fills the soul with heavenly peace and holy joy. He it is who, day by day, pleads with the sinful man; reproves; reproaches; is grieved by his hardness and impenitence; and even yet, while there remains a ray of hope, will not forsake him quite. He it is who comforts the afflicted, and sustains the desponding, and strengthens the weak. He sheds abroad the Love of GOD in the heart, and fills the soul of Man with that Peace which passeth all understanding. Not least is it His office to make men of one mind in a House: to make the husband loving and kind; the wife amiable and complying; the children dutiful and obedient.

His work it is, if the members of a Household come constantly to Church: if the study of God's Word becomes a privilege and a delight: if Prayer is a comfort and a pleasure. No better test could perhaps be suggested as to our state in respect of this Divine guest than the love we feel towards our neighbour, and the appetite with which we engage in Prayer.

Let it suffice us further to remember that if resisted and refused, the Indwelling Spirit will plead less and less forcibly, less and less often. He is declared to be grieved by sin: by hardened wickedness, to be quenched altogether. Here, then, we read our danger. To be by Him forsaken, is surely the most terrible calamity which can possibly befal a living man. Hence that passionate cry of the Psalmist,—'Cast me not away from Thy presence, and take not Thy Holy Spirit from me[a]!'

This great doctrine of the Indwelling Spirit it is which makes the sins forbidden under the Seventh Commandment so grievously offensive to the Holy God. Fornication and all uncleanness, drunkenness and gluttony, are hence declared by St. Peter to be things which 'war against the soul[b].' In proportion as the advantage is great

[a] Psalm li. 11.   [b] 1 St. Pet. ii. 11.

of so blessed a Guest, must the penalty be terrible of rejecting and resisting Him. Thus it is declared of him that defileth the body, inasmuch as it is the Temple of GOD,—'*him shall GOD destroy*^c.'

2. And now for a few words concerning the Body as a Temple. The mere announcement that our Bodies were designed for this magnificent purpose is enough to fill us with lofty thoughts concerning them. Let us at least be warned against indulging in any of those disparaging remarks concerning our bodies which some persons have been prone to fall into. We often hear men speak of their bodies with contempt; contrasting them with their souls: as if their souls were divine, and their bodies human; or as if while the one is destined to live for ever, the other is destined evermore to inherit corruption. Let men remember that they are made up of a human soul and a human body; and that *both* parts are necessary to make up the whole man. Let them remark that their bodies are destined for immortality no less than their souls; and that GOD will not suffer the House which He once condescended to inhabit, to remain for ever ruined and dissolved. GOD will assuredly raise it up;

---

^c 1 Cor. iii. 17.

and respect, even in its very ruins, that which was once His Temple.

This great Truth,—namely, that our bodies are Temples of the HOLY GHOST,—explains why, in Life and in Death, we shew them so much respect and honour. Rather, let it be a prevailing motive with all of us, and reason, why we should shew them *more!* Cleanliness of person, even costliness of clothing, is recommended by nothing so forcibly as the consideration that our bodies are Temples of the HOLY GHOST. . . . The same consideration is the cause why Christian men shew so much reverence towards the Bodies of the departed. The Grave is but a wardrobe, where the poor fleshy mantle is deposited against the requirements of the eternal morning. The soul will then have need of it again. Hence, the cost, (and where it can be afforded, the pomp,) of funerals. Hence it is, moreover, that the Body is laid in consecrated ground,—pointing, (like our Churches,) East and West; because it is itself a temple also; even the Temple of the HOLY GHOST.

And be it observed, that this very word (Temple,) which to us conveys indistinct and different notions, awakened anciently, in the minds of Jew and Gentile alike, the definite notion of *a dwelling place.* The Greek word signifies nothing else; while it is discovered from several expressions in David's Psalms, that he regarded the Temple at Jerusalem as '*an habitation* for the mighty God of Jacob.' '*Here will I dwell,*' (saith the Most High,) 'for I have a delight therein[d].' There, as in the Tabernacle of yet more ancient days, was God to be met with. There was His voice to be heard. There was He seen to dwell in glory between the Cherubims. To a Jewish reader, therefore, consider what a solemn thought the mention of 'the Temple' conveyed! and above all, what solemn thoughts about themselves were suggested by the mention of their *bodies* as Temples! That costly and splendid structure which Solomon had built and garnished under the direction of God Himself, was discovered to be represented by the marvellous fabric of their own mortal bodies.

Yea, a more mysterious thought, by far, was brought before their minds. The Shekinah, or cloud of Glory, which was the visible token of the presence of the Almighty, is known to have disappeared from the Jewish Temple ever since the days of the Captivity. The second Temple, (the same which was standing in the time of our

[d] Ps. cxxxii. 5, 15.

Lord,) had no visible token of Jehovah's presence. During the days of the Son of Man therefore, truly might it be said that 'the glory had departed from Israel.' Yet was it found that in Christ's person, after a spiritual and heavenly manner, all the faded glories of God's chosen people were restored: for in the Temple of Christ's Body dwelt all the fulness of the Godhead; ('*and we beheld His Glory,*' says the Beloved Disciple.) Yea, and in every one of His members also was the same marvel and mercy to be fulfilled and repeated: the Divine presence was to be restored in the person of every individual Christian: for 'as God hath said, I will dwell in them and walk in them[e],' so was it fulfilled at the first Christian Pentecost. Thenceforward, the Apostle could say,—'Know ye not that ye are the Temple of God, and that the Spirit of God dwelleth in you[f]?' Or, as it is said in the text,—'What? know ye not that your bodies are the Temples of the Holy Ghost?'

God give us grace, while we say such things, to seek to realize them likewise! It is a fearful thing which we say, when we claim to ourselves God Himself as our guest: yet do we escape

[e] 2 Cor. vi. 16.   [f] 1 Cor. iii. 16.

nothing by seeking to disguise from ourselves the solemn truth that He does indeed dwell within us, unless we have driven Him away. Rather let it be our pious endeavour to listen for His promptings; to obey His gracious motions: by watchfulness and Prayer, to secure His abiding presence, and His continued Love.

The Fifth Sunday after Easter.

ANSWERED PRAYER.—Part I.

St. John xvi. 23.

Verily, verily, I say unto you, Whatsoever ye shall ask the Father *in My Name, He will give it you.*

With words like these, the Saviour of the World sought to comfort the hearts of His Disciples on the night before He was taken from them. All His wondrous Discourse, from the xivth to the xviith chapter of St. John's Gospel inclusive, is of this character; full, throughout, of tenderness; abounding in words of comfort, in assurances of abiding love, in promises of blessings in store. There can be no doubt that the reason why the Church hath taken out of those chapters the gospels for all the Sundays from the Third after Easter until Whit-Sunday, is because at this season of the year she considers us to be somewhat in the condition of those sad Disciples. We may, or we may not have the hearts to feel it; but it fares with us, at this time, as it fared of old in Israel when the sons of the prophets came to Elisha, and said unto him, 'Knowest thou that the LORD will take away thy master from thy head to-day?' We may, or we may not be conscious of the resemblance; but it is hard to understand how those who have attended to the course of the Christian Seasons, can fail to feel as if they were already on the point of losing Him Whom they have of late beheld tempted, suffering, dead, and buried for their sakes; raised from death; and since, for forty days, (come Thursday next,) walking the earth with His risen body. That some, in every place, have such feelings, we know. Those persons will feed upon the gracious words of this day's gospel, as if they were addressed to themselves; and will derive all the consolation from them which they are meant to convey.

But all alike should be made attentive by the words of a text like this; for *all*, at least, *pray:* and no one ever yet prayed without hoping that GOD would be pleased to grant him the thing he prayed for. Now, the text contains a direct promise, and a plain condition, concerning prayer.

'Whatsoever ye shall ask the Father *in My Name:*' such is the condition. 'He will *give it* you:' such is the promise. Observe how large it is! '*Whatsoever* ye shall ask.' Surely it must concern us all to have a right understanding, as well as a full belief, in what so nearly affects us!

Now, it is this very *largeness* of the Divine promise which here chiefly strikes us.—'Am I to understand then,' (it may be asked,) 'that any thing I ask, of whatever kind it be, will be granted me? Is there no limit? Does GOD really stand pledged in this place to grant me every thing I choose to ask for?'

But there is a clearness of understanding in matters spiritual, even in men of corrupt minds, which plainly forbids any such supposition. The candle of the LORD burns far too brightly within all of us, the Voice of GOD is heard far too clearly, to allow of any very grievous mistake in matters of prime moment to our souls' health, and our eternal Salvation. We know that GOD cannot stand pledged to grant us *every thing* we choose to ask. But there is great danger lest, upon this, we go off into the opposite extreme; and suspect that the promise which has just been read to us, because it does not mean *quite* every thing, therefore means *almost* nothing. Let us especially guard against this fearful mistake. And, that we may make no mistake at all, but obtain wise and correct notions of the whole matter, let us consider the text by the light of GOD's Holy Word; and humbly hope for His blessed guidance, that we may not be so unhappy as to interpret His gracious words amiss.

Above all things, let us seek to impress our hearts with the solemn truth that no words of our SAVIOUR CHRIST are ever to be made light of, or explained away. Let them ever be taken in their plain obvious sense; (and, if there be any doubt as to their meaning, in the sense which the heart rather than the head declares to be the true one;) and we shall scarcely ever go wrong. Especially safe are we, if the threat, or promise, or precept, occurs in many other places of the Bible. Apply this remark to the promise in hand, and its force will be felt at once. Our LORD, for example, says in another place,—'Whatsoever ye shall ask in My Name, *that* will I do.' In another,—'If ye abide in Me, and My words abide in you, ye shall ask what ye will, and it shall be done unto you.' Our SAVIOUR has elsewhere said,—'Ask, and it shall be given unto you; seek, and ye shall find; knock, and it shall be opened unto you.' This is express; and the reasoning which follows immediately after, is quite conclusive. Yet once more,—'All things whatsoever ye shall ask in prayer, believing, ye shall receive.'

From all this, it will appear that we are quite safe in taking the words of the text in their plain literal meaning; and that we cannot interpret them too largely. For it is not to be supposed that any thing which was not entirely *meant*, would have been so often repeated, and in language so *certain* to mislead.

But then, since it is incredible that we are at liberty to ask for anything we happen to wish for, with the entire certainty of its bestowal,—what limits are we to set on the Divine promise? And thus, whereas a moment since, we ventured to assert that the promises of GOD are to be taken *literally*, it might seem as if we were already bent on limiting one of the most precious promises of all.

This matter, nevertheless, admits of a very satisfactory explanation. If a loving parent were asked whether he could deny any thing to his children, he would perhaps answer, Nothing. Yet, ask him whether he would therefore grant them such requests as he knew must certainly work their utter ruin; and who sees not that the inquiry would be treated as ridiculous? Not *those* things, certainly! (would be the indignant language of every heart:) I could not, of course, mean *that!*

We are reminded therefore that there is a limit, well understood though not expressed,—*too well* understood, in fact, to require that it should *be* expressed,—to our common promises: a limit which nevertheless argues no unreality, no insincerity in the speaker. And availing ourselves of the homely but obvious illustration already offered, we shall have no difficulty in perceiving that, however faithful and true in the matter of His promises, yet, if we pray for things *which God knows would be for our hurt,* we have no right *to expect* that God will grant them: and conversely, that if God does not grant the things which we pray for, the reason may well be, and very probably is, because it would hurt us to obtain our petitions.

In no way however can we perhaps better set forth our belief in the efficacy of Prayer, than by adding,—which we do gravely, and confidently, —that if a Prayer for *any* gift, be it what it may, were to be constantly persevered in; if the heart were to resolve on taking no denial, and the lips were never to grow weary of asking; we make little doubt that the person so praying would run a fearful risk of *having his prayer answered,*—let it be for whatever thing it might. This could not, of course, be the case, were he to remember to add to his prayer words like these,—'Yet not my will, but Thine, be done:' or,—'Grant it, LORD, if it be for my good, and Thine own glory: not else!'—With such a clause added, we should have no fear about the issue. Without it, we should tremble for the man exceedingly.—He would probably fare like Balaam when he was permitted by GOD to go with the princes of Moab; and to take a journey, of which every step brought him nearer to his shameful and sinful end.—The result would resemble, again, the result of Israel's supplication that GOD would give them a king. Because they were *determined* to receive of GOD the thing they asked, and because they persevered, GOD at last sent them a king *in His wrath*..... Apply these remarks to a prayer which any of ourselves might be tempted to make for health, for riches, for leisure; or again, for children, for honours, or for the gratification of any favourite scheme of earthly happiness; for power, high office, and the like;—and it will be felt how easily it might happen that the greatest of all calamities would be that a man should have his prayer granted.

The subject of Prayer is evidently one of such extreme importance that, viewed in different aspects, it may well be made the subject of several distinct sermons. We will conclude the subject of 'answered Prayer' in a separate discourse; for it would be scarcely possible, (as well as unwise,) that we should condense into narrow limits all that we are desirous of saying on this head. It shall suffice to have thus opened the subject, on this occasion: to have insisted on the largeness of the Divine promise, and on the literal sense in which those gracious words of our Lord Christ are to be understood. At the same time, we have indicated one obvious restriction upon its amazing fulness; but we have intended to shew that if any limits are set upon it, they are prescribed by Divine Love itself; and that, without them, Prayer would cease to be the prime instrument of winning for ourselves a blessing from Almighty God.

The Ascension-Day.

CHRIST'S DEPARTURE AND RETURN.

Acts i. 11.

This same JESUS, *which is taken up from you into Heaven, shall so come in like manner as ye have seen Him go into Heaven.*

So spake the two men, (that is, the two Angels,) clad in white, whom the Eleven Apostles beheld standing by their side, in the hour of our LORD's Ascension into Heaven. The event itself is very concisely related in the Gospels. He lifted up His hands to bless His chosen ones; and while He was in the very act of bestowing upon them His prevailing blessing, He rose slowly from the earth; and, with the eyes of all intently fixed upon Him, ascended up on high. His retiring form did not grow less and less, until it disappeared entirely; but a cloud from beneath, (it is expressly stated,) withdrew Him from their eyes. The word used is a remarkable one. It conveys the notion that the cloud bore Him up; came from beneath, and carried Him up,—as a chariot might do,—from Earth to Heaven. . . . The Apostles were yet gazing intently after Him, when lo, 'two men stood by them in white apparel; which also said, Ye men of Galilee, why stand ye gazing up into Heaven? this same JESUS, which is taken up from you into Heaven, shall so come in like manner as ye have seen Him go into Heaven. Then returned they unto Jerusalem from the mount called Olivet, which is from Jerusalem a sabbath day's journey[a].'

In this striking narrative, there is one point to which we desire to call attention; a point, which gives it a special meaning as addressed to ourselves; and helps us to realize our private and personal interest in it.

We have seen that the Angels, instead of making any remark on the Ascension of our LORD,—though that great event was even then in progress, and the rest of their glorious choir in the upper Heavens were already shouting, 'Lift up your heads, O ye gates;'—I say, the two Angels spake nothing of our LORD's *Ascension* to the men of Galilee; but declared to them something concerning His *return*. He 'shall so come,' (said they,) 'in like manner as ye

[a] Acts i. 10—12.

have seen Him go into Heaven.' Heavenly likenesses do not strike earthly eyes very forcibly: we can but suggest that *the place* will be the same; seeing that the prophet Zechariah has said that 'His feet shall stand in that day upon the mount of Olives, which is before Jerusalem, on the East[b].' That, as He ascended in the sight of all, so, when He returns, 'every eye shall see Him[c]' likewise. That, as 'God is gone up with a shout; the Lord, with the sound of a trump[d],' so it is expressly revealed that He shall return with like terror: 'for the Lord shall descend from Heaven with a shout, with the voice of the Archangel, and with the trump of God[e].' And further, that as a *cloud* received Him out of the sight of His Church, so in *clouds* He will be sure to reappear. 'Behold, He cometh with clouds!' says the beloved disciple[f]: and Daniel declares, 'One like the Son of Man came with the clouds of Heaven[g]:' and Christ says of Himself,—'All the tribes of the Earth shall see the Son of Man coming in the clouds of Heaven, with power and great glory[h]'.... Still more remarkable, perhaps, when it is remembered that on *a single* chariot-cloud

[b] Zech. xiv. 4. [c] Rev. i. 7. [d] Ps. xlvii.
[e] 1 Thess. iv. 16. [f] Rev. i. 7. [g] Dan. vii. 13.
[h] St. Matth. xxiv. 30.

He was borne up to Heaven, is the discovery that in certain places of Scripture, a *single cloud* is also described as the instrument of His future triumphant return. Thus: 'I looked,' (says the beloved disciple,) 'and behold a white cloud, and upon the cloud one sat like unto the Son of Man[1]:' while, in St. Luke's Gospel, it is written, —'Then shall they see the Son of Man coming *in a cloud*, with power, and great glory[k].'

These points of resemblance, then, it may be thought, were among those which the Angels intended when they prophesied concerning CHRIST's return, that the manner of it would correspond with the manner of His departure. They seem to reprove the Apostles for gazing up with mute wonder at an event which was already past; instead of attending to a great reality which was yet future; a reality which concerned them all very nearly; and which they were taught to connect with the great mystery which they had already been permitted to witness.

This point,— the connexion, namely, of CHRIST's future Coming to Judgment with the great event which we this day celebrate,—is one which we shall do well to set clearly before our minds. The plainness with which Holy Scrip-

[1] Rev. xiv. 14.   [k] St. Luke xxi. 27.

ture itself enforces this connexion is really striking:—'If ye then be risen with CHRIST,' (says the Apostle,) 'seek those things which are above, where CHRIST sitteth on the right Hand of GOD.' But observe how he proceeds;—'When CHRIST who is our life *shall appear,*—then shall ye also appear with Him in glory [1].' . . . 'Our conversation is in Heaven,' (St. Paul elsewhere says;) '*from whence,*'—(mark the connexion established between our LORD ascended, and the same LORD returning to be our Judge,)—'*from whence also we look for the* SAVIOUR, *the* LORD JESUS CHRIST; who shall change our vile body, that it may be fashioned like unto His glorious body [m].' . . . . Just so, do the Angels speak: 'This same JESUS, which is taken up from you into Heaven, shall so come in like manner as ye have seen Him go into Heaven.' And the Creeds all utter the same language; the Apostles', and the Nicene, and the Creed of St. Athanasius, all set the past and future truth in the closest possible connexion; declaring how He who ascended into Heaven, and sitteth on the right Hand of the FATHER, shall come again with glory, to judge both the quick and the dead. . . . And so it stands in the 'Te Deum.' After the words, 'Thou sittest at

[1] Coloss. iii. 4.   [m] Phil. iii. 20.

the right Hand of GOD in the glory of the FATHER,'—it is straightway added, 'We believe that Thou shalt come to be our Judge!'

We are, of course, very familiar with this connexion of the two things, because we are familiar with all the expressions which have been just now quoted; but it does not therefore follow that we have all been at the pains to connect the thought of CHRIST's present glory with nothing so much as our own future Judgment.—For this, however, it has been shewn that we have the SPIRIT's express and repeated warrant. How, then, can we act more wisely at this time than by seeking to realize so great a doctrine; and dwelling, however briefly, upon it?

Let not our backward gaze at the history of what is gone by, distract our attention from an event yet future indeed, but as *certain* as if it formed part of the history of the past. While we meditate on this day's great solemnity, which, save by the eye of Faith, we cannot see; and in which, save through our general membership with CHRIST, we have no interest,—let us not fail to dwell continually on that far grander event which with these bodily eyes we shall every one most assuredly behold; and in which our concern will be altogether private and personal, as well as in the highest degree fearful and momentous. . . . How divinely hath it been ordered that, in this way, every event in our LORD's History should be turned to our edification; and even in the instant when He is taken up out of our sight, the warning should be heard that He will even so return! How does He thus, by the lips of His Angels, gather up the two extremities of the Sacred Year, (Whitsuntide and Advent,) as if they were the two furthest links of a chain; and clasp them together, yea, *rivet* them eternally into one! . . . 'A certain nobleman *went into a far country* to receive for himself a kingdom, *and to return*[n].' That is the sum of the history! His going away, and his coming again,—His Ascension into Heaven, and His Advent back to earth,—these two things GOD Himself hath joined together: and the Sacred Year, the order of the Church's service, exhibits a faithful reflection of *that*, His sovereign mind and will.

We also will seek so to think of our ascended SAVIOUR, as we know that He wills us to think. 'We believe' that He will 'come to be our Judge:' let us *prove* that we believe it, by acting like men who wait for their LORD. Such an expectation is

[n] St. Luke xix. 12.

the best balm for bleeding or for broken hearts, for the sick and sorrowful, the lonely and the afflicted, for as many as suffer wrong, or feel the burthen of their present being. It becomes the very staff and stay of the soul amid change and uncertainty. Such an expectation is moreover a check to Sin and Disobedience: for he who thinks habitually of CHRIST returning to Judgment, will learn by Faith to behold Him as ever nigh. . . . . GOD, of His mercy, grant us so to pass the days of this mortal life, that when His Blessed SON shall come again in His glorious Majesty to judge both the quick and the dead, we may rise to the Life immortal; through Him who liveth and reigneth with the FATHER and the HOLY GHOST, now and ever!

Sunday after Ascension-Day.

ANSWERED PRAYER.—Part II.

St. John xvi. 23.

Verily, verily, I say unto you, Whatsoever ye shall ask the Father in My name, He will give it you.

In a former Sermon, we tried to ascertain with what limitations this glorious promise was delivered by our Saviour to His Church. It was suggested, that although unconditional, yet it must be subject to one obvious limit; namely, that the petition which it would be injurious to us to have granted, God cannot be supposed to stand pledged to us to grant. We would observe next, that there are things which *we ought not* to pray for; and therefore, which we cannot *expect* at God's Hands. It is easy to perceive how many unanswered prayers may be explained in this manner. 'Ye ask, and receive not,' (saith the Holy Spirit,) '*because ye ask amiss.*' On the other hand, 'this is the confidence that we have in Him,' (saith the beloved Disciple,) 'that if we ask any thing according to His will, He heareth us.'

Disappointment in prayer may sometimes be accounted for on another principle: namely, because there is very often an utter want of Faith in the heart of him that prayeth. The prayer unmixed with Faith, cannot expect a reply. The HOLY SPIRIT declares expressly,—'Let not that man think that he shall receive any thing of the LORD.'

Or again,—the lips may draw near to GOD, but the heart be far from Him: and this will fully account for unanswered prayer. Kneeling down and 'saying one's prayers,' is not *praying*. If there is no reaching out of the heart to GOD, there can no blessing follow.—Now judge yourselves, ye who have sometimes complained that your prayer went unanswered. Consider whether it may not have been because you asked for things you *should* not: or because you asked with no lively Faith that GOD could and would answer your petition: or because your prayers are a mere wandering over a form of words; a *form* of godliness without the *power!*

Let me remind you further, that it is plain from Holy Scripture, that our Divine Master sometimes delays to grant our petitions in order to try our Faith. He delivered a parable on a certain occasion 'to this end, that men ought always to pray, and not to faint; saying, There was in a city a judge, which feared not GOD, neither regarded man: and there was a widow in that city; and she came unto him, saying, Avenge me of mine adversary. And he would not for a while: but afterward he said within himself, Though I fear not GOD, nor regard man; yet because this widow troubleth me, I will avenge her, lest by her continual coming she weary me. And the LORD said, Hear what the unjust judge saith! And shall not GOD avenge His own elect, which cry day and night unto Him, though He bear long with them*?' If then none of the cases before supposed, is your case; and you complain of strong cryings to GOD which have yet failed to bring down the promised blessing from on high; consider whether there may not be, in all this, a trial of your Faith: whether it may not be the intention of GOD to see whether *you* have the heart to pray,—not always, but *for a week;* ' and not to faint!'

To the more spiritually minded, nay, to all, we would further remark that we must be content to *trust* GOD with the fulfilment of His own

* St. Luke xviii. 1 to 7.

promises. We have asked for release from suffering, but He keeps us in constant pain: we have asked to be allowed to do Him service, but He causes us to be bed-ridden for years: we have asked for Health, but a feeble frame of body is ours: Rest we have prayed for, but lo, He sends us weariness: and there are plans in life which we have besought Him to bless; but lo, they have not had the issue we expected and desired!

We answer in reply,—But what if, instead of releasing you from suffering in *Time*, GOD answers your prayers by delivering you from the pains of Eternal Death? Would you call Him unfaithful in *that* case?

You prayed to be permitted to do Him service. He keeps you bed-ridden. But what if it should appear hereafter that your patient Life had preached patience to thousands,—your calm Death, resignation, to parents, neighbours, friends; and thus you *had* served GOD effectually; *had* lived to His praise; *had* lived to His glory; *had* drawn a thousand hearts to Him?

You asked for Health. He sent you a weakly frame. But what if the soul grew stronger, the more its earthly tabernacle tottered and trembled: strongest *then* when its tabernacle fell?

How then? Was the prayer answered, or was it denied?

You prayed for rest. He gave you unrest. It was because He knew that rest in life would have been your ruin. You are now to rest with Him, in Abraham's bosom, throughout the ages of Eternity,—for ever, and for ever, and for ever. How then? Has your prayer been answered, or not?

The plans in life which you besought Him to bless, all issued *in a different manner* from what you had asked and expected. Well! but what if the way you had wished and expected would have been ruin and misery; or at least, very imperfect blessedness? What if the 'different manner' in which GOD wrought should prove to be the *best* manner? the issue, the very *best* which could have been imagined? What then?

We have been endeavouring to shew that since GOD's ways are not man's ways, nor His thoughts like ours; it is the part of the creature ·to trust its *prayers*, just as it commits *itself*, to the merciful CREATOR. 'Thou art wise, O LORD, and I am foolish. According to Thy Wisdom, grant me my petitions! I am weak, Thou art mighty! According to Thy strength, not *my* notions of what is strong, confirm Thy gracious promises!

I for Time: *Thou* for Eternity:—fulfil through the ages, O LORD, the things I pray for in the years of my earthly pilgrimage! Thy thoughts are very deep: Thy ways are very wonderful: according to 'the counsel of Thy will' dispose of all my lot! O give me the heart to believe in Thee, to obey Thee, to rely on Thee,—heartily, entirely, implicitly! In Thine own good time, —in Thine own best way,—in the largest sense, (for *that* is *Thy* sense,)—*so* grant me my petition, O LORD my GOD; and *Thy* will, not mine, be done.' . . . This is the language of Faith. GOD make it ever the language of us all!

But O, let us be well persuaded, one and all, that in nine cases out of ten, the simple case is that *what* we pray for, *that* GOD grants: not presently, but *now;* not in some strange way, but in the very way we meant it. O believe it, —young and old, learned and simple, rich and poor, believe it! Rather, *own* that so it is! Why is it that we lack comfort? Simply because we forget to *pray!* Why do our schemes fail? Simply because we take *every step but one* in order to conduct them to a prosperous issue! To what is our disappointment, our long-continued anxiety, our trouble, our calamity,—bodily, spiritual, mental,—to be traced? To the want of *Prayer!* True it is that we sometimes ask and receive not, because we ask amiss; but how much oftener does it happen that we *have* not because we *ask* not! O, if it were the last words of counsel, of warning, of exhortation, we had to deliver with these mortal lips; if we had but one message to deliver to hearts afflicted, or understandings weak,—to a doubting conscience, or a fainting spirit,—to any, under *any* affliction, *any* want, distress, or difficulty,—*that* one message should be;—'Go thou and pray: but ask in Faith, nothing wavering. Go thou, and plead the merits of the Eternal SON before the Almighty FATHER: and be *sure* the LORD will give thee all thou needest, all thou askest! It was not so of old time. To pray to GOD the FATHER through GOD the SON, *this* is reserved for *us*. This prevailing plea, ('through JESUS CHRIST our LORD,') this prevailing Name, is ours. 'Hitherto have ye asked nothing in My Name,' (saith our LORD:) 'ask and ye shall receive, that your joy may be full[b].' O bow down thy heart with gratitude, as often as at the close of Collect and of Prayer that blessed Name recurs, and *the head* is bowed in homage: remember, then, that thou art pleading before the Almighty FATHER the meritorious

[b] St. John xvi. 24.

Cross and Passion, the sufferings and the sacrifice, of the Son of Man; and reminding Him that thou hast anchored thine heart, placed all thy reliance, built up the very pillar of thy Faith, on Him. Then be thou sure that so certainly will He hear thee; so surely will He bless thee; so faithfully will he call to mind those large words of promise,—'Whatsoever ye shall ask the FATHER in My name, He will give it you.' So surely will He *give* thee the very thing thou *askest!*

Whit-Sunday.

GRIEVING THE SPIRIT.

Ephesians iv. 30.

Grieve not the Holy Spirit of God.

In these words, the Apostle must allude to all those actions which are done in despite of the Spirit of Purity, Truth, and Love: and it may be that, on this great Festival, when we celebrate the descent of the Holy Ghost,—that mysterious Third Person in the Blessed Trinity, against 'grieving' whom, the Apostle here warns us,—we cannot act more wisely than by dwelling on a few of the most common of the acts referred to; and reminding ourselves at once of their subtle nature, and of their extreme heinousness.

Since the practice of Love, Divine and Human, is the fulfilling of the whole Law, it might seem enough to speak of violations of the bond of Love; and under that one head, to sum up all our counsel. But though Truth and Love may be conveniently considered together, yet Purity of speech must be spoken of alone: if for no other reason, yet for this; that it is in special connexion with the matter of our *conversation*, that the Apostle's solemn warning is delivered. 'Let no corrupt communication,' (he says,) 'proceed out of your mouth... and grieve not the Holy Spirit of GOD.' A little further on, while He denounces 'Fornication and uncleanness,' as things which are not fit to be even *named* among Saints, he speaks again of filthiness, foolish talking, and jesting, as things unbecoming the Christian character: obviously meaning thereby, *impure* talking; and the making merry with subjects which men are *ashamed openly to name.*

1. Here then we have our first lesson. If we would not grieve the Holy Spirit of GOD, the words of our lips should be *pure.* It would lead us far to consider the reason of this solemn caution. Let it suffice to recollect how Godlike is the faculty of Speech,—by which, indeed, we maintain our place as lords of GOD's Creation, and hold intercourse with GOD and with one another. Let us consider *why* we were entrusted with so glorious a faculty; (doubtless, the setting forth of His praise!) and think what the prostitu-

tion of it to the dishonour of ALMIGHTY GOD, must be. CHRIST Himself is called *the Word;* and surely, there must reside in the thing, of which He has deigned to assume the Name, an especial Dignity!

Then further,—do but consider what a deep impression impure words often make on those who hear them. Who does not know what it is to be haunted by some abominable phrase, or wicked word, which he heard casually, perhaps in very early youth; and, (as it appeared,) could not forget, precisely because the effort which he made to forget it, only imprinted the iniquity deeper on his memory? . . . These things grow old with us. We are ashamed to think that we know them. And yet, it may be that we did not *wish* to know them; (and *that* indeed is our only comfort;) but we were in a strange company, or in the street, or we overheard what was not meant for us; and the Enemy of our souls sent the arrow, through the gate of hearing, into our hearts. . . . How stealthily things of this sort make their entrance; how deep they bury themselves within us; and how they rankle there; few can tell. The point however which we desire rather to call attention to, is the dreadful condemnation which awaits those who have suggested impurity to others by their own unclean language. 'It must needs be that offences come, but woe to that man by whom the offence cometh.' The fear of offending the least of CHRIST's little ones should surely be a constraining motive with us all for great circumspection in this particular. And if any are conscious of a tendency so to offend, and yet sincerely regret and dread it, let them know that their one remedy is prayer to that same Spirit of Purity whom they dread offending that they may be kept from occasions of offence.

2. We will mention next some of the common, but perhaps rather more secret ways, in which mankind are prone to violate the Law of Love. Especially is one here reminded of those unkind stories about one another which persons are so fond of repeating,—generally for want of something else to talk about; and which are so often more than half untrue. Let them be *entirely* true however; we grieve the Holy Spirit of GOD as often as we needlessly reveal, or spread, the story of our neighbour's shame. It may not indeed, and very probably does not, amount to *shame* exactly. And yet it borders thereon; for it is our neighbour's *discredit;* or, (strange to say,) the story would not be repeated.

3. Another matter, which may seem of small importance, but in reality is not so, — is, the putting a bad construction on a doubtful action. Something has been said to us, which will bear two meanings: and we choose to take it in the unkinder meaning of the two. More shall not be said on this subject. We will but remark that it seems to be a very common fault; and that it cannot but be very grievous to the Spirit of Love.

4. Next, *unforgiveness* is a special offence of the class under consideration. How many ways have been invented to evade a duty of which such strong things are spoken by our LORD Himself; even that our forgiveness of others' injuries shall be made the measure of the forgiveness we shall ourselves experience at His Hands!... You will find persons who can forgive every thing but one; but *that* one thing, they declare they can never forgive. They are in perfect charity with all men, except one man; and they cannot forgive *him!* ... Or they say,—'I *forgive,* but I cannot *forget:*' as if it were not perfectly plain that they were strangers to the virtue of forgiveness altogether! No. The proof that one forgives an injury is as obvious as it is unpalatable. It is not, to be willing to confer a favour upon

the offender. Rather is it, to be willing to *incur* an obligation at his hands.

5. Let us call to mind only one other aspect of the same vice, to which some persons are very prone; and which cannot but be a great grief to the Holy Spirit of GOD. We allude to the habit of dwelling in thought upon any wrong which we may happen to have experienced. Some men, if a slight has been put upon them, and still more if they have suffered deliberate injury; if they suspect injustice, ingratitude, or unkindness; and especially, if they have detected a complication of all these: in such cases, it is not a rare thing to find persons going over, in thought or in word, their grievance; enumerating the points of injustice; heightening the ingratitude by description; deepening the unkindness by dwelling upon it. It is easy to be eloquent in such a matter; and the interest, (to the speaker,) never flags. Alas, such things become at last the hardest of all to get rid of! The wrong has been rehearsed so often that it becomes at last a part of oneself. One *cannot*, scarcely, forgive it, if one *would*. To *forget* it is impossible.

In truth, against this way of grieving the HOLY SPIRIT, all had need to be on their guard.

Every one has, (or thinks he has,) something to forgive: and every day brings idle minutes, perhaps leisure hours, during which such things recur; or rather, *are brought* to us by the Enemy of our souls, to see whether we have any pleasure in them. The solitary walk, and the sleepless pillow, the time spent in dressing, or at meals, all these afford him the opportunities he desires . . . Let us dismiss the subject with once more declaring that all such thoughts become our masters or our slaves, as we will. In GOD's strength, let us arm ourselves with the words of a Collect, or a Psalm; (for the Sword of the SPIRIT is the Word of GOD;) and then, resolutely turn away from such dreadful company, to better thoughts. We may be sure that we shall never struggle against such enemies in vain. The SPIRIT Himself, whom we fear to grieve, will have compassion on our infirmities, come to our aid, and effectually help us.

GOD, of His infinite Mercy and Goodness, endue us with all heavenly graces! By the inspiration of His HOLY SPIRIT, (who, as at this time, came to dwell with His Church,) enable us, day by day, both to perceive and to know what things we ought to do; and also give us grace and power faithfully to fulfil the same; for the sake of JESUS CHRIST, His SON, our LORD!

Monday in Whitsun-week.

THE SOUL'S THIRST.—Part I.

St. John vii. 37.

Jesus stood and cried, saying, If any man thirst, let him come unto Me, and drink.

We shall not do amiss, as it seems, on the two days which follow after, and wait upon Whit-Sunday, if we bend our thoughts in the direction suggested by our Lord in the text; for '*this* spake He of the Spirit, which they that believe in Him should receive: for the Holy Ghost was not yet given.' In other words, the Divine Speaker was alluding to the season which has now at length arrived: was proclaiming wherein would consist its blessedness; and was teaching men to long for it, as Eastern Travellers are said to long for the fountain of living water in the waste. Although the meaning of such words must be plain to many, and a matter of blissful experience to some, yet will it benefit all of us to fasten our thoughts, for a short space of time, on these words of our SAVIOUR CHRIST, and to be reminded of their deep and affecting fulness. He speaks of *the Thirst of the Soul;* concerning which we propose, on this occasion, to say somewhat.

Now, consider what 'Thirst' is: a passionate longing from within, and nothing to satisfy it from without. *That* is Thirst. And *who* has not felt it? who does not feel it now?

For example: who does not thirst after *Happiness?* Consider the end proposed by almost all our worldly plans and arrangements. Settlement in life, Holy Matrimony, the careful rearing of Children; the provision we make, or seek to make, against the morrow, against winter, against old age. The whole scheme of our lives is formed with this view. If we were to be asked, Why we do all these things? we should answer, Because we thought it would make for our Happiness. — Now this shews that we thirst after Happiness. There is a passionate longing from within: there is nothing adequate to that longing from without. We therefore seek to find that which may satisfy it.

Once more. Who does not thirst after something to *love?* The heart was meant for affection, and cannot live without it. Like a vine, it must have something to cling to. Observe how Children, (unless they have lost their nature,) cling to their Parents, and Parents to their Children: how the man, (unless he be a wretch,) loves his Wife, and the Wife her Husband. Take notice of the friendships of all ages; the affection which subsists, or ought to subsist, between Masters and Servants. Nay, the feeling is so strong in us that we bestow some of it on the brute creation, the animals which are with us most! Surely, all this shews that we thirst for something to love. There is a passionate longing from within. We require something to satisfy it from without. We therefore reach after that which may effectually quench our thirst.

Again. He must be a miserably degraded being who has never felt a thirst for *Knowledge*. We speak not so much of what is popularly called by that name, as of something far higher and better. To know more of GOD, and of the hidden things of Creation: the nature, and history, and offices of the Holy Angels: the future destiny of man, and all that most concerns him :— we have probably all felt something of this thirst. Still keener must our desire be for greater light in the study of GOD's Holy Word. Our LORD's discourses,—how difficult parts of them are! and

St. Paul's Epistles,—there are sayings in them we can never fathom. Yes, and simpler things than these,—a miracle, or a parable: the whole volume of unfulfilled prophecy, of course; and (what is stranger) many and many a passage in that which has long since found fulfilment: who does not thirst for more light on all these points? So universal is this passion, so keen this thirst, that besides desiring these, the most worthy objects of Man's curiosity, he confesses a thirst for *general* knowledge. He buys books. He passes long studious days and nights in what the wisest of men described as a weariness of the flesh,—aye, and of the spirit too! The health of many a man has broken down, some have destroyed themselves, in consequence of the thirst we are describing. There was a passionate longing from within: little presented itself from without to satisfy it. So they climbed the heavens, and fathomed the sea, and traversed the earth. They were consumed by their thirst!

Only once more. We presume that we are addressing no one who has not done *more* than wish, who has not fairly *thirsted* after *Holiness*. We speak not now, indeed, of those who are simply sorry for their sin as soon as it is committed, and say they wish they were not such wicked persons as they are. No; the class we are more especially intending are Christians of a better stamp. We are thinking of those who begin and end the day with prayer; and who make it their endeavour to keep the thought of GOD before them throughout the day: but who, notwithstanding every endeavour, find it impossible to live so much above the World as they desire. They find that Sin assails them, in some form or other, all day long. A bad thought, unbidden, comes into the heart: or the mind wanders in prayer: or the desire of what is not for them, assails them: or they are tempted to repine at their lot: or they are betrayed into pride: or the World takes up too much of their time. Now, it is not needful to go on in this enumeration. The Christian who knows, experimentally, the pain and grief of any of the things we have been describing, has felt the *thirst after Holiness*. There was a passionate longing, within: there was little or nothing to gratify it, without. His soul was all athirst; and it was *Holiness* for which he thirsted. He cried out with the Psalmist[a], 'As the hart desireth the water brooks, so longeth my soul after Thee, O GOD. My soul is athirst for GOD,

[a] Ps. xlii. 1, 2.

yea even for the living GOD: when shall I come to appear before the presence of GOD?'

Now, a little attention will shew us further how the case stands with the afflicted and unfortunate: the bereaved and lonely: the weary and disappointed: those too who stand lowest in their own estimation, and are half tempted to despair of themselves. It will easily be seen that these are they who are consumed by thirst: whose soul is, as it were, hard at death's door.

For we spoke of the thirst for Happiness: but surely, he whose plans have failed, and whose hopes are blasted;—who finds that every earthly scheme is but the exchange of one set of trials for another;—he who has been struck down by disease, or is afflicted with illness in his family, —a thing which turns his laughter into heaviness, and his joy into mourning: this man, who (we began by saying) thirsted after *Happiness*, surely has had his thirst aggravated a hundred times. He sought for Consolation, but he found it not. Instead of water, vinegar was brought him, and it seemed to him mingled with gall.

We spoke of the thirst for Love: but how must this thirst be aggravated, rendered intolerable, by the death, even by the withdrawal, of the thing whereby it hoped to quench itself!

The Orphan and the Widow, the bereaved and broken-hearted, could tell us something about this matter.

We spoke also of the thirst for Knowledge: but how stands the case with him who with shattered health, and enfeebled powers, is compelled to confess that every advance does but convince him of his ignorance, the more? Like one who climbs a hill; but who, the higher he goes, discovers more and more to wonder at. This is not the way to *quench* thirst. It is, on the contrary, the way to make thirst intolerable. It is a thirst which consumes, and will slay at the last!

And we spoke of the thirst after Holiness: but much worldly business does not supply the thing which such a thirst requires. Much less do daily failures quench the soul's craving for a closer walk with GOD. Hourly falls, countless slips,—with the eye, the tongue, the hand, the heart, the mind;—all these do not quench this thirst. On the contrary, they inflame it. They make the whole heart sick, and the whole body faint. They force the Christian to cry out at last —'O miserable man that I am! who shall deliver me from the body of this death?'

Enough has been said to make our meaning

clear when we speak of 'the Soul's *Thirst;*' and affirm that this is no rare affection of the Soul, but almost the very condition of its being. What remains of the subject will be fitly considered in a separate Discourse.

Tuesday in Whitsun-week.

THE SOUL'S THIRST.—Part II.

St. John vii. 37.

Jesus stood and cried, saying, If any man thirst, let him come unto Me, and drink.

In yesterday's Sermon, we explained that by the *Thirst of the Soul*, we allude to that passionate longing from within which fails in finding from without that which can entirely satisfy it. This, we instanced in four particulars: the thirst after *Happiness*,—after *Love*,—after *Knowledge*,—after *Holiness*. We further endeavoured to shew that, under this point of view, the afflicted and unfortunate,— the bereaved and lonely,—the weary and disappointed,—those who stand lowest in their own estimation, and are half tempted to despair of themselves:—that all these are they who are consumed with Thirst; whose soul is, as it were, hard at death's door. It remains, now, to speak of the remedy mercifully provided for all the cases supposed.

Observe, in passing, that our LORD might have spoken of the Soul's *Hunger*, had He willed; and the meaning would have been the same. He Himself is known to have *thirsted* at Samaria's well; to have *hungered* on the way from Bethany: but it was in His soul that He endured that Hunger and that Thirst. Why then is it 'Thirst' in this place, not 'Hunger?' Plainly because Thirst is the keener want: because, also, it is the manner of Scripture to discourse of the SPIRIT under the image of *Water;* and our SAVIOUR was about to reveal Himself to His Countrymen, fetching water, as on their Feast-day they did, from 'Siloa's brook that flowed fast by the Oracle of GOD,' and bringing it with pomp and ceremony into the Temple, as Himself 'the Fountain of Living Waters*,'—the true source of Spiritual refreshment to Israel. It is Man's *spiritual needs* therefore, of which our LORD here discourses under the image of mere bodily craving: and He takes the severer bodily want, and makes it stand for Thirst and Hunger both.

And surely, we may begin by assuming that every one finds his place in some one or more parts of the picture we have drawn. All have

* Jer. xvii. 13.

longed earnestly for *something*; they have sought to gratify their longing: they have found that the remedy failed to satisfy. And no wonder! for there is *nothing* on this side the grave, that can *fill* the soul! The things of Time cannot satisfy those eternal desires which were meant to find their accomplishment only in Eternity. Lawful they are indeed, one and all, so far as we have noticed them: calculated also to solace the heart, and minister to all its innocent desires. But they cannot,—they were not meant,—to satisfy. Their office is to lead on to something higher, and purer, and better. The thirst after Happiness guides us to GOD's Right Hand: and of Love, to Him who is perfect: and of Knowledge, to the presence of Him 'in whom are hid all the treasures of Wisdom[b]:' and of Holiness, to Him who alone maketh holy. But this is not found out at first; or, it is known, but not believed; or, it is believed, but not acted upon, (which is one and the same thing with disbelieving it.) Hence it is that we *have* thirsted; it may be, that we still thirst! We are resting in that which is close at hand, and have not yet so much as sought to look beyond it. There *are* therefore, who, could

[b] Col. iii. 2.

we hear them, even now cry out,—'Yea, my tongue cleaves to my very jaws. I do, as it were, die, under a thirst, which I cannot control or remove.' To all men, but to such an one, in particular, does our SAVIOUR address the words of the text; 'If any man thirst, let him come unto *Me* and *drink!*'

We heartily invite you to ponder over the words of this gracious invitation, and most loving promise. 'Let him come unto *Me:*' *there* is the invitation! 'Let him drink:' *there* is the promise! ... What is it but to say:

O ye who have longed for Happiness, and sought it, but have failed to find it:—who have pined for Love, but have never been satisfied:—and grasped at Knowledge, but have discovered that it did not fill your soul:—who have sighed for a closer walk with GOD, but have sometimes felt as if you were cast out of His very presence, and must surely learn to despair of yourselves at last:—come hither unto Me! 'He that believeth on Me, shall *never* thirst.' Ye have sought for things which will not satisfy. The joys of Earth are short-lived and deceitful: and 'whosoever drinketh of *that* water, shall thirst again; but whosoever drinketh of the water which *I* shall give him, shall *never* thirst!'

With Me, and with Me only, dwells a satisfying portion. 'Come unto *Me*, and drink!'

Freely slake your thirst in *Me! I* will give you abundance of Peace and Joy; for I am 'the Father of mercies and the GOD of all comfort[c].' 'Come unto Me, and drink!'

My Love thou wilt find sufficient for thee; and in Me only wilt thou discover a worthy object of thy Love. 'Come unto *Me*, and drink!'

Study My Word; ponder over My perfections; yea, give Me but thine heart: come unto Me, and seek to do My will, and verily thou shalt be made wise unto Salvation! 'Come unto Me, and *drink!*'

Pray to Me daily,—many times a day,—for larger and larger supplies of My Spirit: and they shall not be denied thee. But remember thou faint not; remember thou *fail* not. 'Blessed are they which do hunger and thirst after righteousness; for they *shall* be filled[d].' 'I am Alpha and Omega, the beginning and the end. I will give unto him that is athirst, of the fountain of the water of Life freely[e]:' and 'with joy shall he draw water out of the wells of Salvation.' 'If any man thirst, let him come unto *Me*, and drink!'

[c] 2 Cor. i. 3.   [d] St. Matth. v. 6.   [e] Rev. xxi. 6.

TUESDAY IN WHITSUN-WEEK.

You will perceive the drift of what has been spoken, and recognise that it amounts to a declaration that CHRIST is the Believer's *only satisfying portion:* the only thing which can *satisfy* the desires and longings of the human heart. You will see that the text wraps up, and contains within itself, this great secret: much in the same way as a single corn of wheat contains the fulness of a future harvest. This is the truth which we have been labouring to illustrate: the one thing of which we desire that GOD Almighty may convince all our hearts!

Let us not suppose that we know this *already*, if we are quite contented with this life and this world, and desire nothing beyond either: if the sight of Sin, in any form, offend us not. Or, on the other hand, if worldly trouble and anxiety weighs us entirely down. Or, if again we *feel* much, but *do* little: allow ourselves in slanderous words and uncharitable thoughts, impure desires, unholy imaginations, and the like. No. Let us not be deceived. He only understands, by experience, the matter of our present Sermon who tries to live *in* the World without being *of* the World: who makes it his whole business to build his nest, and lay up his treasure in Heaven: who, in the midst of sorrow can think upon GOD with comfort; and, like Hope amid billows, anchor his soul upon *Him*. Who craves nothing so much as the knowledge of God and of His perfections: who makes it the great business of his life, to be holy!

'Jesus stood and cried, saying, If any man thirst, let him come unto me and drink.' May He who spoke those blessed words, bring home their heavenly teaching to the hearts of all! Lift us up above our trials, and comfort us with His abounding Love, and fill our souls with heavenly Light, and make us abound in every Christian Grace!..... May He keep us in constant remembrance that here below the moth and rust corrupt, and the flower fadeth, and nothing satisfieth, and the flesh is weak: but that it is not so in Heaven where He is. Yea, in *this* life will He come to us, and with supplies of His Grace will quench our thirst. But the Christian's hereafter is far more glorious; his portion, I mean, in 'that great City, the Holy Jerusalem,' which the disciple whom Jesus loved saw 'descending out of Heaven from God; having the glory of God; and her light like unto a stone most precious, even like a jasper stone, clear as crystal[f].' For *there* shall the Saints of God 'hunger no

[f] Rev. xxi. 10, 11.

more, *neither thirst any more;* neither shall the sun light on them, nor any heat. For the Lamb which is in the midst of the Throne shall feed them; and *shall lead them unto living fountains of waters;* and GOD shall wipe away all tears from their eyes[g]!'

[g] Rev. vii. 16, 17.

Trinity Sunday.

THE SUGGESTIONS OF TRINITY SUNDAY.

PSALM xc. 12.

So teach us to number our days, that we may apply our hearts unto Wisdom.

THIS day sets a crown on the Christian Year, by rehearsing the mystery of the glorious and undivided Trinity. The seasons which we observe as members of CHRIST's Church are not reckoned in the same way as the seasons which the World observes. The World begins its year with January; and reckons by months, and days of the month: but the Church begins her year with Advent; and reckons by the events in the Life of her LORD. And thus it happens that the Sacred Year begins in the Winter, because our LORD was born in the Winter; and ends in the Summer, because it was *then* that the last events recorded in the Gospels took place. Advent and Christmas, Epiphany and Lent, Holy-Week and Easter and Ascension-Day,—these are the great Festivals by which the Church takes note how Time is going. Now all these have reference to the *second Person* in the glorious Trinity. But we learn from the Acts of the Apostles, how that ten days after our LORD had ascended into Heaven, the HOLY GHOST, (the Third Person,) descended, to dwell with believers for evermore. Accordingly, last Sunday we commemorated the descent of the HOLY GHOST: and on this day, we gather up the whole mystery of so many Sundays into a single commemoration, and call the day *Trinity Sunday*.

It is obvious to notice how the services for the present Festival all point in one direction. The first lesson describes the work of Creation, in which we find the Three Persons of the Trinity mysteriously associated. 'In the beginning, GOD created the Heaven and the Earth:'—*there*, the FATHER is mentioned. 'And GOD *said:*'— *there*, the SON is spoken of; (for 'by the Word of the LORD were the Heavens made[a]'). 'And the SPIRIT OF GOD moved upon the face of the waters.' *That* completes the mention of the Holy Trinity. And surely it is a striking fact that the three first verses in the Bible should contain so express a notice of this lofty Doctrine! ...... At the end of the second Lesson, a Voice proclaiming the mind of the FATHER is heard

---

[a] Ps. xxxiii. 6.

from Heaven; while the HOLY GHOST descends upon the Eternal SON. Thus the mystery of the Trinity is exhibited in a single chapter both from the Old and the New Testament.

Equally appropriate will the afternoon lessons be found to be. One gives the history of the appearance of the SON of GOD with two angels to Abraham; which was emblematic of the Trinity. The other,—a glorious chapter from St. John's First Epistle,—speaks of the three Witnesses; and contains passages which bear so remarkably on the day, that the reason why that Chapter was chosen becomes apparent the instant we hear it read. The Epistle and the Gospel likewise look in the same direction. All must be struck with the glorious account of what St. John saw in Heaven: how he heard the cry of thrice Holy,—which is the portion of Scripture appointed for the Epistle. While, in the Gospel, we behold the Eternal SON discoursing to Nicodemus of GOD the FATHER and GOD the HOLY GHOST.

So then, the services of to-day are all meant to guide our thoughts to the great and crowning doctrine of Christianity; the three Persons in One GOD: and Trinity Sunday comes at the end of so many great Festivals, because the mystery

TRINITY SUNDAY.

which it commemorates was not fully disclosed till after all the other Festivals had passed away. There had been *hints* given, every now and then, in the Law and the Prophets, of the Blessed Trinity: for instance, Aaron had been commanded to bless the people by saying three times ' the LORD bless thee, and keep thee[b].' Isaiah, in like manner, heard the Seraphim worship GOD, by crying ' one to another, *Holy, Holy, Holy*[c];' as if they had said,—Holy is the FATHER, and Holy is the SON, and Holy is the HOLY GHOST. But these are *hints* only. The Doctrine is nowhere expressly laid down either in the Law or the Prophets. In the fulness of time, however, when GOD sent His SON into the World, *that* which had been taught before darkly, was shewn openly. The Second Person in the Blessed Trinity was then expressly revealed. Then was He ' seen of Angels[d].' Men heard Him, and saw Him with their eyes; looked upon Him, and their hands handled Him. St. John even lay upon His breast at Supper. But the whole of the mystery had not yet been fully revealed. Our LORD must leave the world before the Doctrine could be seen in all its completeness. ' It is expedient for you that I go away,' (He said :) ' for if I go

[b] Numb. vi. 24—26.   [c] Is. vi. 3.   [d] 1 Tim. iii. 16.

not away, the Comforter will not come unto you; but if I depart, I will send Him unto you.' So He died, and rose again; and fifty days after, the HOLY GHOST was sent. This did indeed complete the mystery. When, on the first Christian Pentecost, the HOLY GHOST was poured out,—(the HOLY GHOST which proceedeth from the FATHER, and the SON,)—then, all was plain. Then was it understood that there is one Person of the FATHER, another of the SON, and another of the HOLY GHOST: though the GODHEAD of the FATHER, of the SON, and of the HOLY GHOST is all One: the glory equal, the majesty co-Eternal. All this, became plain *then*. And hence we see why, immediately after Whitsuntide, comes Trinity Sunday.

Thus much it is right to say on a day like this, in explanation of the Church Services. The Festival itself is a day of leave-taking; a kind of farewell. We must all feel that we have reached a limit, and can go no further. The Sundays which follow to-day, look back and point to today; being reckoned from it. We trace no longer the footsteps of our REDEEMER, whom we have watched through Infancy and Manhood, through Suffering and Death,—to Resurrection, and Ascension into Heaven. The History of His earthly Life ended on Ascension-Day. The outpouring of His Spirit occupied our thoughts last Sunday. All is over now; and we seem called upon to go forth, and do His work, until His coming again,—which will be at Advent. We seem to drift away from the shore, as on this day; and to have a wide and a dreary ocean before us. So that the present Festival, with all its grandeur, brings some sad thoughts with it. All our glorious Sundays are passed and gone. Our great Festivals are all over; and the sacramental half of the year may be considered to come to a close with the last words of this afternoon's service.

A day like this, invites us to great *thoughtfulness*. Above all things, we cannot help being struck with the wonderful privilege we enjoy, in the largeness of the Revelation vouchsafed to us. Before *our* eyes, the whole mystery of the Trinity hath been set. That which the prophets knew but dimly, *we* see in the full blaze of Gospel Light. It is not a dark type, an obscure image, a mysterious saying which we have to feed upon: but the very substance itself is ours, of which all those were but the shadows. We look upon no Paschal Lamb at Easter. Lo, CHRIST Himself hath been sacrificed for us; and the benefits of His most precious Death are communicated to our souls as often as we celebrate His Death in the Sacrament. Instead of Circumcision, we have the gift of the Spirit in Holy Baptism, cleansing the heart, and bringing us into such an union with our LORD as that covenant in the flesh of Abraham's natural seed was never able to accomplish. All Prophecy, by the coming of CHRIST into the world, has in like manner been made plain. Whereas the Prophets of old studied their own prophecies, and saw but dimly the meaning of that which the HOLY GHOST inspired, —we have heard the SON of God Himself, His Apostles and Evangelists, apply and expound their meaning. What things the very Angels desired to look into, but could not quite understand, have all been freely laid open to us. Surely the greatness of such a privilege should make us tremble! How shall we escape if we neglect so great Salvation! The thought is surely an amazing and a perplexing one, that every village child knows a hundred things which Abraham, and Moses, and David, and the Prophets would have rejoiced, beyond all telling, to know; and yet they were not allowed to know them!

It is natural for Christians who are in earnest in the matter of their Salvation, to desire to gain a practical lesson from every Sacred Season: secretly, to turn every Festival, as it comes round, to some special use. If *a pious practice* growing naturally out of Trinity Sunday, is asked for, we would suggest the following: namely, that we henceforth seek to realize more fully the *Christian* character of the Psalms of David, and of the Old Testament Lessons. Let every prophecy, henceforth, be more closely connected in our minds, with its fulfilment: every history, bring to view its prophetic aspect, as well as its obvious literal interpretation. If every allusion to our SAVIOUR in the Psalms, filled us with secret pleasure; if every reference to His Humiliation or to His Glory, brought before us the History of Passiontide and Easter,—how dear would the lengthiest portions of our Morning and Evening service become! No longer deemed a tedious exercise, they would be found, (what they were designed to be,) a relief and a solace to the weary soul; and the events which we have been celebrating since Advent, would retain unwonted freshness until the last of the many 'Sundays after Trinity' had run out, and Advent again sounded its note of solemn warning.

The First Sunday after Trinity.

THE PARABLE OF LAZARUS.

St. Luke xvi. 19.

There was a certain rich man.

THIS is like no other of our LORD's Parables: for it belongs neither to this life, nor to the life to come; but to that mysterious life which lies between the two;—a life concerning which, by the Light of Reason we can discover nothing; while from Revelation itself, we know but very little. It relates to two persons,—the one, rich: the other, a beggar. And concerning these two persons we must take care to notice exactly what is said; and not to *invent* things concerning them which are not set down in Scripture. For instance, many think that the rich man was a hardhearted wretch, who denied a few crumbs to the beggar who lay suffering at his gate: whereas not a syllable of the sort is said in Scripture. Some, again, seem to suppose that the one went into torment because he was rich; while the other was comforted because he was poor. But the Gospel says nothing of the kind.—It will be well therefore that we should seek to obtain some truer notions on the subject.

All that is stated concerning the rich man, is, that his clothing was of the most luxurious kind; and that every day of his life, he fared sumptuously. The beggar who was laid at his gate full of sores, and who desired to be fed with the crumbs which fell from the rich man's table, *may* (for aught that appears to the contrary,) have sometimes even been pitied by the rich man as he went out and in. We must not invent a worse character than we find set down. Our safest course is, to reason backwards; and say, —Since the rich man was in a state of torment after his death, it is certain that he had led an evil life: and in like manner, the beggar's comfort after death must be regarded as a sign that he had been accepted in his lifetime. And when we have got so far, it seems that we should debate *thus* with ourselves :—' I perceive then that the parable sets forth a state of abject misery, (utter destitution, hunger, and a loathsome disease,) as favourable conditions to future blessedness: a state of great bodily enjoyment, on the contrary, (fine linen, purple, and sumptuous fare *daily* partaken of,) as dangerous to the soul's welfare throughout eternity. To which of these two classes, then, do *I* belong? Am I rich? O then, my soul, let us think well of our danger; and look to it closely that *we* incur not the rich man's misery, after death. We will not fail at least to be compassionate towards our poorer neighbours. No, nor will we fail to interrupt our luxurious living, now and then, for a single day. The Church recommends those who *can* feast always, to *fast* sometimes. We will obey her counsel.—But I am perhaps sick, suffering, and poor. What fruits of holiness then do I bear? What virtue hath sickness wrought? What blessed effect hath suffering had upon me? My misery is somewhat like that of Lazarus. O my soul, what fruit have we therefore to shew? Let us beware that we shall therefore be *required* to win *a crown!'* .... *This* is the true, as well as the wholesome, way to reason:—a method which turns Riches into a warning-note that danger is at hand: Poverty and Sickness, into an incentive to Holy Living and the patient waiting for CHRIST.

For, so far from thinking that the rich man in the Parable was a hard-hearted wretch, we suspect that he was a man with kind family feelings. It is observable that in the depth of his own misery, he called to mind the case of his five brothers, who were living as he had done,—sumptuously and carelessly. He implored that they might have a timely warning given them. He dreaded lest they should become partakers of his own misery. He was so much in earnest, so bent upon this scheme of saving them from suffering what he himself suffered, that he argued the case; and tried to prove that a witness from the dead would convince their obdurate hearts, and work in them greater seriousness; repentance, and amendment of life. . . . The rich man in the Parable, therefore, seems to have been rather one of Esau's stamp: an amiable kind of person; easy, and full of what the world calls 'good feelings:' but wanting in all those more important qualities which GOD requires and approves: such, for example, as strict integrity, purity of speech, earnestness in working out our own Salvation, zeal in our calling, and that living sympathy which not only relieves the beggar lying in sickness and misery, but tries to view the SAVIOUR in that sick and suffering member of CHRIST's Body.

Of Lazarus, very little is said. We are left to conjecture that he not only hungered after meat and drink; but also, (and it may be, *in consequence of* his bodily need,) after heavenly things. We may not doubt that he was patient in suffering, and became perfected even by the very process of his pain: for his poverty made him lowly in his own eyes; while his loathsomeness bred in him the most abject sense of his vile condition. He was, in his own estimation, forlorn and an outcast. Wherefore, He who putteth down the mighty from their seat, but exalteth the humble and meek; filling the hungry with good things, but sending the rich empty away; ALMIGHTY GOD, for these reasons, caused Lazarus after death to be comforted, and the rich man to be tormented.

In the meantime, the end of these two persons is recorded; and the record is conveyed in very striking language. 'It came to pass that the beggar died, *and was carried by the angels into Abraham's bosom.* The rich man also died, *and was buried.*' The contrast is strongly marked. The one was conducted therefore to the place where Abraham is; the place where GOD's Saints are waiting for their perfect consummation and bliss, both in body and soul. Of the rich man, on the contrary, it is declared that after death, he found himself in Hell and in torments; and lifting up his eyes, he saw Abraham afar off, and 'Lazarus in his bosom.' Without entering into any of the curious questions which this narrative suggests concerning the state of the departed, let us bend our thoughts on a far more practical concern. Let us call to mind that amid excess of meat or drink, the tongue is particularly prone to sin. If not to filthy conversation, there is an inducement to profane speech; at least to sinful talking,—whether quarrelsome, or slanderous, or untrue. Doubtless, souls in pain feel the anguish most in *that* member wherewith they have most offended. Let us observe then that the man who had fared sumptuously every day, being in torment, *felt* the torment chiefly *in his tongue.* 'Father Abraham,' (he cried,) 'have mercy on me, and send Lazarus that he may dip the tip of his finger in water and cool *my tongue!*' . . . O, when tempted to sin; whether with the tongue, which is, (saith David,) '*the best member that we have;*' or in any other way with the body; let us think of the misery of suffering *through our Sin* to all eternity! GOD grant that this thought may check us; and save us, it may be, from ruin.

The only part of the Parable which yet requires notice is the close of it. We gather from the concluding portion a very important fact concerning the Life to come; namely, that a great gulph is eternally *fixed* between the wicked and the just; so that there is no passing from the one to the other. And oh, if so it be, let us dwell often and anxiously on the misery of those who shall find themselves hopelessly separate from the society of the Saints; and that, not for a brief season, but for ever and for ever! Take notice how keen a touch of despair, is conveyed by those words,—' Nay, Father Abraham; but if one went unto them from the dead, they *will* repent!' As if the speaker had said,—The history of what is passing here, the torture of this flame would so terrify, even in description; that *might* a departed spirit but rise up from the fiery lake, and go back to earth, and preach to mankind,— the most sinful *must* repent; the most obdurate *must* be softened!

Ah, my friends, this anticipation here finds its answer in the words,—' If they hear not Moses and the prophets, neither will they be persuaded though one rose from the dead.' The saying may not be doubted nor misunderstood. It means,— If the Old and New Testaments; the Gospel of JESUS CHRIST; the means of grace by GOD Himself provided, Sacraments and Confirmation and

Prayer; if the services of the Sanctuary, and the instruction of the Prayer-book; if the HOLY SPIRIT pleading with us invisibly; and the countless opportunities vouchsafed to Christian men in a Christian country:—if these all prove unavailing to awaken to a life of Holiness, to produce Repentance, to carry the soul to GOD; *nothing* could achieve the blessed end: no, not though the grave should give up its dead; though the lips which had long since forgotten speech, and the limbs which had forsaken motion, and the eyes which had closed on the things of sense, were each to do its several part to awaken, to terrify, and to persuade: though the tongue should tell of horrors which might sicken; and the hand and the eye enforce what was spoken, with their dumb but more expressive eloquence; —*they would not repent, they will not be persuaded!* no, not *though one rose from the dead!*

The Second Sunday after Trinity.

THE PARABLE OF THE GREAT SUPPER.

St. Luke xiv. 16.

A certain Man made a great Supper, and bade many.

It is worth observing that this parable was delivered to a single individual. The Divine Speaker intended doubtless that *all* should listen; but His words were addressed to *one*. He therefore invites the personal and private attention of every Christian to the narrative which the words of the text introduce.

The circumstances under which the parable of the Great Supper was delivered, were as follows. Our Lord was sitting at meat with one of the chief Pharisees. There were several persons present; and it seems from what is said of the way they behaved, (all trying to get the best places,) that they were very far from being of the temper which God approves. Our Lord therefore delivered some heavenly teaching concerning Humility, and the Hospitality which seeks no return,—ending with the promise that He who does such things shall be recompensed 'at the Resurrection of the just.' 'And when one of them that sat at meat with Him heard these things, he said unto Him, Blessed is he that shall eat bread in the Kingdom of God.' What he meant was,—Yea Master, *his* reward will be a reward indeed. Our Fathers have taught us to think of the Resurrection of the just, as of a heavenly banquet which is to usher in God's Kingdom. Blessed indeed will he be that shall find his recompense *then;* that shall eat bread in the Kingdom of God!

Our Lord proceeded at once to deliver the Parable which forms this day's Gospel.—There was a Man who made a great Supper, and invited many persons to come and partake of it. But at supper-time, instead of coming, they all began to make excuses. One had bought some land; another some oxen; another sent word that he had married a wife. Two of them said, 'Pray excuse me:' the third said roundly, 'I *cannot* come.' The giver of the Feast was displeased, (as was natural;) declared that none of those men should taste of his Supper; and commanded that 'the poor, the maimed, the halt, and the blind,'—nay, as many as were found in 'the highways and hedges,' should be compelled to come in, that the House might be filled .... These are the main parts of the Parable.

THE PARABLE OF THE GREAT SUPPER.

Although the persons to whom it was spoken, did not understand it, *we* at least are aware of its meaning. The man had exclaimed, 'Blessed is he that shall eat bread in the Kingdom of God!' Our SAVIOUR's answer comes to this,— *Thou* art the man! or rather, Thou *mayest be* the man; *thou* mayest eat bread in the Kingdom of God; *thou* mayest be 'blessed' if thou wilt! For *I* am He who, in the parable, made the great Supper; that is, I have provided all things which the soul's hunger and the soul's thirst can desire: even the Gospel of the Kingdom; the way of Salvation; the knowledge of Myself! I 'bid many,' for I invite *all!* It is 'supper-time' *now;* the evening of the day; the latter time. I am come into the World: I have ordained My Apostles: I have chosen My Disciples: My Ministry already draweth towards a close; and I Myself am prepared to be offered up a Sacrifice for the sins of the whole world. Come, therefore; for all things are now ready!

Such was the gracious invitation of our LORD. He invited all who sat at the Pharisee's table to come to Him. His blessed voice sounded in their ears, and cried aloud to *them!* He had put on the form of a servant; and called 'the guests to come to a better feast than that of which they had been partaking. But they understood Him not: and so they gave no heed to His words. *Why* was that?

Our LORD Himself leaves us to infer the probable reason. There was land, or there were oxen, or there was a wife: property, which must be looked after; possessions, requiring activity; family ties, claiming the affections:—there was *something* in the way. But however this may have been, let us consider what is at least certain:—here was a large company of persons quite unconscious that they were listening to the Invitation to come to the great Supper; in whose ears, nevertheless, the incarnate SON was proclaiming the message, 'Come, for all things are now ready!' They may have all thought that the parable which our LORD delivered was nothing to them: but, in fact, (as we have seen,) *theirs* was the invitation; *theirs* was the opportunity. To every one at table, singly, it might have been truly said,—'*Thou* art the man! CHRIST is speaking unto *thee!*'

And can we fail to perceive that if the invitation was *theirs,* so is it *ours* also? If the cry was to *them,* so is it also to *us?* And do we not run the same risk, incur the same danger, as they? Is it not to be feared that some of *us* also may be unconscious of the solemn truth that every day, every Sunday, on *this* Sunday especially, when that parable has been read to us, that the invitation is personal and private: that there hath been a banquet made ready; and that we are invited, yea entreated to come and be partakers?

We, at least, are aware, we are even now reminding one another, that a summons has been given us by GOD to come to Him. He has prepared the highest delight for our souls: the knowledge of Himself, for those who desire the best knowledge; for those who thirst after righteousness, large supplies of His Holy Spirit, abundant stores of Grace: His Word, revealing Him to our understandings: His Sacraments, conforming us to His image: His public Service, bringing us before Him in the manner which He loves: Prayer, which admits us to wondrous nearness with Him. 'Come,' (He says,) ' for all things are now ready!'

... Opportunities of obedience: occasions for the exercise of Faith, and Hope, and Love: all these are freely offered us at different times; and they all come to us from GOD, whose Heavenly Kingdom is composed of such as are exercised in the practice of all Heavenly graces.

How then do we receive the message? In

too many cases we act precisely as the men in the parable acted. We put off our obedience: at all events, we yield it not. And the reason is that there is another thing, which we care more about, in the way: oxen which must be proved, a piece of ground which must be seen after, standing for *all* property whatsoever; (the worldly calling, the means of support, however splendid, however lowly, it may happen to be:) a newly married wife, again, standing for all fleshly ties, because Marriage is the closest and most mysterious of any. These things, then, in some form or other,—the Land, the Oxen, the Wife; the things of time and the things of sense, the things which concern this life present,—*these* things it is which stand between us and GOD. The parable before us reveals us to ourselves. It tells us why we are so cold and so seldom in Prayer; why our service in Church is such a barren service; why our Communions are so few and so unworthy; why our obedience is generally so imperfect; our efforts after Holiness so feeble; our appetite for Heaven so impaired. It is because the cares of this World engross too much of our time and thoughts; and because our hearts are given away from GOD, and given up entirely to earthly ties. We are shewn to ourselves in this parable, as in a mirror. We see the reflexion of our life: the very image of our inner man is here shewn us by Him who knoweth what is in man!

Let it be well observed that neither Land to be seen, nor Oxen to be proved, nor Wife to be cared for,—that *none* of these are blameable. It is not that these things are wrong in themselves. Quite the reverse. They are God's ordinance: God's own appointment. But the best things may be abused; and God's own gifts may be made to stand between us and God.

If worldly trouble, (anxiety, disappointment, and the rest,) keep us from Prayer: if the duty of providing for those most near and dear to us, is suffered to engross the whole of our thoughts and of our time :—if schemes of pleasure, and plans for our families, are suffered to run out into results which keep us from the House of God, and the narrow path of Duty :—as often as the claims of God are balanced against the claims of the World, and made to give way :—as often as the Love of God is thrown into the shade by the love of any of His created things,—let that thing be what it may :—so often do we, in effect, reject the Divine invitation; declare that we have bought land, and must go and see it; have bought oxen, and must go to prove them; have married a wife, and therefore *cannot* come!

And if it be true that nothing concerns us more than to know what it is which keeps us from our greatest good,—how can we over estimate the importance of the present parable? This danger once known, if we honestly desire to serve GOD and to please Him, we shall know how to guard against it. The first approach of the evil will alarm us. The darkening sky, and the fading embers; the flickering Faith, and feeble Hope, and lukewarm Charity,—*these* will rouse us to a sense of our impending danger; and we shall know in what quarter to look for the cause of that which is bringing our souls so very low. Aye, and we shall seek amendment and restoration also; seek it, with many a prayer, many a strong endeavour; seek it, as men who see Danger, aye, *Death* before them: and the joys of GOD'S many mansions, *our* promised Inheritance, the Kingdom prepared for *us*, very far away! For CHRIST Himself hath said it, concerning as many as rejected the Heavenly Feast, —'None of those men which were bidden shall *taste* of My Supper!'

www.ingramcontent.com/pod-product-compliance
Lightning Source LLC
Chambersburg PA
CBHW020306240426
43673CB00039B/724